"Culture" and the Problem of the Disciplines

"Culture" and the
Problem of the Disciplines

Edited by John Carlos Rowe

COLUMBIA UNIVERSITY PRESS
NEW YORK

COLUMBIA UNIVERSITY PRESS
Publishers Since 1893
New York   Chichester, West Sussex

Copyright © 1998 Columbia University Press
All rights reserved
Library of Congress Cataloging-in-Publication Data
"Culture" and the problem of the disciplines / edited by John Carlos Rowe.
p. cm.
Includes bibliographical references and index.
ISBN 0-231-11242-4 (cloth). — ISBN 0-231-11243-2 (pbk.)
1. Culture. 2. Cultural policy. 3. Multiculturalism. I. Rowe, John Carlos.
HM101.C89554 1998
306—dc21   97-44499

Casebound editions of Columbia University Press books are printed on permanent
and durable acid-free paper.
Printed in the United States of America

c 10 9 8 7 6 5 4 3 2 1
p 10 9 8 7 6 5 4 3 2 1

"Culture" and the Problem of the Disciplines

Introduction

John Carlos Rowe

From the fall of 1992 to the spring of 1995, the Critical Theory Institute at the University of California, Irvine, worked on the topic " 'Culture' and the Problem of the Disciplines." This volume reflects that work and consists largely of essays by members of the group and invited guests that were presented, discussed, and revised during that period. Work on this research project actually began as early as the spring of 1991, when the members of the group began to discuss possible topics for a new research project to follow "Critical Theory, Contemporary Culture, and the Question of the Political," which was published as *Politics, Theory, and Contemporary Culture* (Columbia, 1993) and edited by the previous Director of the Institute, Mark Poster.

In the spring of 1991, we were unable to agree on an appropriate topic and focus, even though it was clear to most of us that some consideration of the renewed importance of concepts and theories of "culture" would be central to our work for the next three years. Our discussions that spring undoubtedly resembled those of many other scholars in the humanities and social sciences in the first half of the 1990s as they struggled to come to terms with the dramatic changes in their respective disciplines as a consequence of internal institutional and professional crises, some of which were provoked by larger social, economic, and political forces. Our common interest in the changing meaning of "culture" as a concept and term was matched by our interest in how the institutions of teaching and research—universities, professional organizations, research centers, foundations that fund research—were changing in response to both intellectual movements and often-contrary social forces.

Our disagreements were fundamental and appeared in some cases to be insurmountable; they reflected basic differences in our respective conceptions of what constitutes "critical theory" today. For some members, critical theory had achieved prominence in the United States primarily as a suite of practices concerned with the fundamental operations of language and thus focused on reading, writing, and interpretation. To speak of "culture" in any generalized manner thus raised for these scholars urgent questions regarding the status of the object of study. How could "culture" possibly constitute an object of study, as a discrete text can be said to be, when we know that "culture" is composed of a vast number of different, competing representations? These same scholars knew well enough the complex systems of representation and hermeneutic problems involved in a single, putatively "discrete" text—itself an elaborately intertextual complex—so the task of examining "culture" as a "text" or even as a suite of interrelated texts struck these scholars as both quixotic and Sisyphean.

Other members of the group argued that we really had no choice in the matter of focusing on "culture," because the most influential new methods of scholarship—variously named cultural studies, cultural criticism, colonial and postcolonial studies, feminism and gender studies, ethnic studies, and minority discourse—had already defined their respective projects as critical investigations of the ways in which dominant ideologies maintained their powers through culture and the ways oppressed and marginalized peoples had asserted their own cultures as part of the politics of emancipation. All of these intellectual approaches derived at least in part from the language-based theories identified primarily with structuralism and poststructuralism, as well as with the traditions of ideological criticism established by the Frankfurt School, the Birmingham and Manchester Schools, and so-called "post-Marxian" approaches in which "culture" played an increasingly important part in our understanding of ideological effectiveness.

Those members who worried about the difficulty of determining any credible "object of study" for something as vast and inchoate as "culture" were also concerned that our small research group did not represent sufficient expertise in the necessary disciplines to investigate any topic involving the study of "culture" and the many new disciplines claiming "culture" to be central to their intellectual work. Indeed, the Critical Theory Institute in 1991 was composed primarily of humanists from the several language and literature departments at Irvine and from such related disciplines as history and film studies. "Culture," some argued convincingly, cannot be studied exclusively from literary, historical, and philosophical perspectives; anthropology, sociology, art history, and visual culture are indispensable for any reconsideration of the subject.

Our disagreements were profound enough—in a group that exists only by virtue of its ability to work collaboratively—that we decided to take a sabbatical from our usual research activities. First, we agreed to suspend all our public lectures and discussion groups. If we could not agree on a topic, then there was certainly no good reason to invite distinguished scholars to the campus. Second, we decided to select a variety of books and articles that we would read together in hopes of discovering some common ground and thereby formulating a workable research project. Each member of the Institute was invited to suggest a book or essay, and we narrowed the proposed texts down to a manageable group. We then met regularly to discuss readings from such collections as *Nation and Narration,* ed. Homi Bhabha; *Culture Theory: Essays on Mind, Self, and Emotion,* eds. Richard A. Shweder and Robert A. LeVine; *Conflicts in Feminism,* eds. Marianne Hirsch and Evelyn Fox-Keller; and *Cultural Studies,* eds. Lawrence Grossberg, Cary Nelson, and Paula A. Treichler, with Linda Baughman and assistance from John MacGregor Wise.

We found our own disagreements, hesitations, and anxieties often reflected in the essays and chapters we read; we also discovered that the transformation of "critical theory" from a primarily Eurocentric tradition to an increasingly global movement opened great new possibilities even as it involved obvious risks. Challenged, revised, and sometimes rejected outright by scholars around the world in its Eurocentric and idealist manifestations, critical theory has nonetheless had a profound influence on cultural studies. As a cultural "import" that represents European and U.S. intellectual canons, critical theory can reproduce in other cultures many of the problems for which it has already been criticized in Europe and the U.S.: its failure to articulate issues of race and gender, its adherence to a restricted canon of theorists from Plato and Aristotle to Foucault and Derrida, its legitimation of modernity even by its critique, its avoidance of mass and popular culture.

On the other hand, critical theory is being transformed by cultural studies and other approaches that have challenged its institutional authority and Euroamerican antecedents. Our readings together made clear that cultural studies as represented in several different disciplines assumes that culture is based on discursive practices and that the subjectivities involved in making it are themselves socially constructed. Concerns among some members of our group that cultural studies had ignored critical theory's many warnings about essentialisms and universalisms of all sorts—the first targets of deconstruction—were exaggerated. The critique of universalism and essentialism has resulted in a dialectical exchange that has transformed both critical theory and cultural studies. Despite the fear that the justifiably oppositional politics of newly emergent groups to the ideologies that dominated them might itself become a neonationalism, most cultural studies approaches depend on a crucial distrust of nationalist ideologies of all sorts, even as such approaches seek to define necessary group and community affiliations in ways conducive to politically effective collective action.

Critical theory and cultural studies also register effective resistance to the transformation of universities into technological training centers for multinational corporations. The essays included in this volume effectively "write back" against this tendency to universalize different ideas of "culture" into a global "monoculture" defined by the first-world economies that control production, labor, markets, and consumption and thereby hold the patent on the definition of "culture." Throughout the essays in this volume, there is special emphasis on the hybridity and *métissage* fundamental to many different cultures and thus the inappropriateness of speaking in any general way about what constitutes "culture."

Despite continuing disagreements about methodological and disciplinary approaches, we discovered from our collaboration promising means of criticizing the political, economic, and intellectual forces of the present historical moment. The "culture wars" of the late 1980s and early 1990s are by no means over; they have simply warped into new and less publicly visible struggles for control of educational funding, curricula, "standards" (or "competency levels"), and pedagogical authority. Whether understood as historically discrete movements or as profoundly interrelated names for the same kinds of intellectual approaches, critical theory and cultural studies have traditionally called for institutional changes that would be emancipatory for students and would take the social function of education into account. Today, as public universities in the United States and abroad drastically "downsize," discontinue affirmative-action programs for student admissions and faculty appointments, and stress privatization of funding, we are at grave risk of forgetting the fundamental purposes of educating students to think critically: to enable them to become active agents in creating just and diverse societies.

If "culture" then appears as an undecidable term in our collective research, this in no way means that specific cultural formations cannot be interpreted with the various intellectual tools developed by critical theory and cultural studies. Even in the most focused examinations of historically and socially specific cultural productions, however, it is clear that traditional disciplines must work in complementary ways in order to comprehend what constitutes social reality. Thus the concern of some members of the Institute regarding our respective disciplinary limitations in studying anything as vast as "culture" is overcome when we realize the study of culture can no longer be understood as the work of a single scholar or even that of a particular discipline, such as anthropology or sociology or history. "Culture" as a term immediately poses a disciplinary problem that must be solved before the work of understanding "it" can begin, and this problem may well be seen as a positive motivation for doing the sort of collaborative research we have gathered in this volume.

Our year of reading and discussion led to an inevitable redefinition of our project. We agreed that our own institutional situations had to be starting points for reimagining "culture," especially because the term is so commonly identified as an educational goal: students enter the "culture" of liberal education; students "acquire" the "culture" offered by the best education. In the popular imagination, a college education still promises some command of "culture" (however the term is defined) that can be traded for social, economic, and political authority. Understanding education's role in not only the transmission but also the definition of culture led us to give special consideration to new scholarship concerned with the ideological consequences of the formal organization of knowledge and thus the political functions of educational institutions.

The results of our research thus begin appropriately with "Foundations of Diversity," David Lloyd's reflections on the university's role in the production of culture and of citizens who help legitimate a specific set of otherwise arbitrary practices that are recognizable as "national culture." Lloyd argues that conservative attacks on multiculturalism, postmodern theory, feminism, ethnic studies, and cultural studies are based on the recognition that the university continues to "organize crucial social functions" and thus enjoys real social power. For Lloyd, those social functions include citizenship and the ability of subjects to transfer "from one sphere to another within the complex differentiations of capitalist societies." What he considers a "radical multiculturalism," which must be distinguished from a liberal, assimilationist notion of "cultural pluralism," threatens to disrupt this customary educational purpose of producing obedient individuals who reproduce everyday social and national norms. The contemporary university is "modeled accordingly on a European system that promoted not so much a mono-ethnic culture as . . . a universalist culture which . . . is assumed to supercede local or ethnic values or knowledges." This model of the university has a continuous history from the Enlightenment to the present and thus is informed by what Lyotard has termed the grand narratives of emancipation and enlightenment.[1]

As a result, the classroom itself is often "a focal point for the experience of assimilation and marginalization" for those students who do not already belong to the normative culture. No matter how dramatically we change the texts taught, Lloyd suggests, the work of assimilation and related marginalization will still be done by systemic features of the modern university. For cultural studies and radical multiculturalism to succeed, they cannot accept their current positions at many colleges and universities as mere "additions" to the existing educational structure; they must actively *change* that structure. Such educational change will also transform, and thus must take into account, the larger ideology that forms "subjects for states based on representative democracy and formal political rights." To achieve this revolution, Lloyd calls for a "postpolitical critique," which would question "the very formation of the political" in the educational and cultural practices he begins to analyze in his contribution to this volume.

The modern university helped legitimate the nation-state by defining the "culture" appropriate to that state, but the postmodern university may already be following a different narrative of legitimation. As J. Hillis Miller argues in "Literary and Cultural Studies in the Transnational University," the postmodern forces transforming the modern university are the end of the cold war, the globalization of capitalism, and the new communications technologies. Miller warns us not to accept too hastily the terms of a new "cultural studies," if in fact its approaches merely repeat in a different age the essentialisms and universals by which national ideology legitimated its fictions in the modern era. In this regard, cultural studies threatens to become a mere extension of the older nation-, group-, identity-specific disciplines, rather than achieving the interdisciplinarity required in a global situation. Thus when individual examples of a culture are made unproblematically "representative," we have forgotten the lessons taught by critical theories attentive to the general problem of representation in both its aesthetic and political senses.

Such cultural texts rendered unproblematically "representative" can be all too easily assimilated into the usual ideal of the university. Like David Lloyd, Miller finds strong evidence for this danger in the ways new programs in ethnic and women's studies have been "added" to the existing university's structure without significantly affecting the structure that had for so long excluded these disciplines. Miller thus warns us to beware of the "double contradictory gesture" so typical of both the modern liberal university and the "liberal pluralist" social ideal it upholds: the other is other and must be kept separate, but the other is not really other and can be made part of the usual family of disciplines.

Miller's solution to this problem is for cultural studies to rely on the self-conscious and self-critical disciplinary moves already available in various critical theories. Following postmodern theory's reflection on the problem of representation as well as on the discursive media of representation, cultural studies would thereby avoid being co-opted by the dominant ideology (and its educational agents) and begin the work of building a university based on "dissensus" rather than "consensus," in keeping with the educational reforms proposed by Lloyd. To be sure, Miller's appeal for cultural studies to be more conscious of its own methodologies, in the manner of previous critical theories, assumes a distinction between the two, as if cultural studies is not already shaped by the methods and values of what was once termed critical theory.

Sacvan Bercovitch's "The Function of the Literary in a Time of Cultural Studies" helps foreground the special role played by literary works in this transformation of the university proposed by both Miller and Bercovitch. There is, of course, no essential "Otherness" for either Miller or Bercovitch, but an insuperable, inarticulable, even *sublime* otherness is often just what we experience in the greatest literary texts. This literary uncanniness may well be the challenge to enlightenment rationality and instrumentality that we are losing at our peril as we abandon literary texts for the many other cultural texts that are addressed by cultural studies. For Bercovitch, literature is unique in its ability to put us in touch with multiple ordinary meanings and is thus an inherently "counterdisciplinary" way of understanding the world. Great literary texts, like *Paradise Lost* and *Light in August*, are universal because they do *not* transcend. That is, they problematize the historically and socially particular in ways that cannot be easily overcome. In this regard, literature differs from philosophy, which claims some transcendence of such particulars.

Bercovitch's definition of literature's disciplinary transgression sounds much like definitions of critical theory, and it is clearly the social and political criticism inherent in literary functionality that would equate the literary and critical functions for him. In an interesting suite of rhetorical moves that tell us much about his training and interest in American Studies, Bercovitch links this "literariness" with such "new beginnings" as the discovery of the New World and the foundational ideas, such as American individualism, of democracy in the United States. In this way, he obliquely links older ideals of American Exceptionalism with a literary function that is always challenging universals, disciplinary borders, and cognitive certainties. Both Miller and Bercovitch show how this literary function effectively replaced the authority of philosophy in the modern American and European university, and there is thus an understandable nostalgia in both essays for a literariness that may be complexly intertwined with other and more dominant discursive functions in the production of postmodern cultures.

Miller's and Bercovitch's efforts to salvage a literary ideal for culture are challenged implicitly by Linda Williams's essay on contemporary film and Leslie Rabine's essay on popular women's fashions. In view of the tremendous influence of such contemporary media as fashion magazines, photography, and popular films in shaping our ideas of culture, it is hard to imagine how literature might still claim to "direct" a culture so centrally shaped by these and other nonliterary media. Not only do these new media reach more readers and viewers—and far more *quickly*—than most novels, plays, and poems, but fashion and film seem more integrally involved in the speed and flexibility of the cultural "flows" Marshall McLuhan and Jean Baudrillard have judged characteristic of postmodern experience.

Williams carefully interprets the divide between modern and postmodern cultures in terms of the shifts in viewers' expectations from classical Hollywood cinema to the postmodern cinema that begins with films like Alfred Hitchcock's *Psycho* (1960). Rarely treated as a postmodern film, *Psycho* nevertheless plays upon the audience's fascination with the fluidity of gender roles and sexual identities that reflects new, postmodern social circumstances. Williams argues that postmodern film plays upon "specific regimes of spectatorial pleasure" that previous theories had understood as pornographic and outside the proper disciplines of reason and understanding. Anticipating horror films in which certain destabilizations of social conventions (such as gender, sexuality, and race) are designed to give us an emancipatory pleasure, not unlike the gratifying "terror" of an amusement park ride, *Psycho* announces a new, postmodern regime of the *unstable.*

Williams calls for different methods of interpretation to comprehend such "spectatorial pleasure," which she analogizes to postmodern and thus postanalytical modes of cognition that incorporate aleatory and affective dimensions generally bracketed by the moderns. The new "sensuality" of film requires a new "body" for the viewing audience, and Williams shows how Hitchcock disciplines these new bodies not only by *Psycho*'s formal techniques and thematics but also by means of the film's *marketing*, in which audiences willingly contributed to their own re-education. Departing from older theories of the audience's ideological determination by the cinematic apparatus, Williams shows how the postmodern audience actively participates in the construction of its own identity, adding a crucial performative dimension to the theory of cinematic reception in the postmodern age.

Gender roles and sexual identities are represented as playfully flexible in Hitchcock's postmodern film, but Leslie Rabine argues that such fluidity may be available only to certain subject-positions that are specific to the familiar hierarchies of race and class. Challenging the usual critique of oppositional logic in cultural studies, Rabine argues that our eagerness to avoid essentialisms and binaries of all sorts may prevent us from recognizing their reemergence in the cultural situations we choose to analyze. She argues that "the possibility exists that a postmodern fluid white feminine identity depends for its production upon the image of a fixed black feminine identity," and she proceeds to investigate this possibility in the photographic and prose essays of contemporary women's fashion magazines.

Rabine's interpretation of the different cultural consequences of representing African American women and their fashions in a magazine like *Essence*, marketed to the black community, versus *Mirabella*, marketed to the white, middle-class community, reminds us that we should not too hastily conclude that the "postmodern condition" applies equally to those occupying different socially constructed categories such as race and class. Our tendency to speak of "women" as if they belonged to the general category "Woman" is an old problem of which postmodern theory and cultural studies have often warned us, but there may be a similar propensity in the work of these same approaches. Showing how fashion works complexly as an ensemble of discursive practices by which cultural identities are constructed, Rabine also demonstrates how this cultural work is often done by reinscribing racial, gender, and class hierarchies.

Neither Williams nor Rabine reflects explicitly on the pedagogical implications of her arguments, but each scholar treats her "object of study" as a suite of social practices that perform their own educational work. Women are taught to *choose* certain styles of dress, related body postures, and physical disciplines (diet, exercise), in order to emulate ideals of beauty or sex appeal. Williams argues that viewers of postmodern film are encouraged to *play* with certain subject-positions and to assume *postures* of terror and titillation for the sake of their entertainment and thus the film's "meaning." What, then, should be our own pedagogical strategies in the classroom when the objects of study are themselves *instructionally* coded, especially when the educational ideals of the classroom, the magazine and boutique, and the movie theater may be drastically different? For Miller and Bercovitch, the literary text is often a *model* for our own instructional practices by virtue of either the "otherness" it encourages us to experience or its refusal to answer the basic human questions it poses. The implicit compatibility of the instructional method and the value of the high-cultural text is challenged by mass-cultural texts, like film and fashion, that often teach very different lessons from what many liberal educators would advocate.

The teacher may respond to this situation by retreating to familiar educational ideals and values, tacitly condemning by exclusion the "lessons" of popular and mass culture and cleaving even more desperately to the "classics." Williams and Rabine suggest another response (or range of responses) that would begin by questioning the certainty of the teacher's cultural authority. James Boon's contribution to this volume expands this challenge to include the "canons" (either traditional or avant-garde) of disciplinary knowledge, and he tries to offer an example in his own teaching of the hybrid, postmodern subjectivity that is variously constructed by postmodern film and fashion in Williams's and Rabine's essays. In his own work as a critical theorist, anthropologist, and cultural critic, Boon happily locates himself in the midst of the cultural confusions that academics describe as "inter-" or "postdisciplinary" and that ordinary people experience as "postmodern." Stressing the *performative* aspects of teaching that derive directly from the everyday use of language, Boon playfully and thus seriously returns liberal education to the ordinary complexities of real life. Education, the teacher, and the student are always already "hybridized" by the disciplinary networks in which they are constructed. Contemporary as such an approach may be, Boon warns us against historical egotism by pointing out equivalent hybridities in such a venerable figure as Edward Sapir, whose seminal book *Language* (1920) helped effect the paradigm shift from a cognitive to a language-based model for knowledge.

Boon wants us to respect those precursors who helped frame the intellectual projects of critical theory and cultural studies. He also wants us to understand how intellectuals continue to shape dominant ideas of culture, even if they do so by *transgressing* the boundaries of such popular conventions. Pointing out how Sapir's understanding of language's fundamental hybridity led Sapir also to reject all nationalisms as contrived fictions, Boon stresses the continuing importance of the language model for anthropology and the other disciplines basic to cultural studies. There is, of course, a long tradition in anthropology, which can be traced at least back to Franz Boas's "On Alternating Sounds" (published in the *American Anthropologist* in 1889), that the anthropologist should be wary of his or her own "sound-blindness," or the "inability to perceive the subtleties and actual semantics of the speech, the cultural sounds, he was hearing" in another culture.[2] Learning how to "listen" to the sounds we ourselves produce as we interpret other cultures is one of the difficult lessons Boon teaches in this essay, and recognizing the fundamental hybridity of any effort to comprehend "culture" is another.

Boon achieves this teaching by way of a rhetorical performance that is self-consciously marked in the published version of the lecture he delivered at Irvine, but we can hardly capture the vitality of that lecture, as it involved Boon's readings in different languages, dialects, and accents in live voice and from audio recordings. In such a performance, Boon embodied (disembodied?) the postmodern teacher who challenges repeatedly the presence of his institutional authority.

Williams, Rabine, and Boon deal variously with ways contemporary culture colonizes the postmodern subject. Cultural studies is for many inextricably related to, for some indistinguishable from, colonial and postcolonial studies. What was once termed "the critical study of colonial discourse" continues to shape cultural studies, attentive to the subtleties by which contemporary cultural powers transform individuals into "subjects" of new regimes. Focusing on more traditionally recognizable colonial and imperial histories in Africa and the Caribbean, Suzanne Gearhart adds to this work by insisting that the critique of imperialism by cultural studies take into account the psychoanalytic processes of internalization by which imperial power legitimates itself and colonized subjects may resist it.

Criticizing Frantz Fanon's work for lacking such a psychoanalytical dimension, she proposes the work of Albert Memmi, especially *The Colonizer and the Colonized* (1957), as a better model for contemporary cultural critics. Adding this important psychoanalytical dimension to our criticism, Gearhart is able to explain why cultural studies remains interested in colonialism and imperialism long after they have been nominally disestablished. Because the psychic effects of colonial domination on both the colonizer and the colonized continue to shape their respective understandings of social reality long after colonialism has formally "ended," then cultural critics may justifiably continue to speak of the need for "decolonization" in independent states.

Gearhart's revival of Memmi's significance for contemporary cultural studies also involves Memmi's recognition that colonialism itself relies on the sorts of *métissage* and *créolisation* that are sometimes unreflectively celebrated by contemporary cultural critics. Gearhart argues that Memmi helps us distinguish between the sorts of cultural hybridity that maintain colonial rule in both the state and the subaltern's psyche and those forms of hybridity that may well resist and ultimately transvalue such social psychologies. The postcolonial project must, then, not only complete the work of decolonizing subjugated nations but add to it the task of decolonizing the subjected citizens (or "citizen-subjects").

Mark Poster provides an appropriate conclusion to this collection of essays, reconsidering the implications of the new cultural and social changes that have in part motivated critical theory and cultural studies in the scholarly discipline of history. Poster's reconsideration of historiography in terms of the new forces of our postmodern cultural situation is unusual among historians, because they have traditionally relied on the apparent self-evidence of their subjects and objects of study. But just as the presumed objectivity of historical data has been challenged by modern historians, so the supposedly discrete and autonomous agent of history (and historical authorship) has been challenged by postmodern theories.

Taking one of the few recent efforts by historians to contend with this postmodern challenge, Appleby, Hunt, and Jacob's *Telling the Truth About History,* Poster shows how these historians caricature the postmodern theories derived from Foucault and Derrida. Trying to negotiate the equally unacceptable extremes of "absolute truth" and "postmodern relativism," the authors offer a "practical realism" that Poster considers inadequate to the multiple realities of our postmodern condition. Poster's effective defense of Foucault and Derrida against misreadings by Appleby, Hunt, and Jacob also helps historicize the work of these theorists in terms of recent intellectual debates, including Derrida's own turn to a more explicitly political position.

Reading carefully Derrida's *Specters of Marx* (1993) as a critical response to the conservative triumphalism of works like Francis Fukuyama's *The End of History and the Last Man* (1992), Poster shows how postmodern theory, at least as it is represented by Derrida's work, aligns itself with the Marxist project of emancipation and more recent theories of "radical democracy." In both respects, Poster argues, Derrida refutes the charges of "relativism" and "nihilism" leveled at postmodern theory and articulates a political position that has a venerable tradition of radical praxis and the potential for coalitions with contemporary feminisms, cultural studies, and ethnic and minority discourses.

Concluding that "the postmodern world will be one of multiple realities, virtual realities, little narratives, cyberorganisms, nonlinearities," Poster challenges historians to reconceive of their discipline in light of such changes to the object of study. Recognizing that the individual subjects constituted by these new realities will be unavoidably complex, multiple, and hybridized subjectivities, occupying on any day multiple identities and in a lifetime a dizzying myriad of subject-positions, Poster also challenges historians to develop methods of representing history that are more adequate to this lived experience.

Poster's appeal to other historians applies as well to the audience of scholars we hope to reach with this volume. We have the good fortune of knowing that those reading these essays are likely to be multidisciplinary, polyglot, hybridized intellectuals whose own work will provide added support for the arguments offered here. It is appropriate we conclude this collection with Mark Poster's enthusiasm for the emancipatory challenges and promises of the new age, even as we share his recognition of the many dangers that face intellectuals as they try to retheorize their pedagogical and scholarly work in an age of rapidly changing social, economic, technological, and cultural conditions.

Readers of this volume will have to judge for themselves the validity of our hypothesis that these essays represent the various ways in which critical theory has been transformed in recent years by its encounter with cultural studies. We who have experienced the full four-year process during which this research project developed from basic disagreements over topic and method to the engaged essays in this collection can say confidently that we have been significantly influenced and changed by the scholarly and political work of cultural studies.

[handwritten margin note: Critical Theory & Cultural Studies]

NOTES

1. Jean-François Lyotard, *The Postmodern Condition*, trans. Geoff Bennington and Brian Massumi (Minneapolis: University of Minnesota Press, 1984), 31–34.

2. See Eric Sundquist, *To Wake the Nations: Race in the Making of American Literature* (Cambridge: Harvard University Press, 1993), 5–6, for a more developed account of Boas's critique of "alternating sounds."

Foundations of Diversity:
Thinking the University in a Time of Multiculturalism

David Lloyd

In a brief but suggestive essay, Jürgen Habermas has analyzed the crisis of the university in Germany in terms of a discourse on "the idea of the university" and its loss of relevance in the face of the increasing differentiations that follow scientific rationality.[1] But strikingly, the crisis of the university as it has manifested itself recently in the U.S.A. has been cast in terms of the debate around Western culture and multiculturalism, rather than in relation to the universities' increasing subordination to the needs of the state's military-industrial and corporate complexes—a subordination that indeed profoundly affects the traditional autonomy of the university. Rather than argue that the public focus on multiculturalism represents, as it doubtless may, a noisy displacement of attention from crucial shifts in the educational sector, I want to add the different claim that simultaneous with this shift, and as another aspect of the present stage of capitalist rationalization, the debates around multiculturalism do engage and are symptomatic of a more profound educational and social crisis than can be articulated simply within the logic of rationalization. This involves my claiming, against Habermas to some extent, that the "idea" of the university, though conceived in slightly different terms than he elaborates from within the German tradition, continues to organize crucial social functions: precisely those over which conservative ideologues are so exercised. Those functions involve the formation not simply of citizens for the political sphere but of subjects capable of transferring from one sphere to another within the complex differentiations of capitalist societies. Later in the essay, and by way of Kant's foundational essay on the university, *The Conflict of the Faculties*, I argue that it is in its very differentiation *from* other social spheres that the liberal educational apparatus functions *with* them, and that this is quite distinct from the oppositional, utopian function that is for Habermas the "idea of the university." I also argue that the possibility of a radical version of "multiculturalism" can interrupt the functioning of the university and by extension the educational apparatus as a whole in ways that have important implications for fundamental elements of modern political subjectivity.[2]

This essay can be no more than a gesture toward rethinking the foundation or idea of the university for a multicultural society, a gesture aimed at achieving the disequilibrium of all those singular terms rather than the elegance of finality. I begin by discussing one highly contested gesture of intervention in the curricular, pedagogical, and disciplinary structure of a university, namely the institution of the American Cultures Breadth Requirement at the University of California at Berkeley, with which I was practically involved as a member of the Committee on Education and Ethnic Diversity. Taking the evident conceptual and practical limitations of that measure as a starting point, I use that very situated intervention as a means to elaborate the ideological and practical constraints that constitute the apparent parameters of institutional transformation within the present structure of the university. Holding in mind these parameters, which are effectively the university's ethical self-representation or sense of mission, I seek to explore how this ethical purpose, specifically its role in producing citizens over and above the functional production of trained professionals, determines the limits of any multicultural intervention but also produces a continually destabilizing excess of multicultural projects.[3] Finally, I suggest some theoretical considerations for dislodging the ethical and therefore political assumptions that underlie and hamper such interventions, in the hope of making space for a more radical set of multicultural projects.

I

The history of the American Cultures Breadth Requirement (ACBR) at Berkeley is fairly simple and probably analogous to that of similar measures elsewhere. Principally in response to the pressure of students for greater intellectual diversity, in faculty as well as curricula, a pressure that had been strategically applied by continuing to mobilize the political energy of the divestment campaign of the mid-1980s, the administration and the Academic Senate appointed a Committee on Education and Ethnic Diversity. The committee, chaired by the anthropologist William Simmons, was charged with considering appropriate measures to respond pedagogically to the increased ethnic diversity of the student body. As may become clearer later, the committee was already significantly contained in scope by being focused on the pedagogical rather than either the hiring or research agenda of the university. Nonetheless, it was clearly composed of faculty and student representatives who were from the outset committed to introducing measures designed to address to some extent the general indifference of departments to issues of racialization and ethnic differentiation in American history and culture. In many respects, this clear commitment at least to reform provides for a valuable case history of debates and outcomes within the left-to-liberal grouping of proponents of multiculturalism in some form. I want to focus on the differences that emerged in thinking through the logic of a possible requirement, differences at once political and academic, but will sketch first the general ground of agreement within which those differences emerged.

There was extensive discussion as to the parameters of the requirement, but several guiding principles emerged early on: that it should not be an "Ethnic Studies requirement," both because that would create appalling staffing problems for the relevant departments and because we wanted a requirement that would effect changes in departmental teaching across the campus; that it should be comparative (a formulation to be discussed further below); that it should focus on the main "minority" groups as currently defined (a commitment that met, as we shall see, with profound opposition); that it should foster and would require interdisciplinary and team-taught courses. Some of this thinking was of course designed to use the committee's deliberations to move beyond our narrowly pedagogical charge and to use curricular demands to effect, however indirectly, changes in the research and hiring goals of departments.

It is important to stress, all the more since one of the strategies of opponents of the requirement is to term it the American Cultures *course*, that what was finally recommended was not *a single and uniform course*, but *a flexible requirement* fulfillable in many ways, including within the structure of many existing majors—i.e., it can double with another major requirement, such as the English "Cultural Varieties," or can be used simultaneously to fulfill a breadth requirement, e.g., sociology or humanities for engineers. Its official title is the American Cultures Breadth Requirement: it was designed to be integrated with the existing structure of Berkeley's undergraduate education, much as is the assumption that a breadth of knowledge across disciplines is necessary, or that all students should have a knowledge of American history and institutions, be literate (take Composition 1A and 1B), and be capable of some quantitative reasoning. Tailored as it is to existing structures, a requirement that addresses cultural differences remains peculiar in that it cuts across disciplines formed from an assumed universal-ist perspective, rather than asking merely for an acquaintance with other, no less discrete disciplines, a point to whose larger implications I will return. To call the Requirement "a course" or "the course" misrepresents it, furthering the assumption that a single course is being demanded in order to transmit or impose a single ideological version of ethnic relations. What we aimed for instead was a requirement that would have a definitive if indirect effect on Berkeley's conception of its educational role, within and across departments, by insisting that the courses be furnished from within or between those departments. In this respect, it differed in conception from more publicized measures taken, for example, at Michigan and UC Santa Cruz, as it differed from the CIV requirement virtually contemporaneously instituted at Stan-ford. It was neither, on the one hand, a single course or set of courses on eth-nicity or race, largely independent of and correspondingly uninfluential on existing departments, nor a move to supplement courses on Western civi-lization with readings from non-Western writers. Hence, of course, much resistance from faculty centered on this apparent encroachment on and attempt to redefine disciplinary concerns.

No less than the principle of seeking to transform the curriculum of existing majors, the principle of comparison was never really at issue on the committee; it was rapidly assumed as fundamental because we all agreed that students—and faculty—needed a deeper sense of historical interactions among different ethnic groups as these have affected the formation of Amer-ica. There were different emphases, however, whose political significance is crucial. Some felt that a comparative approach would further the realization that American culture integrates many different cultures and would place more emphasis on positive contributions by minorities. Others, including myself, felt that the importance of a comparative approach was that it encouraged focus not simply on the different kinds of cultural and material disadvantage faced by various groups historically and currently, but on the ways in which those differences are constituted historically and actually in the relations between groups. Such an approach might better have been described as *differential*, engaging both the persistence of power and class differentials among ethnic groups and the the processes through which racialized social formations are continually reproduced.

Significantly, however, the term was evidently at odds with the "com-mon sense" of university discourse and had an effect of "defamiliarization" that was persistently resisted even in committee. Whereas the notion of "comparison" has historically been congruent with the ultimately integrative function of the disciplines, the concept of differentiation or of differential studies insists rather on the relations of nonequivalence that structure social processes. Accordingly, though these differences of opinion affected the tone of the report, there is no doubt that it was the former emphasis that was encapsulated in what became the virtual motto of the recommendations, *e pluribus unum*. In other words, the social model inscribed in the requirement was one of cultural pluralism rather than cultural difference.

The other major point of contention, which led to the defeat of the recommendations at the first Academic Senate discussion of them in Spring 1988, concerned the explicit inclusion of white ethnics or European Americans. The first report (1988) called for the comparative study of the four major minority groups, and remarked that this would obviously involve studying their interactions with the European Americans. It also required only two groups as the basis for comparison. The redrawing of the recommendations in the following year concentrated largely on this issue (and was as much a matter of rephrasing as anything else) in response to faculty opposition. The opposition was tactical, succeeding in exploiting the self-interest and, indeed, self-regard of white faculty, but it touched on a crucial issue to which I will return since it affects profoundly the fundamental structures of the university in its self-conception: the mobilization of white anxiety that the longstanding identification of white privilege with ethical status has been fundamentally challenged and reframed as a contradiction by what we might term, in the broadest sense, "critical race theory."[4] For this reason, the opposition of students to the explicit inclusion of European ethnic groups, which they saw as an attempt to dilute the requirement and to reduce its potential for analyzing racial oppression rather than espousing ethnic diversity or pluralism, was both philosophically and politically well grounded. In the end, more or less all the groups involved in our discussions accepted the political necessity of including Euro-Americans explicitly, though it meant increasing the number of required groups to three. The requirement would probably not have got through the Academic Senate without that wording; however, to have maintained the basis of comparison as two groups would have permitted, if not encouraged, the very intellectual habit that the requirement was shaped against: the conception of ethnic interrelations around a white-other axis. In keeping with the *e pluribus unum* tendency signaled above, the main effect of this amendment was to institute a principle of equivalence among ethnic groups, including that oxymoronic category "white ethnics." It is precisely that principle of equivalence that grounds the pluralist version of American culture and history.

One primary ground of defense of the requirement, which regarded its ethical ends as in conformity with those of the university in general, was that it might answer to some extent the often-expressed need of students of all ethnicities to know more of each other's cultures and accordingly to shape a more tolerant population. Such a project is no more than an extension of one of the traditional roles of universities and schools, namely the formation of citizens able to participate fully and responsibly in society. This apparently minimal goal, which could be accepted even by those who fear that too much emphasis on non-Western cultures will undermine the Western institutions of the state, could be accepted precisely because of its merely supplementary role in the larger context of university policy.[5] Contained within this conception of the university's function and hampered by the contradiction between the desire to influence or even "infect" the existing disciplines, and a consequent parasitic dependence on those disciplines, the ACBR was in fact captured both by the political exigencies its passage necessitated and by the limitations the fundamentally liberal values that framed it presupposed. Indeed, the exigencies both reinforced the limitations and were produced by them, insofar as both support for and opposition to the requirement were almost entirely framed within liberal discursive parameters. Each of the objections, no less than the formulations and reformulations of the report, are symptoms of those constraints. For neither the immediate structure of pedagogical relations nor the larger social ends of the university embedded in its founding presuppositions could be challenged. It is to each of those levels of the university—the classroom and its mission—that I turn in the following sections.

Summarily, we may say that until very recently, until, that is, the advent of what has been termed the "Western Culture Debate," the American university had tended unquestioningly to shape its curricula around an assumption of Western cultural centrality. Although culture is the determining domain here, it includes the sciences inasmuch as these are defined by priorities and procedures that are Western in formation and history.[6] The university is modeled accordingly on a European system that promoted not so much a mono-ethnic culture as, in conformity with the longer history of state-formations, a universalist culture which, though mediated through national differentiations, is assumed to supercede local or ethnic values or knowledges. The disciplinary structure of the university further reinforces this model by dividing the sciences from the humanities and from the social sciences, a division that corresponds to a postenlightenment (that is, Western and modern) division of a universal human reason into "faculties," and in turn into the larger differentiation of spheres of practice within Western society: the technological/economic, the political, and the cultural. The disciplinary as well as the curricular structure of the university is profoundly "Western" and conforms in all respects to the West's notions of modernity, academic objectivity, relevance, and hierarchy of bodies of knowledge. In this sense, the terms "Western," "European," and "white" all designate in fact not merely another ethnicity, equivalent to that of racialized minorities, but a principle fundamentally antagonistic to the social formations it has designated differentially as "ethnic." That is to say, the antagonism between the university structure (or indeed the structure of the state) and ethnic minorities is not simply a confrontation between the disavowed ethnocentricity of the dominant culture and the cultures of the dominated, but actively and continually produces irreconcilable categories. Ethnic and minority positions as such always emerge in differential relation to the unifying tendencies of the state and its apparatuses, and this differential formation of positions produces the contradictions in which the pluralist model founders: the *plures* out of which the *unum* should emerge are in fact constitutively, not merely accidentally, antagonistic to it.[7]

The minimal but common pluralist solution of adding a dose or two of ethnic materials to the present disciplines' curricula to make them a little more hospitable to ethnic minorities is neither adequate nor able to prevent an effect of "excess" from breaking the limits of pluralism. For the remedy is designed to alter little except on the surface: in this familiar situation, by no means confined to academic spheres, a minority's culture is skimmed off and in one way or another consumed and celebrated while the social and economic conditions that provide the "life-world" of those cultural forms are destroyed. Minority students' assimilation to Western norms would merely be a little cushioned by the attention given to "their cultures" in academic reservations—curricular and institutional. But the important moment of contradiction, which prevents this narrative from achieving closure, lies in the recognition that in various forms and manners, cultures relegated to marginality, residuality, "underdevelopment"—in short, non-Western cultures—can contain the basis for a very radical critique of the Western cultural norms by which they are judged. Just as civil rights-based affirmative action has radically changed the demographics of the university in ways that enable challenges, rather than merely assimilation, to its fundamental structures, so the "intellectual affirmative action" of bringing even a minimal representation of minority cultural works into the curriculum produces effects that exceed the assimilative ends of pluralism.

II

The foregoing arguments call for some provisional reflections on the implications of a more radical version of multiculturalism. In this section I want to broach the question of how "the transformation of hegemony" can take place in the university by way of the very unilaterality of its declaration of universality.[8] The obligation of the university, on the basis of the liberal democratic values that are intrinsic to its legitimation, is to assimilate individuals into a single culture. As Martin Carnoy has argued, this process involves at once an extension of that culture's hegemony and the production of the terms through which its unilaterality is to be challenged by subordinated cultures.[9] The resistance of subordinated cultures to such institutions is articulated through their very production as subordinate or intellectually marginal by the hegemonic assimilation. That is, the university, as the state-formation in general, continually constitutes its minorities as different from its cultural norms. In the daily life of university culture, the resistance this produces is generally envisaged as failure, lack of adaptation, or inadequacy until such a point as the present, when a combination of numbers and political articulateness on the part of some faculty and students transforms dispersed resentment into a concerted demand for rights.[10] Nonetheless, the intrinsic limitations of measures like the ACBR signal the need to go beyond a discourse of rights and representation to a more fundamental critique of the function and form of the university and its disciplines as critical ideological state apparatuses. Minority discourse and the theoretical work of people of color accordingly present a critical challenge to the representative functions of the university at all levels, in the composition of the faculty and student bodies, the classroom, curricula formation, and the structure of disciplines.

This challenge to the dominant paradigm manifests itself insistently in the classroom. The various terms that have been evoked, from all sides, to deal with conflicts around race and ethnicity, sexuality, the structure of the curriculum, or the bias of given methods and assumptions, indicate the extent to which the multicultural classroom points beyond the liberal paradigm of proportional representation within a single model for representation itself. What the multicultural classroom plays out is something more problematic than a question of equal access or inclusion. On what can loosely be described as the left, unease is expressed in a suspicion of essentialism. Resistance to one or another paradigm in the name of, say, a black, chicana/o, or lesbian perspective is seen to run the risk of reducing all members of those categories to identity and losing specificity, even in the name of specificity. Diana Fuss's "Essentialism in the Classroom" is an excellent summary statement of this position, where the interventions of apparently marginalized students appear as effective, authoritative interruptions of an uninterrogated decorum of the classroom:

It is the unspoken law of the classroom not to trust those who cannot cite experience as the indisputable grounds of their knowledge. Such unwritten laws pose perhaps the most serious threat to classroom dynamics in that they breed suspicion amongst those inside the circle and guilt (sometimes anger) amongst those outside the circle. In its most extreme incarnation, the guilt of the outsiders is exploited by the insiders to keep everyone in line—that is, to regulate and to police group behavior. . . . When provoking guilt in "the enemy" becomes the prime motivation for one's politics, we have to begin to question what negative effects such a project might possibly have, especially in the classroom. The tendency to psychologize and to personalize questions of oppression, *at the expense of* strong materialist analyses of the structural and institutional bases of exploitation, poses one such undesirable effect.[11]

I will come back momentarily to a "materialist" analysis of the dynamics of the classroom that this passage overlooks and later to an analysis of the assumptions about the place and intent of the invocation of "experience" implied here. Liberal and conservative arguments, in keeping with the historical function of education as an apparatus of expanding and consolidating nation-states, render such conflicts either by metaphors of localism and inadequate development that reduce the significance of such interventions, or in terms of a correlative suspicion of "relativism." This latter term, which can be expressed as the dissolution of presumed regulative concepts, emerges when a proliferation of cultural perspectives ceases to be containable within the significantly entitled "marketplace of ideas," wherein differing perspectives represent exchangeable equivalents or options subject to an identical law of evaluation, and instead produces incommensurability, heterogeneity, and nonequivalence.

But the question of "relativism" draws attention to the fact that, beyond all the terms generally used to characterize the conflicts, what is at stake is precisely the nonequivalence of given groups or subjects as opposed to the production of equivalence or identity through the geography of the classroom. In the traditional classroom, the teacher occupies the apex of a virtual pyramid and is the point of orientation for students not only as learners but as subjects in formation. The importance of the predominance of white males in such positions lies not in any particular quality inherent in whiteness or maleness, but in the white male's assumption of a position unmarked sexually and racially. The white male as teacher or the teacher as white male accordingly comes to stand for the formal political or civic Subject against the particularities and insufficiencies of other, marked positions. His function is to produce the disposition to disinterest and formality in his students by representing it to them. The play or exchange of multiple perspectives is always regulated by the ideal of what Kimberle Crenshaw has termed "perspectivelessness," located in the teacher as disinterested Subject.[12] This is, as against Fuss, "the unwritten law of the classroom" and constitutes its virtually ineradicable "common sense." The production of such a disposition, however, depends upon the subordination of bodily particularities, upon a certain disembodiment of both teacher and knowledge so that identification can take place. Such a regulative disembodiment is the fundamental "essentialism of the classroom" that guides critiques such as Fuss's.

To displace such concepts, we have to think of the classroom as a crucial transitional site in the movement of individual subjects from ethnic cultures to minority status, as an institution aimed at producing the Subject at the same time as it produces the "local" or "particular" as its residue. The classroom is a focal point for the experience of assimilation and marginalization simultaneously, since marking happens only in relation to the unmarked. Resistance that can be typed at a primary level as essentialism or relativism must therefore be reconceived as differential and as reinvoking the body in the place of disembodiment. In this way, the body of the white male becomes an issue, where it formerly functioned as the sign of its own disappearance. For this reason, of course, the most recurrently problematic classroom issues are those concerning ethnicity or race and sexuality, since these issues thematize the body of the teacher. Resistance in the classroom that invokes identification with a minoritized group is effective precisely because it raises to consciousness the partiality of the white male body rather than representing, for example, Latina lesbian identity, which in itself remains an instructively problematic claim. For even in the act of claiming a certain representativeness, it problematizes the very disembodiment that representation requires. It draws attention at once to the processes of formation that produce the teacher as Subject and to those that produce the ethnic subject as minority.

If such dynamics have the effect of displacing the teacher from the site of truth and representation, they also give rise to the notion of a certain *constitutive* ignorance on the part of the teacher that is both a disability and a possibility. That is to say, the common ignorance of the teacher with regard to particular ethnic cultures is not merely contingent and to be overcome by study, but is intrinsic to the formational disposition of the teacher as Subject, which finds expression in but is not limited to the canon or the standard curriculum. The multicultural classroom demands in effect that that constitutive ignorance, as well as contingent ones, be acknowledged and brought into play in the critique of educational formation and in the pursuit of a differential understanding of both ignorance and knowledge. This goes beyond the common liberal attempt to democratize the classroom by confessions of professorial limitation, as it makes the formations, and not just the personalities—authoritarian or otherwise—of teacher and students objects of critical discourse. But it also implies that "experience" is not merely a knowledge or attitude brought to the classroom, that the classroom is itself a crucial site of experience and, moreover, one constitutive of the categories of experience.[13] To this point we will return later.

The radical multicultural classroom is equally to be conceived as a space in which the apparent contradiction between particularity and theory dissolves. This remark is to be taken as critical both of those theorists who see particularity as reductive and as politically and pedagogically disintegrative, and of those who see theory as a reduction of the particular to the universal—as indeed an idealist theory would be. For idealist theory seeks to furnish transcendental grounds for its concepts, and after this fashion the university divides the objects of its knowledge into the quasi-permanent or canonical form of the disciplines. Within each discipline, and within each disciplinary classroom, representative objects of knowledge, including the multiple perspectives of students, are to be subordinated to regulative concepts. But precisely because theory—which we might usefully conceive as a concern with the regulative ends of given practices—is thus bound up in the movement of the university toward the universality it claims, because theory attempts to subsume particulars into universals by grasping specific instances formally and gathering them into concepts, passage through the theoretical will be indispensable to any disestablishment of the university that is not merely rejectionist. That is, the critique of individual practices and sites of practice within the university has to be thought of in relation to the ends that name those practices as either normative or deviant. The interruptive negation of classroom dynamics by the minority student becomes from this perspective not an appeal to raw or unreflective experience but an historically located articulation of a contradiction that emerges in the very formation of the subject as at once particular and representative.

What this means is that recognizing the assimilative function of the university at all levels requires rethinking the status of the "particular" in relation to theory. The residual instance of particularity that it is the logic of all assimilation to produce, whether the recalcitrant student body or differing bodies of knowledge that resist representation, becomes a crucial theoretical locus of intervention. And here it is not a question of what appears as merely the inert resistance of the object, but of a redisposition of the relation between objects of knowledge and the concept of the Subject. For where, in Kantian terms, the concept represents the "unity of the manifold,"and either regulates or constitutes the internal relations of the elements of the perceptual "manifold," the task of a critical theory is to give back mobility, reformulating the elements that constitute any "given" concept or body of knowledge so that its content differs, and rethinking the relation of the elements within their conceptual matrices so that the differential significance of their subordination registers. In the pedagogical sphere, the "essentialism of the classroom" has here a crucial role to play so long as the bodies in question are thought differentially rather than essentially. That is, in relation to the disposition of the subject formed through the representative function of the teacher, the sexually or racially "other" body is seen at once as a negatively marked residue and as a site of complexly resistant formations constituted by pedagogical practice itself. Thought in terms of differentiation rather than identifications, the incommensurability of bodies in the classroom has the double effect of returning the formalism that protects even the critical Subject to its material grounds in the geography of social relations, and of transforming the conceptual field by enforcing a constantly adjusting alignment of perspectives and priorities into new dispositions. The frequent response "That's not how it looks from here" comes then to transform both the subjects and objects of pedagogy, principally by taking the classroom experience itself as an object of inquiry and refusing to reify texts or concepts as the objects of a neutral method or theoretical approach.[14]

In the next section, I want to explore some of the political implications of these arguments in a fashion that will tend to disturb the concept of the political itself. Traditionally the function of pedagogical practice and disciplines has been to stabilize subjectification and the objects and modes of inquiry respectively. The vehement conservative reaction to challenges to the traditional authority of the teacher and to genuinely interdisciplinary work is encoded in terms of respect and standards, but is nonetheless an acknowledgment of the potential force of transformations whose outlines are only just emerging. What I want to suggest, through a brief genealogy of the foundational assumptions and ends of the Western university, is that such reactions emerge within the terms of a formation of "power/knowledge" that the dynamics of multiculturalism have thrown into question at a moment when the rationale of the formation has become virtually exhausted. For as we shall see, the rationale for the autonomy of faculties was itself originally political, attempting to secure a space for free inquiry within more or less autocratic states and to permit critical thought outside the limits of dogmatic religion. This formal autonomy of the university, like that of aesthetic culture, comes gradually to have a crucial if covert political significance for the emergent bourgeois state, one that is seen most clearly in the university's role in forming citizens. An autonomy whose initial function was to preserve critical thinking against one state form has now become the alibi of subordination to another state form, and critical thinking an observation of disciplinary formalities. Objectivity becomes the code word for a positivistic acceptance of the status quo and the recirculation of unquestioned and immobilized objects of knowledge. The transformation of bodies and modes of knowledge that is taking place outside or across the traditional disciplines is a scandal to the self-evident truths of such objectivity and is accordingly denied "scientific" status. The new constructions of knowledge deny the "common sense" that guides the division of the faculties within a regulative concept of human identity and refuse to see the equivalence of Subjects as the highest ethical moment. They challenge fundamentally the formal basis on which representative democratic states claim universality and pose the differentiation of the material construction and consequences of such concepts as race, gender, and sexuality in place of the multicultural pluralism offered by the university. Not least, they challenge the fundamental differentiation of spheres that constitutes the space of education as apart from the economic and the political, a challenge that leads me, at the limits of the essay, to propose the need for thinking the possibility of a "postpolitical" moment. By this I do not mean "the end of ideology" or, for that matter, of history, but the need to think through the implications of a general redistribution of practices in late capitalism that has profoundly disrupted given assumptions about the inside of the academy and the outside of political activism.

III

At the beginning of this essay, I suggested that Immanuel Kant's late essay, *The Conflict of the Faculties*, regarded by some as the unacknowledged blueprint of the modern university,[15] suggests a subtly different conception of the university than is inscribed in Habermas's somewhat utopian understanding of it as an exemplary community. *The Conflict of the Faculties* opens with a significant analogy that implies that different conception:

> Whoever it was that first hit on the notion [*den Gedanken*] of a university and proposed that a public institution of this kind be estab-

lished, it was not a bad idea to handle the entire content of learning (really, the thinkers devoted to it) by *mass production,* so to speak—by a division of labor [*Es war kein übeler Einfall . . . den ganzen Inbegriff der Gelehrsamkeit (eigentlich die derselben gewidmeten Köpfe) gleichsam fabrikenmässig, durch Vertheilung der Arbeiten zu behandeln*].[16]

The analogy is significant both for the logic embedded in it formally and for its descriptive content. The fiction entertained here of a punctual moment of foundation for the university asks us to engage in a thinking [*Gedanken*] that is in fact governed by the ends rather than the origins of the institution and that attributes its actual disposition to a certain logic rather than to the contingencies of history.[17] Accordingly, the logic of the analogy between the university and a factory, between the division of its faculties and the efficient deployment of labor, is at once revealed as a crucial historical index and simultaneously dehistoricized or naturalized. Historically, Kant—fully conscious, as the second essay emphasizes, of his moment as one of transition from autocratic states to republican constitutions—presciently grasps the form of the university as he is *re*thinking it in its relation to the larger "organism" of an emergent bourgeois society. I take this notion of the organic society from Kant's own description in the *Critique of Judgement*:

> Thus in the case of a complete transformation, recently undertaken, of a great people into a state [i.e., the American Revolution], the word *organization* has frequently, and with much propriety, been used for the constitution of the legal authorities and even of the entire body politic. For in a whole of this kind certainly no member should be a mere means, but should also be an end, and, seeing that he contributes to the possibility of the entire body, should have his position and function defined by the idea of the whole.[18]

What is said here of individual subjects holds equally for the spheres in which they act: the relative autonomy of each sphere as an end in itself "contributes to the possibility of the entire body." It is not simply that the university functions like a factory, but that both constitute relatively autonomous domains whose differentiation as social spaces within the larger organization of society simultaneously requires the commensurability or analogy of their forms.[19] Without such commensurability, the passage of the increasingly formalized subject between domains would be attended with precarious inconsistency. This is in large part what is meant by a process of rationalization whose simultaneous but by no means contradictory aspect is atomization. The same formal rationality is required of the subject of judgment in the university as of the subject of abstract labour coevally emerging within political economy. The ends of an identical reason govern the division of spheres and objects of practice and furnish the rationale for the redisposition of the human being as Subject.

I emphasize this analogical structure from the outset, as Kant does in his essay, for two reasons: one, it allows us to emphasize the latent assumption of the possibility of a transfer between discrete domains of society instituting a principle of equivalence; and two, in formally embedding that possibility in the very structure of its logic, the passage opens simultaneously the reactive and the projective dimensions of Kant's thinking on the university. For, as is well known, *The Conflict of the Faculties* is a reaction to the threat of censorship by the Prussian state of Kant's essay on religion, *Religion Within the Limits of Mere Reason* (1793), and argues for the autonomy of a critical philosophy in relation to the major faculties (theology, law, medicine), all of which have an instrumental relation to the state and for which, in effect, philosophy in its very noninstrumentality becomes the "censor." At the same time, however, Kant's essay, by conforming to and expounding the logic of an "idea" of the university, exceeds by far the occasion of its publication in order to foresee the forms and the ends of the modern institution of higher education.[20] As a "blueprint" for the university, not merely a description of it, *The Conflict of the Faculties* undertakes a delicate negotiation between what a still-autocratic state allows and what can already be envisaged: it is in this sense no accident that the second essay, on law, engages with the emergence of a republican constitution in France and its impact for thinking the universal historical ends of humanity. For what Kant is proposing in the idea he sketches of the university is both, once more, an analogical "constitutional republic" of the intellect and the form of university that would be required of such a republic. Indeed, the very impossibility of realizing either seems to accentuate the clarity of conception of what *might be*.

For it is clear from the rhetorical covertness and the irony with which Kant presents what would be otherwise quite radical propositions that his argument proceeds under the insurmountable constraints of the state. In what must be the most delicately poised ever of worlds turned upside down, philosophy, by virtue of its very ineffectiveness within the political sphere, is seen as the minor or inferior faculty, compared to others through which state power in its various domains of interest is communicated. But by virtue of precisely the same condition, philosophy is also seen as crucial to the efficacy of those faculties, for it continually tests the truth of their propositions. And while in the first instance, "the faculty whose function is only to look after the interests of science is called lower because it may use its own judgment

about what it teaches" (25–27), as Kant's argument progresses, that autonomy of judgment becomes with increasing explicitness the grounds for the
primacy of philosophy:

> It is absolutely essential that the learned community at the university
> also contain a faculty that is independent of the government's com-
> mand with regard to its teachings; one that, having no commands to
> give, is free to evaluate everything, and concerns itself with the inter-
> ests of the sciences, that is, with the truth: one in which reason is
> authorized to speak out publicly. For without a faculty of this kind, the
> truth would not come to light (and this would be to the government's
> own detriment); but reason is by its nature free and admits of no com-
> mand to hold something as true (no imperative "Believe!" [*crede*] but
> only a free "I believe" [*credo*]).   (27–29)

A little later, the function of the faculty of philosophy attains its explicit primacy:

> Its function in relation to the three higher faculties is to control [*con-
> trolliren*] them and, in this way, be useful to them, since truth (the
> essential and first condition of learning in general) is the main thing,
> whereas the utility the higher faculties promise the government is of
> secondary importance.   (45)

The logical turn thus far is almost literally deconstructive in its delineation
and inversion of a hierarchical opposition. It has, however, a constructive or,
better, constitutive end that turns on the concept of autonomy itself as this
logic governs, explicitly, the proposed autonomy of the university and of its
faculty of philosophy, and, implicitly, that of the enlightenment subject itself
as it is to be constituted by the university. This involves two substitutions.
The first is that of the state as an idea of reason for the state as an instrument
of arbitrary power with attendant institutional divisions. This substitution is
implicit in Kant's argument that the model of freedom philosophy provides
is superior for government itself to security based in the unquestionable
authority of a ruler:

> For the government may find the freedom of the philosophy faculty,
> and the increased insight gained from this freedom, a better means of
> achieving its ends than its own absolute authority.   (59)

The second, which follows from the substitution of the state as idea for the
state as absolute (but contingent), is the displacement of the arbitrary claims
of monarchical power by the claim that the ground of security is freedom.

This second substitution subtly moves philosophy from an advisory role within the autocratic state to a founding role for what is, in effect, to be an entirely reconstituted state. The perpetual conflict of the faculties is now rewritten as the motor of a process governed by the final end of human society rather than an irresolvable territorial dispute. Once again, it is in the analogy (with the political sphere this time) that the final significance of the claims for the university is embedded:

> So this antagonism, that is, this *conflict* of two parties united in [their striving toward] one and the same final end (*concordia discors, discordia concors*) is not a *war*, that is, not a dispute arising from conflicting final aims regarding the *Mine* and *Thine* of learning. And since, like the political Mine and Thine, this consists in *freedom and property*, with freedom necessarily preceding property as its condition, any right granted to the higher faculty entails permission for the lower faculty to bring its scruples about this right before the learned public.   *(59–61)*

This freedom that precedes property as its very condition is at once the freedom of subjects under a just political constitution *and* the self-regulating autonomy of the subject to whom property accrues, the subject of law and of enlightenment. Just as the autonomy of the philosophy faculty can only be guaranteed by a state that acknowledges the value of discursive freedoms, so also, and more profoundly as it turns out, philosophy provides the conditions for a political freedom predicated on this autonomy of the individual. This is so in a double sense: first, philosophy is exemplary in relation to the exercise of autonomy generally precisely because its critical interventions are ultimately subservient to the ends of the state; second, philosophy derives the primacy of freedom both from the pure forms of reason itself as universals and from what is designated in the second essay as universal history (141).[21] This corresponds to the divisions of the faculty itself between two departments:

> A department of *historical knowledge* (including history, geography, philology and the humanities, along with all the empirical knowledge contained in the natural sciences), and a department of *pure rational knowledge* (pure mathematics and pure philosophy, the metaphysics of nature and of morals).   *(45)*

Comprising what we would now generally term the humanities, Kant's "philosophy" is concerned not with the contingencies of instrumental state power but with the effects of human freedom as manifested in "historical knowledge," that is, with universal history as a progressive narrative predicated on reason. In effect, the two departments are reunited in a conception of the historical as the realization of the ends of human reason, as the synthesis of historical knowledge with "pure rational" knowledge.

As the second essay, "The Conflict of the Philosophy Faculty with the Faculty of Law," elaborates, the actual historical form of that synthesis is, for Kant in his moment, the French Revolution and the republican constitution that is its ideal: it is the event that universal history requires to point "to the disposition and capacity of the human race to be the cause of its own advance toward the better, and (since this should be the act of a being endowed with freedom), toward the human race as being the author of this advance" (151). In that sense, the advance is less important as actual and concrete than "as an intimation, a historical sign (*signum rememorativum, demonstrativum, prognostikon*) demonstrating the tendency of the human race viewed in its entirety" (151). It is, as the temporality of the historical sign suggests (*signum rememorativum, demonstrativum, prognostikon*), a representative moment in the fullest sense, instantiating a tendency of human nature that it at once recalls and prefigures. At the same time, however, the very precariousness and contingency of such an event gives back to philosophy its status as a kind of permanent instantiation of human ends, dependent on a logical rather than a contingent historical temporality:

> For such a phenomenon in human history *is not to be forgotten*, because it has revealed a tendency and faculty in human nature for improvement such that no politician, affecting wisdom, might have conjured out of the course of things hitherto existing, and one which nature and freedom alone, united in the human race in conformity with inner principles of right, could have promised. But so far as time is concerned, it can promise this only indefinitely and as a contingent event. *(159)*

In this reduction of the historically representative moment to "inner principles of right," Kant not only protects his own text from censorship, as a philosopher who as an "enlightener" risks being decried as a person "dangerous to the state," but also, beyond these contingent and prudent considerations, establishes philosophy—or the humanities—as the locus of exemplary representations (161). He retrieves, in effect, from the stymied and constrained situation of the critical philosopher in the autocratic state the very form in which that critical philosophy will become institutionalized for, and in a state newly conceived around, "freedom and property." On the already contested margins of the old state, and by the inversion of its protocols, the institutions of the new state become apprehensible. Hence the possibility of Kant's apparent prescience.

Kant's account of the faculty of philosophy assumes, if not its "privacy," at least its extreme separation from "the people, who are incompetent" [*das Volk*, "*welches aus Idioten besteht*"] and even from the "businessmen or technicians of learning" [*Geschäftsleute oder Werkkundige der Gelehrsamkeit*] who, as "tools of the government" [*Werkzeuge der Regierung*] must forget much they have learned philosophically in order to be able to fulfill their essentially conservative functions for the state (25). As tools, they are mere *means* in the machinery of state and therefore lack the autonomy given to members of a state organized on republican principles. The tendency of his argument, which is after all an attack on state censorship, is to give back to the philosopher a more public role through the "enlightenment of the masses," which consists in "the public instruction of the people in its duties and rights vis-à-vis the state to which they belong" (161). In the century following *The Conflict of the Faculties*, the function of the humanities in "public instruction" became not simply the fulfillment of this quite narrowly delimited task of citizen formation, but more complexly, and in line with Kant's larger argument, the representation of (in the fullest sense of the term) the exemplary subject whose simultaneous formality and autonomy make possible the individual's movement among the increasingly differentiated spheres of human society, and whose ethical disinterest makes the necessary conjunction of the individual's freedom and instrumentality under capitalism conceivable.

This function of education, and in particular of the university as its "highest" representation, is elaborated variously in different Western contexts throughout the nineteenth century and down to our own moment. The subsequent elaborations of the ethical ends of education by von Humboldt, Schleiermacher, Fichte, and others, cited and traced by Habermas down to the present debates on the German university, have influence on and counterparts in the British and American traditions, especially in the seminal work of Coleridge, Mill, Arnold, and Newman.[22] What I think needs to be emphasized here is that a close reading of Kant's argument allows us to see in these traditions a different logic than that assumed by Habermas, one that defines the "idea of the university" in crucially different terms. This is not to pose Kant as an authoritative source, but to trace in the form of his argument another function than that of pure origination or constitution that is embedded in the idea of foundation.

Habermas's guiding assumption is that the exemplary function of the university has been believed to lie in its embodiment of an ideal and, moreover, in a representative function by which its unity as a community and as an organic form prefigures an ideal lifeworld:

The functions the university fulfills for society must preserve an inner connection with the goals, motives and actions of its members. In this sense the university should institutionally embody, and at the same time motivationally anchor, a life form which is intersubjectively shared by its members, and which even bears an exemplary character. What since Humboldt has been called "the idea of the university" is the project of embodying an ideal life form. Moreover, this idea does not limit itself to one of the many particularized life forms of early bourgeois society, but—thanks to its intimate connection with science and truth—to something universal, something prior to the pluralism of social life forms.   *(3)*

Accordingly, once the high levels of differentiation and specialization of the modern university, particularly in the sciences, manifest themselves, the idea of a normative and unifying ideal permeating the institution as a whole becomes difficult to sustain (4). We can see, however, from reading Kant, that another understanding of the idea and function of the university is not only possible but necessary, even granting the desire of some thinkers to see the university as an exemplary community. For Kant, the issue at stake is precisely not the actual unity or community of the university, but the conflicts predicated on its internal differentiations and on its differentiation as a social sphere from other spheres. This notion of a constitutive differentiation is embedded in his founding analogy between the university and its divisions and the factory and the division of labor, and is sustained in his later analogy of the university with political society. And what is presumed in the analogy that founds the university as if it were merely a "thought" is the objective existence of other spheres through which the institution of the university gets its sense. It is in fact the increasing differentiation of modern society that gives the rationale for philosophy's production of the autonomous Subject as one whose capacity to judge is transferable from sphere to sphere. The unity of that Subject makes possible the presumptive universality of the narrative of modernity within which the circulations of scientific knowledge and rationality take place.[23]

In a context "nearer to home," if less insistently contemporary, John Dewey clearly grasped the fundamental relation between the unity of the subject and the ethical function of education. His essay on "Ethics and Education" (1903)[24] stresses that what constitutes the "scientific" is properly its method, as it involves the disposition of a subject who judges: "The generic propositions of science can take effect, in a word, only through the medium of the habits and impulsive tendencies of the one who judges. They have no *modus operandi* of their own" (40). This means that the distinction between the ethical and the scientific moments in the acts of the subject lies merely in the self-reflexivity of the former, in which "the judger is engaged in judging himself" (44). At the same time, however, this capacity for self-reflection as an ethical subject is inseparable from the foundation of the truth values of science. Just as much as ethics can be given a scientific foundation, science requires the ethical. These propositions are, for Dewey, connected to a fundamental "postulate of continuity of experience"(60). This postulate has a double bearing which in some senses makes explicit for us propositions only implicit in Kant. The first concerns the integration within a hierarchical frame of ethical and intellectual judgment:

> This principle, on the one hand, protects the integrity of the moral judgment, revealing its supremacy and the corresponding instrumental or auxiliary character of the intellectual judgment . . . and, upon the other, protects the moral judgment from isolation . . . bringing it into working relations of reciprocal assistance with all judgments about the subject-matter of experience, even those of the most markedly mechanical and physiological sort.   *(60)*

The second concerns what we have been calling the transferability of the subject through different spheres of practice: "Since human life is continuous, the possibility of using any one mode of experience to assist in the formation of any other is the ultimate postulate of *all* science—non-ethical and ethical alike" (56). This postulate allows for the unity of experience while at the same time assuring respect for the "*distinctive* traits of any type of experience"(56). That is, it preserves the differentiation of spheres while allowing for transfer between their domains.

As is well known, Dewey's whole philosophy of education is predicated on an organicist notion that extends from the individual child to society as a whole and includes the "intellectual whole" that constitutes the differentiated bodies of knowledge.[25] Within these assumptions, the "postulate of continuity of experience" takes on at once a temporal and a spatial axis. The formation of the subject is seen as a constant process of assimilation and sedimentation of knowledge and experience while the very continuity of that history, the identity of the intellectual processes involved in discrete judgments, permits the passage of the subject entire from one sphere of society to another: each domain of human practice redeploys the same capacities so that the subject can be formed within the distinct institutions of education for practice in other, equally discrete domains of society.[26] The process of formation, indeed, requires the forgetting of accumulated experience as part of its socialization within that complex whole, so that much of human behavior may proceed unconsciously or by habit:

> As physical science has brought about an organization of the physical world along with an organization of practical habits of dealing with that world [what he calls above, in referring to technology, "so much precipitated and condensed knowledge" (57)], so ethical science will effect an organization of the mental habits through which the individual relates himself to it.   *(58)*

It is hard to imagine a better articulation, from a liberal and positive perspective, of what Althusser will come to term the formation of subjects "who work by themselves."[27]

The deeply embedded temporal and spatial assumptions in Dewey's philosophy of education, assumptions that continue to structure liberal notions of the assimilative function of education, return us to the problematics of the classroom discussed in the previous section. Two founding presuppositions are crucial: the constitutive equivalence of subjects, which permits their exchangeability within and across social sites, and the continuity of the subject's formation (and, by extension, of society's formation). Instructive here is Dewey's account of "unconscious" processes which, both for the individual and for society at large, are conceived of as matters of forgetting and sedimentation. Self-evidently, this has nothing to do with a Freudian and Lacanian conception of the rhythmic disruptiveness of unconscious processes that are "repressed" precisely because of their inassimilability to conscious formation. What we can most significantly derive for critical purposes from these models of the unconscious is their insistence on the mutual constitutiveness of the subject and the unconscious and the topology of subjectivity that follows. That is, whereas Dewey assumes the continuous formation of the subject and of society to involve a progressive integration into an increasingly complex whole, any mode of social analysis or cultural critique alert to the models of psychoanalysis must recognize that subject formation entails the mutually constitutive emergence of incommensurable and logically antagonistic spheres both within the individual and across the social formation. The moment of the subject within the individual requires not simply the forgetting but the repression—that is, the displacement into other domains—of modes of cultural formation incompatible with the subject.

It becomes accordingly all the more difficult to subscribe to the identification that Fuss, among others, poses between the invocation of experience and identity politics, and in turn between these and an authoritarian exclu-

siveness.[28] The contradictory space of pedagogy in the wake of the achievements of the civil rights movement asks for the production of a different
political imaginary and an alternative critical subjectivity rather than a repetition within the minoritized subject of the identity politics of representative democracies. For failure to grasp adequately the dynamics of the classroom leaves leftist critics like Fuss with an all-too-reductive conception of
the category of experience that remains within the purview of a Deweyan
understanding of subject formation. What the correlation between experience and identity repeats is Dewey's powerful conception of experience as
the identity of the formed subject. Experience is a process of sedimentation
whereby individual constitutive instances—examples, lessons, imperatives—settle into the ground for identity. The very forgetting that allows for
their absorption into the unself-conscious consistency of the subject assures
the identity of that subject in several modalities. The subject's history
becomes continuous, without interruption or, correspondingly, het-
eronomous: its processes of formation are so thoroughly appropriated as to
become its own unquestioned property. By the same token, as we have been
seeing, the identity of the subject is preserved both across various social
spaces and within the various modes of activity, intellectual and moral, that
it assumes. And insofar as Dewey insists everywhere on certain homologies
between the history of nation formation and that of the subject, it is clear
that the citizen-subject formed by ethical pedagogy subtends the nation-
state by being in formal identity with it. The ideological function of the educational state apparatus is given in the very form of its processes and might
be described quite accurately as furnishing the conditions for the identity
politics of the nation-state. Dewey's formulations at the level of the subject
interestingly replicate Renan's now celebrated remark that nations are
formed as much by what they have to forget as by what they collectively
remember: crucial to both is the process of canon formation, which insti-
tutes national and individual identity.[29]

But such a notion of experience and of formation is clearly impossible
for the minority subject, not least at the moment when she interrupts the
dynamics of a classroom which, as Fuss magnificently and unwittingly
demonstrates, is all about forgetting. For what the minority subject is asked
to forget, what it is impossible to forget, is the very process by which she is
forgotten by the Subject in relation to whom she is simultaneously being
constituted. As we saw before, her very interpellation in the classroom
demands her identification with a Subject that simultaneously produces her
as what it must either annul or localize. This contradictory, disjunctive
"experience" of the classroom cannot be redeemed by inclusivity, however

liberal, precisely because it is in no way a question of the commensurability of opinions or perspectives in the marketplace of ideas. It is a constitutive contradiction of the educational apparatus. Accordingly, the "experience" of difference strategically invoked as a means of interrupting the unacknowledged indifference of the pedagogue counts less than the disjunctive experience that this difficult and inassimilable interruption brings into the open. And if, as Fuss asserts, what often follows is silence, we may well ask if it is the silence of censorship or the silence that follows the slippage of the terms by which voice itself is regulated.

Certainly, what is at stake here is the institutional ground on which the political subject emerges as citizen of the nation-state. For if the identity of that subject is inseparable from its equivalence with other subjects, an equivalence that gives the very possibility of pluralist solutions, the dream of commensurability founders here. The force of minority political and legal interventions against the systemic or constitutive racism of the liberal democracy is predicated precisely on the disjunctive nature of an experience radically at odds with the politics of identity that subtends the republican constitution. Thus, for example, the appeal to experience made by exponents of critical race theory, "grounded in the particulars of a social reality that is defined by our experiences and the collective historical experience of our communities of origin," entails no foreclosure of historical analysis.[30] On the contrary: from the differential construction of racialized communities vis-à-vis the state, it derives a critical position that at once invokes the complex history of racial differentiation and the traditions of radical thought and teaching in those communities. Within such traditions, the abstract critical subject that was founded in the radical critique of autocracy but came gradually to represent the formal Subject of the state is displaced by a critical subjectivity that emerges precisely in the contradictions of the state-formation. But that critical subject is simultaneously located within the social and cultural formations of minority communities which, in the long history of racialized America, have always been at odds with the state, neither supplementary to nor replicative of its institutions. Accordingly, the theoretical and practical work of these scholars may necessarily be addressed to the state, since it concerns the question of the law but emanates from positions constitutively outside the discourse of the state. This signifies the emergence of a radically different mode of critical subjectivity.

These reflections put us in a position to understand why, at least in "multicultural" America, the "crisis" of the university has been most virulently expressed not in relation to the quiet corporatization of scientific research but in relation to the "return" of minority politics. This crisis, artic-

ulated through the humanities for reasons now obvious, regards the very formation of the subject, which has not ceased to be the social function of the
universities above, beyond, and in their very specializations and engagements with "interested" spheres. Nor is it resolvable by measures that would,
like the ACBR, seek to expand the content of the formation while maintaining the equivalence of the subjects in pedagogy. What remains to be
thought is the possibility of a pedagogy and a political project founded in the
assumption of nonequivalence predicated on the ineradicable contradictions
of subject formation. This involves passing beyond the assumptions of an
educational system directed toward the formation of subjects for states based
on representative democracy and formal political rights, and accordingly
requires what we might call a "postpolitical" critique, insofar as what is in
question is the very formation of the political. We will need, at least, another
temporality for our histories and another geography of social spaces.

NOTES

1. Jürgen Habermas, "The Idea of the University—Learning Processes," trans. John
R. Blazek, *New German Critique* 41 (Spring–Summer 1987): 3–22.

2. Jacques Derrida's essay "Mochlos; or the Conflict of the Faculties," in Richard
Rand, ed., *Logomachia: The Conflict of the Faculties*, 1–34, explores terrain similar to that
of Habermas's essay. See especially 13–17, where he discusses the "borders" of the university in relation to its "outside." Derrida's emphasis is more on the epistemological than
the political legitimacy of the university.

3. Lisa Lowe has succinctly formulated the paradoxes and possibilities of such projects within institutions:

> At the same time, institutionalizing fields like Ethnic Studies still contains an
> inevitable paradox: on the one hand, institutionalization provides a material
> base within the university for a transformative critique of traditional disci-
> plines and their traditional separations; yet, on the other hand, the institu-
> tionalization of any field or curricula which establishes orthodox objects and
> methods submits in part to the demands of the university and its educative
> function of socializing subjects into the state. While institutionalizing inter-
> disciplinary study risks integrating it into a system which threatens to appro-
> priate what is most critical and oppositional about that study, the logic
> through which the university incorporates areas of interdisciplinarity simulta-
> neously provides for the possibility that these sites will remain oppositional
> forums, productively antagonistic to notions of autonomous culture and dis-
> ciplinary regulation, and to the interpellation of students as univocal subjects.

See "Canon, Institutionalization, Identity: Contradictions for Asian American
Studies," in David Palumbo-Liu, ed., *Revisions of the Ethnic Canon* (Minneapolis: University of Minnesota Press, 1994).

4. I refer here to the group of legal scholars who have been working under this rubric to suggest that their interventions in the legal sphere have important implications in other areas. See, for example, Mari J. Matsuda, Charles R. Lawrence III, Richard Delgado, and Kimberle Williams Crenshaw, *Words That Wound: Critical Race Theory, Assaultive Speech, and the First Amendment* (Boulder: Westview Press, 1993). See also Neil Gotanda, "A Critique of 'Our Constitution Is Color Blind'," *Stanford Law Review* 44 (1): 1–68.

5. Out of the normative 120 units required for graduation, the ACBR will demand only 4, that is, less than 3.5% of any undergraduate's work. This is a tiny measure, but one whose wider and long-term implications (which will only be realized by further struggles throughout the education system) could be of very great importance if they are fully elaborated and theorized.

6. On the Westernness of scientific rationality, see Partha Chatterjee, *Nationalist Thought and the Colonial World: A Derivative Discourse?* (London: Zed Books, 1986), 14–17.

7. This is not, of course, to say that cultures designated "minority" or "ethnic" have no existence or dynamic outside of their relation to state or university formations. On the contrary, it is precisely the inassimilable difference of such cultural formations that causes the anxiety of pluralists. I have tried to spell out this dynamic in "Ethnic Cultures, Minority Discourse and the State" in Peter Hulme, et al., eds., *Colonial Discourse/Post-colonial Theory* (Manchester: Manchester University Press, 1994), 221–38.

8. I borrow the phrase "transformation of hegemony" from Lisa Lowe, "Heterogeneity, Hybridity, Multiplicity: Marking Asian American Differences," *Diaspora* 1 (1): 24–44, esp. 28–29 and 40. It is Frantz Fanon who describes Western hegemony as a "unilateral declaration of universality" in "Racism and Culture," in *Toward the African Revolution*, trans. Haakon Chevalier (New York: Grove Press, 1967), 15.

9. See Martin Carnoy, "Education, State and Culture in American Society," in Henry A. Giroux and Peter McLaren, eds., *Critical Pedagogy, the State and Cultural Struggle* (Albany, NY: State University of New York Press, 1989), 3–23.

10. There is, of course, a quite fundamental reason to continue to support affirmative action, which is that it raises the number of minority students and faculty and causes trouble by doing so. Michael Soldatenko-Gutierrez puts the case succinctly and boldly:

> When reading many contemporary critics of higher education, we find that the real problem has to do with what Allan Bloom calls the "openness" of the university. Stated vulgarly, the university has *too many* African-Americans, Chicanas/os, Asian-Americans, Native Americans, feminists, and working-class whites. While these students have always been around, they had been held within respectable limits and were typically forced to acknowledge, if not accept, the dominant tradition. Now, though still few, they threaten to form a potential critical mass that could rebut the dominant intellectual paradigm. This, I believe, is the "crisis" that these scholars fear—the problem, therefore, is not necessarily with the curriculum or the lack of humanities courses or the need for an effective liberal arts program, the problem is simply too many "non-traditional" factors in higher education.

See Michael Soldatenko-Gutierrez, "Socrates, Curriculum and the Chicano/Chicana: Allan Bloom and the Myth of U.S. Higher Education," *Cultural Studies* 4 (3): 303–4.

11. Diana Fuss, "Essentialism in the Classroom," *Essentially Speaking: Feminism, Nature, and Difference* (New York: Routledge, 1989), 116–17.

12. See Kimberle Williams Crenshaw, "Foreward: Toward a Race-Conscious Pedagogy in Legal Education," *National Black Law Journal*, 11 (1): 2–3. I have discussed the emergence and disposition of the teacher as Subject, and its relation to "common sense," in "Kant's Examples," *Representations* 28 (Fall 1989): 34–54.

13. I owe these reflections in part to Ronke Oyewumi.

14. On the issue of embodiments in cultural studies and pedagogy respectively, two particularly useful recent essays have been Janet Wolf, "Reinstating Corporeality: Feminism and Body Politics," in *Feminine Sentences: Essays on Women and Culture* (Berkeley: University of California Press, 1990), 120–41, and Peter L. McLaren, "Schooling the Postmodern Body: Critical Pedagogy and the Politics of Enfleshment," in Henry A. Giroux, ed., *Postmodernism, Feminism and Cultural Politics: Redrawing Educational Boundaries* (Albany: State University of New York Press, 1991), 144–73. Both draw attention to the culturally constructed nature of the body, and I want to add here that it is one of theory's functions to give back to the body's phenomenological appearance of immediacy its historically constructed dimension.

15. See Preface to Rand, ed., *Logomachia*, vii: "In *The Conflict of the Faculties*, Kant spells out the blueprint for the modern research university."

16. Immanuel Kant, *The Conflict of the Faculties/Der Streit der Fakultäten* (1798), trans. and intro. Mary J. Gregor (New York: Abaris, 1979), 23.

17. Kant later makes this assumption quite explicit:

> Whenever a man-made institution is based on an Idea of reason (such as that of government) which is to prove itself practical in an object of experience (such as the entire field of learning at the time), we can take it for granted that the experiment was made according to some principle contained in reason, even if only obscurely, and some plan based on it—not by merely contingent collections and arbitrary combinations of cases that have occurred [*nicht durch bloss zufällige Aussammlung und willkürliche Zusammenstellung vorkommender Fälle*]. (*31*)

18. Immanuel Kant, *The Critique of Judgement*, trans. James Creed Meredith (Oxford: Clarendon Press, 1952), II:23.

19. Cf. Derrida, "Mochlos": "Kant had multiplied his rhetorical precautions, or rather he had somehow guaranteed the analogical statements with, so to speak, a real analogy: the university is analogous to society, to the social system it represents as one of its parts; and the teaching body represents, in one form or another, the goal and function of the social body."(5). This, however, seems to me closer to a Habermasian reading of the idea of the university than the one I am seeking to develop here, which does not see Kant as positing the social as the ground for an analogous structure of the university as "goal," but rather sees him grasping an analogy among equivalent parts as the structure of the social, of which the university is part.

20. The actual publication of the work brings together very disparately written essays, those on law and medicine having in fact been written before the essay that effectively gives its name to the collection. It would take a longer and different essay than this to elaborate the connections between these occasional pieces and the systematic elaboration of the major critiques with regard to the question of the subject. I will attempt here only to draw out the thinking implicit in these essays on the form of the subject that a critical philosophy, as core of the university, presumes and would produce. On the order of their writing and the process of their publication, see Gregor's introduction to *The Conflict of the Faculties*, vii–xxviii.

21. This subservience is borne out in an otherwise mystifying Appendix in which, after asserting morality, as opposed to orthodoxy or dogma, to be "the mainstay on which the government must be able to count if it wants to trust the people" (109), Kant goes on to cite at length a letter from a former student, C. A. Wilmans, which points to the coincidence between Kantian religious philosophy and what he describes as contemporary Mysticism. The reason for Kant's interest in this convergence between the philosopher and these "merchants, artisans and peasants" lies less in an inclination to Rousseauian republicanism than in Wilmans' assertion that the Mystics' indifference to established religion is conjoined with an "exemplary conduct and complete submission to the civil order"(139).

22. For an interesting analysis of this tradition in England, see Robert Young, "The Idea of a Chrestomathic University," in *Logomachia*, 97–126; on the movement from such ideas as developed in England to the American university, see William V. Spanos, "The Apollonian Investment of Modern Humanist Education: The Examples of Matthew Arnold, Irving Babbitt, and I. A. Richards," *Cultural Critique* 1 (Fall 1985): 7–72.

23. I should note that the celebrated disintegration of the subject in postmodernity is greatly exaggerated. Like Habermas, even Lyotard emphasizes the proliferation of "language games" and of opportunities for consumption rather than the question of the form of the subject of modernity as it persists into the present. There is some difference between a multiplicity of subject positions and an internal disintegration of the subject. Properly understood, the theory of minority discourse has argued for that internal disintegration rather than for any simple celebration of multiplicity. See the critique of Lyotard in the Introduction to *The Nature and Context of Minority Discourse*, and also my "Ethnic Cultures, Minority Discourse and the State," which is a more sustained attempt to elaborate some of these issues.

24. John Dewey, "Ethics and Education," in *John Dewey on Education: Selected Writings*, ed. with intro. by Reginald D. Archimbault (Chicago: University of Chicago Press, 1964).

25. These assumptions are fairly clearly spelled out in "Ethical Principles Underlying Education," in ibid., 108–38.

26. It is perhaps for this reason that in "Ethical Principles," while geography is seen as a fundamental science in depicting the interaction of humans and nature, a version of universal history, the history of "typical epochs" is seen to have "ultimate ethical value." History demonstrates that "social forces in themselves are always the same" and accordingly subsumes geography as an illustration across time of the ubiquity, universality, and continuity of human experience (123–27).

27. Louis Althusser, "Ideology and Ideological State Apparatuses" in *Lenin and Philosophy and Other Essays*, trans. Ben Brewster (London: New Left Books, 1971). This process of "forgetting" is close to that described by Ernest Renan as being essential to nation formation; see *Nation and Narration*, ed. Homi Bhabha (New York: Routledge, 1990).

28. Fuss, in "Essentialism in the Classroom," writes, "Personal consciousness, individual oppressions, lived experience—in short, identity politics—operate in the classroom both to authorize and to de-authorize speech" (113).

29. Renan, *Nation and Narration.*

30. Matsuda et al., *Words That Wound,* 3.

THREE

Literary and Cultural Studies in the Transnational University

J. Hillis Miller

In memory of Bill Readings

Something drastic is happening in the university. Something drastic is happening *to* the university. The university is losing its idea, the guiding mission that has sustained it since the early nineteenth century when, in Germany, the modern research university was invented. Newman's *The Idea of the University* expounded for English readers both this concept of the university and, among other things, the place of literary study in such a university.[1] "Idea"—the word has a Platonic resonance. It names a transcendent form—presiding, generative, paternal—on which particular material embodiments are modeled. The new university that is coming into being lacks such a supervising concept. In place of the university governed by an idea is rapidly being put what Bill Readings calls the university of "excellence." Such a university is the locus of technological training that is more and more in the service not of the nation but of transnational corporations. "Excellence"—the word, as Readings observes, in this case names an empty tautology. "Excellence" is whatever the different disciplines name as excellent. What good is literary study now in this new university without idea? Can we still study literature? Should, ought, or must we still study it? What is the source now of the obligation to study literature—who or what addresses to us a call or demand to do so? Why should we do it? To what purpose? Can literary study still be defended as a socially useful part of college and university research and teaching, or is it just a vestigial remnant that will vanish as other media become more and more dominant in the new global society that is rapidly taking shape? This essay attempts to confront and answer these questions.

I

A provocative passage toward the end of Marcel Proust's *A la recherche du temps perdu*, that huge database of provocative passages, proposes an analogy between the understanding of individual people and the understanding of politics. Literature, for the most part, deals with imaginary characters. It usually approaches larger political, social, religious, or philosophical issues only by way of these characters' stories. The passage I shall cite from Proust might therefore serve as a defense of literary study at a time when its social utility is not always evident to everyone. Some students these days in programs in literature, for example, seem more at ease when they are reading works of theory, more confident that they are doing something important, than when they are reading the literature those works theorize. That is understandable. The political import of literary works is indirect. It has to be worked out through a laborious process of reading and deciphering, while theoretical works these days talk directly about race, class, gender, and other urgent political or social issues. Reading theory, so it may appear, saves you the hard work of reading literature.

George Eliot was already, in 1871, worrying uneasily about the apparent triviality, provinciality, and lowness of the characters in *Middlemarch*. Do not be anxious, she tells her readers, in an admirably ironic passage, you may take my narrative of middle-class people as a parable. You can then transfer what I say to higher and more important levels of society: "Since there never was a true story which could not be told in parables where you might put a monkey for a margrave, and *vice versa*—whatever has been or is to be narrated by me about low people, may be ennobled by being considered a parable. . . . Thus while I tell the truth about loobies, my reader's imagination need not be entirely excluded from an occupation with lords."[2] I have discussed this passage in detail elsewhere.[3] What is important for my purposes now is the contingency and reversibility of the analogies affirmed in parables. "Monkey" just happens to sound like "margrave," just as "looby" alliterates with "lord." This accidental and senseless linguistic similarity justifies putting one in the place of the other, but in either direction: monkey for margrave and vice versa. Reading the political import of literature is like decoding a parable or an allegory. It takes special training, since it depends on certain cryptological assumptions. Proust indicates what those might be.

The passage in Proust makes use of an analogy somewhat like Eliot's. It would seem implicitly to confirm the choice of those who prefer literature to theory. Marcel has been talking about the way "life with Albertine and with Françoise had accustomed [him] to suspect in them thoughts and projects which they did not disclose." This experience of deception has led him, transferring personal experience to a national level, to doubt assertions of "pacific intentions" by Germany, Bulgaria, or Greece. These nations are personified as single living persons, that is, as each having a unity like that of an organism or a consciousness. Moving from this, as he often does, to a high level of generalization, expressed by means of a brilliant metaphor, Marcel asserts that individual life is to national life as a single cell is to the large living body of which it is a part:

> Of course my quarrels with Françoise or with Albertine had been merely private quarrels, of interest only to the life of that little cell, endowed with a mind [*cette petite cellule spirituelle*], that a human being is. But just as there are animal bodies and human bodies, each one of which is an assemblage of cells as large in relation to a single cell as Mont Blanc, so there exist huge organized accumulations of individuals which are called nations: their life does no more than repeat on a larger scale [*répéter en les amplifiant*] the lives of their constituent cells, and anybody who is incapable of comprehending the mystery, the reactions, the laws of these smaller lives, will only make futile pronouncements [*ne prononcera que des mots vides*] when he talks about struggles between nations.[4]

This is wonderfully reassuring to a lover of literature. If you want to understand national politics and the conflicts between nations, study individual human lives, such as those endlessly proliferating details Marcel gives us about his relation to Albertine or those stories about loobies George Eliot tells in *Middlemarch*. If you do not understand people you will never understand politics. Why? Because they can be counted on to correspond exactly, and the study of people is easier, closer to home, and more immediate than the abstract study of politics. Happily, each repeats the other on a different scale, so that to study one is indirectly to study the other. To adopt George Eliot's language, each is the parable of the other, or, to use a word more present in Proust's lexicon, each is the allegory of the other. The claim is that an understanding of nations cannot be approached directly, whereas individual human lives can be comprehended in themselves. If you try to approach national politics without a detour through the analogy with individual lives, you will be sure to speak empty words. Such pronouncements are not only false but ineffective. They have no performative purchase on the real world. The study of literature will allow you to intervene successfully in society and deflect the course of history. An example is the way the diplomat Norpois, in a splendid comic episode in the *Recherche*, succeeds, through his understanding of individual psychology, in getting a man he casually names to Prince Foggi appointed Prime Minister of Italy: "Why has no one mentioned Giolitti?"

The passage in Proust is a little less reassuring, however, to the reader who notices that he says what must be learned about individuals in order to understand nations is not just "the laws of these smaller lives," but their "mystery" and the fact that most of the time they are lying. To "comprehend a mystery" may mean to penetrate it, but it may also mean understanding that it is impenetrable. The phrase is possibly an oxymoron. Marcel's account of his life with Albertine is one of the great investigations into the impenetrable mystery of the lie. Just why a lie, for Proust, can never certainly be found out is a complex matter. A lie, contrary to what appears to be the case, is a matter of bearing false witness, not just a contrary-to-face statement. It is therefore as much a performative use of language as a constative one. To the degree it is a speech act, it is not open to cognition. It belongs to another domain of language, that of doing things with words rather than that of conveying true or false knowledge. If Germany, Greece, and Bulgaria characteristically lie, as do Albertine or Françoise, then what we may need to know about international politics is that understanding it is based on the science of the lie, another oxymoron.

In the continuation of the passage I have been discussing, Proust proposes another striking figure for the relation between individuals and nations. This figure has a strong current resonance tying it to two main topics of this essay: the effects of the cold war's end on the university and the effects of new communications technologies on the study of national literatures in the university. I call this figure the "fractal mosaic." Just as an organic living body repeats on a larger scale the life of each of the cells that makes it up, and vice versa, so, says Marcel, "la grande figure France" is like a huge geometric shape "filled to its perimeter with millions of little polygons of various shapes," while Germany is "another figure filled with an even greater number of polygons" (F4:350; E3:795). Let me explain how the figure of the fractal applies. A nation, France or Germany, is a huge spatial array with the integrity of a certain geometric shape, outlined with definite borders and filled up from border to border with millions of little polygons of various shapes. It is like a mosaic made of many small tesserae set side by side to make a pattern. Each of these little polygons is what we today would call a subjectivity, a subject, a subject of the nation-state where it is located. France is filled to the edges with Frenchmen, Germany with Germans. But the peculiarity of this mosaic, as Marcel tells the reader, is that the total pattern of the nation, the slightly irregular hexagon that outlines France, repeats "on a larger scale" all those smaller polygons, even though the repetition is always repetition with a difference. It follows that if you understand representative examples of the smaller polygons, you will understand the large one.

The figure Proust describes is like a spatial design of which he could have had no knowledge, the fractal. Fractals are characterized by what mathematicians call "self-similarity." Smaller parts, at whatever scale, repeat the larger pattern of the whole, though in the most interesting fractals never exactly or predictably. The unpredictability, approaching that studied in chaos theory, occurs if an aleatory element is included in the generating formula. An example is the way the general design of a coastline is repeated, on a statistical average of irregularity, in ever smaller and smaller segments, down to the outline made by a few feet of beach, with its rocks, sand, and pools. The coastline of the state of Maine, where I spend my summers, is an example of this. My 420 feet of shore repeat, with a difference, the general irregularity of bays, islands, necks, and peninsulas characteristic of the whole Maine coastline many hundreds of miles long. Or rather the coastline of Maine is, like all fractal borders, in a sense infinitely long, since any segment of it can always be inspected at a smaller scale and further refined in its irregularity. Each new level of irregularity of course makes it longer.[5]

Proust's two figures—of the body made of many cells and of what I am calling the fractal mosaic—not only justify the study of literature as politically useful. They also indicate presuppositions that would allow the rational organization of such study. A nation, Proust's figures suggest, is a living, organic unity, with definite edges. It is the embodiment of a unified national culture, a culture as definite and unique as the biology of a single species with one exemplar. Each human being is also a unity that mirrors in a special way the unique configurations of that national unity. The validity of the trope of synecdoche, part for whole, allows the study of the whole by means of the part. As George Eliot says somewhere in *Middlemarch*, the larger waves are made of smaller waves and both have the same pattern. If a work of literature may be assumed to be like a human individual, the fractal image of its author, as Proust repeatedly and eloquently argues in the *Recherche*, then the study of literature, it would follow, should be organized as the separate study of each national literature's most important works, that is, the works that most directly embody that culture's self-understanding of its tradition. Each major national author is a little polygon mirroring in a special way the whole nation. The work of each author will mirror in fractal self-similarity the unity and specificity of the national culture—what makes France France, Germany Germany, the United States the United States. Moreover, the law of fractal self-similarity means that study of a limited number of carefully chosen representative works from different historical periods will allow the reader to understand the unified culture of the whole nation.

A further support for the current applicability of the mosaic figure would come from the way this image is often proposed these days by scholars of United States multiculturalism as an appropriate replacement for the traditional figure of the United States as a melting pot transforming immigrants from many lands, cultures, and languages into homogeneous monolingual "Americans" (as by metonymy we habitually call them, forgetting that the United States is only one part of America). The United States, in the now-outmoded figures, after the melting pot has done its work, is filled with millions of little polygons repeating with a difference the unified shape of the national culture as a whole. But in a multicultural nation the tesserae remain distinct, juxtaposed side-by-side and never assimilated to universal sameness. The term "mosaic" is a focus for the battle among different notions of what United States culture is or ought to be.

II

The passage by Proust gives an apparently natural inevitability to the way the study of Western literature has traditionally been organized in our universities, that is, in a number of discrete departments, each devoted to the separate study of a single national literature, with the dominant one being, of course, the one representing that language and literary tradition of the nation in which the university is located. Does this well-established paradigm still hold? Can we accept the figure of the fractal mosaic both as a true description and as a heuristic pattern indicating how the study of literature ought to be organized in the university and of what use such study is? What is happening today with the study of national literatures? By "today" I mean the time when new communication technologies—computers, e-mail, fax machines, VCRs, videos, CD-ROMs, hypertext, and "surfing the Internet"—are fundamentally changing the ways humanistic scholars are related to one another and do their work. I mean also the time of the end of the cold war, the weakening of the power and integrity of nation-states, the globalization of economic and cultural systems, and the consequent transformation of the university's mission.

Vincent Cable in "The Diminished Nation-State" emphasizes the way new technologies have globalized business.[6] He distinguishes two different technological drives: "First, and more sedate, transport costs have fallen with improved physical communications: better cars; jet aircraft; containerization; motorways. Second, and more spectacular, advances in computing power and in telecommunications—digital systems, satellite technology, and, more recently, fiber optics—have transformed the ease, speed, quantity, and quality of international information flows" (26). This end is particularly conspicuous in the globalizing of international finance and therefore of the flow of capital that funds transnational corporations. Especially interesting is the way Cable, citing Richard O'Brien, sees money as transformed in the computer age into "an information product": " 'The essence of money is . . . the information it conveys, whether as a store of value or medium of exchange."[7] Thus Richard O'Brien begins his explanation of the ways in which computerization and advanced telecommunications (involving almost instantaneous linkages) have transformed international finance. "There are now global markets for currency transactions and all forms of marketable securities. Competition is intense and capital is highly mobile" (26). It used to be that banking was, with unconscious irony, called an "industry," as though it actually produced something of use value. Now money is rather "information," and banking is an information service. Money flows back and forth at the speed of light on the Internet along with all the other cultural information, including, but of course by no means limited to, all those works of literature available "online" as "electronic texts." Money and literature or other cultural artifacts become no more than somewhat different forms of "information," available at any point where there is an appropriate computer terminal. This new ubiquity "ends geography" in the sense of penetrating all borders and local enclosures. It does not matter where I am as long as I have a computer terminal connected to the Internet. When both money and literature, along with other cultural artifacts, are turned into information, Wallace Stevens's somewhat enigmatic aphorism in the "Adagia," "Money is a kind of poetry,"[8] is fulfilled in an unexpected, hyperbolic way. If money is a kind of poetry, "poetry," in the broad sense of cultural forms generally in various media, is also a kind of money. Vincent Cable recognizes this when he stresses the new value assigned to intellectual property and telecommunication rights: "information, per se, has become tradable: management consultancy; films, records, and compact discs; television news; telecommunications services; software systems, design, and programming. It is no coincidence that the Uruguay Round [an international economic 'summit' meeting held in Uruguay] had some of its most testing moments over 'Information' issues that were scarcely thought of five years earlier: intellectual property protection, market access for films, and telecommunications" (26).

One result of this globalization in the United States and to various degrees in many other nations in the West is that those responsible for funding higher education no longer believe that their nations need the university in the same way as they once did. The primary evidence for this is the cutting off of funds, almost always justified by budget stringency, as has been the case in the past few years for the University of California. The University of California was until quite recently arguably the greatest research university in the world. Now it is being rapidly weakened by budget cuts and through early retirements made for many professors irresistibly attractive by "golden handshake" offers of benefits—a procedure borrowed from the corporate world. On the one hand, there is no longer confidence in the need for basic research in the university as something directly funded by the nation-state or by its subdivisions. Such research was in any case always largely supported as ancillary to the military buildup. With the end of the cold war came the end of the apparent need for many kinds of basic research. It is difficult for most professors in the humanities in the United States to accept the fact that their prosperity in the sixties, seventies, and eighties was as much a result of the cold war as the flourishing of aircraft and weapons manufacturers, or the space race that put men on the moon. Nevertheless, such was the case. The expensive development of humanities programs was an ancillary part of our need to be best. Now that the cold war is over, humanities programs are being downsized along with scientific parts of university research and teaching. The job situation for newly trained physicists, I am told, is even worse than it is for new Ph.D.s in English. What those in charge (legislators, trustees, granting agencies, university and college administrators) in the United States need, or think they need, and therefore demand, is immediately applicable technology. The weakening of our space program and the killing of the Superconducting Supercollider project are salient examples of this. Applied research can often be done just as well by computer or pharmaceutical companies and the like. These have been increasingly funding research inside the university, co-opting the university's scientific skills and laboratory facilities (often originally paid for by federal money, that is, by part of the military-industrial complex) for research that in the end has to be defended as the potential discovery of patentable procedures that will make the companies profitable. The university in response to these radical changes became more and more like a bureaucratic corporation itself; for example, being run by a corps of proliferating administrators whose bottom-line business, as in the case of any bureaucracy, is to perpetuate themselves efficiently, even if this sometimes means large-scale "administrative cutbacks."

At the same time, "society," in the concrete form of legislators who give money to public universities and of trustees who manage private universities and colleges, also no longer needs higher education in the way it once did—that is, to transmit national cultural values, however much such authorities may still pay lip service to this traditional role of humanities departments. The work of ideological indoctrination and training in consumerism, it is tacitly understood, can be done much more effectively by the media, newspapers and magazines, radio talk shows, and television and cinema.

Moreover, after what has happened in humanities departments from the 1960s on, those in charge now no longer trust the professors of literature to do what they used to do or even, they might claim, what they are hired to do. The cat is out of the bag. These academic bureaucrats and legislators are by no means stupid. Whatever their protestations about the eternal values embodied in the Western canon, the news has got through to those in charge of the universities that the actual culture of the United States is multitudinous, multicultural, and multilingual, as well as disunified in other ways. Moreover, they know now that you can no longer trust professors to teach Chaucer, Shakespeare, Milton, and the rest in the old ideological ways. These authors, read in certain ways, as professors seem perversely inclined to do and to teach their students to do, are what seems to them dynamite that might blow up the social edifice. So the more or less unconscious strategy is to welcome the self-destruction of the traditional literature departments as they shift to cultural studies and then gradually cut off the money, in the name of financial stringency and the need to build more prisons and support welfare programs.

Though some of these changes in the university are being imposed from the outside, most obviously the drastic reduction of funding, the changes are also happening on the inside, with the conscious or unconscious complicity of university and college teachers and administrators. These changes are irreversible. They affect all branches and departments of higher education, especially the research university, but in different ways in different parts of the curriculum. Those who teach and do research in departments of national literatures have hardly begun to be aware of the way these changes alter their work or to develop the conceptual figurations necessary to grasp the changes, though a growing number of books and essays are addressing this task from many different perspectives.[9]

III

In exploring this further, I shall take the study of English literature in the United States as my example, since it is my own "field of expertise." It should be recognized from the start, however, that the choice is hardly innocent. English literature is not just one national literature among others. One main feature of the globalization I have mentioned is the way the English language, primarily of course by way of the United States, is gradually, for better or for worse, becoming a universal language. English is already spoken everywhere in the world as the second language of millions and millions of people for whom it is not the mother tongue. With the study of the English language goes the study of its literature as one of the most potent instruments to spread capitalist ideologies. Or at least we used to be confident that this was the case: it is not quite clear, when you think of it, how the study of Shakespeare or Hardy will aid the economic imperialism of the United States.

What has happened, as a consequence of these societal changes, to the traditional discipline of the study of separate national literatures, for example the study of English literature in the United States? For one thing, it is gradually being swallowed up by increased offerings in American, that is, United States, literature. Most universities now have departments of English and American literature, whatever they may be called, and American literature has become more and more dominant within such agglomerations. Moreover, a "crisis in representation," as Brook Thomas calls it, exists in our writing, teaching, and curricular design in departments of national literatures. In various ways most teachers in American colleges and universities used to believe in the validity of a part-for-whole or synecdochal relationship in literary study, in another version of Proust's fractal mosaic. A good literary work was presumed to be an organic whole, so the study of a part could be a means of understanding or teaching that whole. Teachers could use with a clear conscience the detailed study of a citation. Such a procedure could be brilliantly exploited as a method of reading, for example, by Erich Auerbach in *Mimesis*. The whole work, carefully chosen and explicated on the assumption that each part of it mirrored the totality, could then be used as a way of understanding what was assumed to be a homogeneous circumambient culture. One citation from Virginia Woolf's *To the Lighthouse* could represent, for Auerbach, the entire modernist practice of realistic representation. It was possible to claim, without seeing the claim as all that problematic, that study of *Moby-Dick* would give readers a full understanding of mid-nineteenth-century American culture. Of course such claims were not always made quite so blatantly, but some version of this assumption operated widely as an unquestioned ideologeme (but an ideological element is by definition unquestioned). The ideologeme may have been all the more powerful for being an unspoken assumption guiding the choice of the canon and the devising of curricula.

Few people any longer have an unshaken confidence in this paradigm, even those who most stridently assert it. We recognize, as I have said, that the United States is a multicultural and multilingual nation. A given work or canon represents only one part of a complex, nonunifiable whole. To choose to teach *Moby-Dick* rather than *Uncle Tom's Cabin,* or even to choose to teach both of them together, cannot be based on a proof that they are in some way objectively representative. The choice is motivated and unjustifiable—which does not mean it is necessarily bad. It means those who devise syllabuses and curricula must take responsibility for their choices, not defend them as based on universal criteria of excellence. Nor can we any longer have recourse to some standard of intrinsic superiority allowing us to say that *Moby-Dick* is a better work than *Uncle Tom's Cabin,* or vice versa, since that standard too, we have been persuaded, is the result of ideological bias. This loss of confidence in the possibility of justifying a syllabus on the basis of its objectively verifiable representative status is almost as much of a disaster for those trained in the old ways of teaching literature (me, for example) as a loss of confidence in the power of elected representatives to stand for them would be for citizens of the United States.

The crisis in representation in the humanities leads to enormous problems in establishing curricula, in practical work of teaching and writing about literature, in making decisions about appointments and programs. One reason, for example, that so much time is spent in theoretical speculation these days is that we have no consensus about just how we ought to proceed. Everyone is likely to feel he or she has to reinvent the whole institution of teaching literature in the university from the ground (or lack of ground) up. Bernard Bergonzi has written a polemical book about this change as it affects the discipline of English literature, the title of which tells what he feels about these effects: *Exploding English.*

IV

This crisis of representation for literature departments accompanies a larger crisis of representation for the university as a whole, in particular for the humanities as an element in a new kind of university in a different world, a world of global economy and global communication. The old nation-state university is being replaced both by an internationalization of university research and by a recognition, in the United States, that we are not and never have been a nation-state with a unified culture, not as that concept has supervised the European sense of citizenship from at least the Renaissance on. For many people in the United States, as a result of our recognition that we are to a considerable degree the "disunited states," the old mission of the university no longer has persuasive force. We have not yet, however, invented a new paradigm for the nature and function of the university.

The loss of this special role for the study of English literature puts English departments especially under stress in the new kind of university that is developing. Those of us who are professors of English have been deprived of our traditional role as preservers and transmitters of the unified culture of a homogeneous nation-state. There was always something of an anomaly in basing the values of the United States on the study of English literature, that is, on the study of the literature of a foreign country where they happen to speak a version of our own language. It takes only a moment's thought to realize how different it is for a British citizen, of whatever class, gender, or race, to read Shakespeare, Milton, or Dickens, from what it is for an American to read them. These authors do not belong to us or express our national values or even the values of our hegemonic class in the same ways as they do for British citizens. Nevertheless, English literature was still the basis of a literary education in the United States when I got my undergraduate and graduate degrees not all that many decades ago. My graduate English qualifying examination for the Ph.D. stopped with Thomas Hardy and included no American literature at all, much less any theory.

The study of English literature in the United States is in one major way like its study in Korea, Norway, Taiwan, Germany, or Italy. In another important way it is unlike. To study English literature in the United States, Korea, or Norway, to take it seriously as a source of values and humanistic understanding, is in all those cases to study the literature of a foreign country, a small and increasingly less important island nation off the coast of Europe. The difference of course is that a version of English also happens to be the dominant and even the official language of the United States, whereas it is a second language in Korea, Norway, Taiwan, Germany, and the rest. The dominance of the American version of the English language in the United States, however, perhaps only makes more invisible to us what is problematic about basing American training in humanistic values on a literature that is not native to our soil. American literature and English literature are by no means parts of one homogeneous whole, even though the former has traditionally been taught as subordinate to the latter, as at my own university and at the other two universities at which I have taught: Johns Hopkins and Yale. These days, however, radical changes in society, in the university's relation to society, and in the actual study of literature in the university are putting in question the traditional English major. I mean by that the more or less sequestered study of major canonical works by English authors from "*Beowulf* to Virginia Woolf," organized in courses devoted to historical "periods": the Renaissance, Romanticism, the Victorian period, Modernism, and so on. Just what are those changes, and just why have they occurred?

The research university in its modern form as an institution in the West originated with the founding in the early nineteenth century of the University of Berlin. It was established according to the plan devised by Wilhelm von Humboldt. Such universities had as their primary role service to the nation-state, conceived as an organically unified culture with a single set of ideals and values enshrined in a unified philosophical tradition and national literature (or in a certain way of appropriating Greek and Latin literature). The university was to serve the nation-state in two ways: 1) as the place of critical thinking and research, *Wissenschaft*, finding out the truth about everything, giving everything its rationality, according to the Leibnizian formula that says nothing is without its reason; 2) as the place of education, formation, or *Bildung* where male citizens (they were all male then in the university) are inculcated, one might almost say "inoculated," with the basic values of a unified national culture. It was the business of the university to produce subjects of the state, in both senses of the word "subject": as subjectivities and as citizens accountable to state power and capable of promulgating it. For Humboldt and his colleagues, following Kant, the basis of *Bildung* was the study of philosophy. That is why we are all still called "doctors of philosophy," whatever the discipline in which we received a higher degree. This is a pretty complete absurdity these days, if you think of it, since philosophy proper is an increasingly marginal part of the university, with most professors of philosophy engaged in arcane problems of logic while most Ph.D.s in other fields know little or nothing about philosophy.

With some support from works like Schiller's *Letters on Aesthetic Education*, Anglo-Saxon countries in the mid-nineteenth century, first England and then the United States, deflected this paradigm in an important way by substituting literature for philosophy as the central agent of cultural indoctrination. Grounds for this shift already existed of course in the importance granted to literary edcucation by many of the German theorists: the Schlegels, Schelling, and Hegel, for example, as well as Schiller. This shift occurred in England and in the United States to a considerable degree under the aegis of Matthew Arnold's formulations about culture and anarchy, about the study of poetry, and about the function of criticism. The modern American research university has inherited the double mission of the Humboldtian university. This allegiance was explicit in the founding of The Johns Hopkins University in Baltimore in 1876. The Hopkins was based explicitly and self-consciously on the German university rather than on the English university model, though with some influence from the scientific universities coming into being in England. Thomas Henry Huxley spoke at the founding of Johns Hopkins. The admirable proliferation of both public and private research universities in the United States followed thereafter.

The combination of gathering scientific knowledge or *Wissenschaft* (which includes knowledge of history, cultural history, and literary theory, as well as of biology and physics) and at the same time teaching a nation's unifying values seems coherent enough. Nevertheless, a tension has always existed between these two goals as charges to the department responsible for doing research and teaching in a country's national literature. On the one hand, the mission is to teach students, by way of literature, the central ideas and values of a national culture. These are presumed to be enshrined in unalterable fixity in the nation's canonical works—*Beowulf*, Chaucer, Shakespeare, and the rest for English literature. On the other hand, scientific research is supposed to be critical and "disinterested" (Arnold's word), a search for truth independent of subjective bias. Research is value free, *Wertfrei*. It is organized according to a universal methodology of research. This methodology is applicable *mutatis mutandis* to the human sciences as well as to the physical sciences and to the life sciences.

A touching confidence that these two enterprises would achieve the same results for a long time made it possible for departments of national literatures to believe they were fulfilling both missions and reconciling the two contradictory charges the university or college had given them. A professor of English could pursue research of the most positivistic kind into the minutiae of an author's life, or do the most mind-numbing bibliographical and editorial work, and at the same time teach undergraduate classes extolling the ethical virtues contained in works by Shakespeare, Johnson, Browning, and the rest. The first activity made him (they were almost all male then) feel he was doing something useful to aid his university's scientific devotion to truth-seeking. The second made him feel he was fulfilling his responsibility to *Bildung*.

The strange use of the literature of a foreign country as the basis of national culture in the United States is a symptom, however, of a fundamental change in the Humboldtian model of the research university when it was institutionalized in the United States. William Readings is right when he says that the concept of a unified national culture in the Unites States has always been a promise or hope for the future, something always yet to be created by contractual agreement among the free citizens of a republic, rather than something inherited as an inescapable tradition from the nation's historical past.[10] English literature was co-opted by American schools and universities as the basic tool for the creation of a national culture that has always remained something evermore about to be rather than a given. Recent books have shown that the creation of English literature as a pedagogical discipline occurred in the nineteenth century as part of British imperialism. Franklin Court, in *Institutionalization of English Studies*, and Robert Crawford, in *Devolving English Literature*, have shown the way English studies were devised in Scotland as a way of putting down Scots and making Scotland more part of a unified Great Britain.[11] Gauri Viswanathan in *Masks of Conquest: Literary Study and British Rule in India* has shown how English studies were used as an instrument of colonial domination in nineteenth-century India.[12]

It appears that the young United States did not need to be coerced into acting still like a colony, at least in submitting its cultural ideals to English literature. Nevertheless, Shakespeare's ringing affirmation in *Henry V* of England's island unity and the glories of victory at Agincourt has a hollow sound in a country that established itself in a revolutionary war by defeating the British. For us the words "Lexington," "Bunker Hill," "Yorktown," and "Valley Forge" have more resonance than "Agincourt." It might be argued that over the past fifty years we citizens of the United States have come to recognize that we have an indigenous national literature that serves to unify us and make us all Americans. On the contrary, the rise of American literature and American studies as separate disciplines in United States universities and colleges demonstrates just the point I am making. The important books on American literature, from those by Matthiessen, Feidelson, Lewis, and Perry Miller down to more recent work by Pearce, Bercovitch, and Harold Bloom[13] have been devoted not so much to describing as to attempting to create the unified national culture we do not in fact have. They characteristically do this by a complex performative scholarly ritual masking as objective scholarship, and by the appeal to such general concepts as the frontier ("Go West," young man!), the American Renaissance, the American Adam, a certain use of symbolism, a special kind of Romance, the Puritan ideal, the internal coherence of a canonical poetic tradition from Emerson and Whitman through Stevens to Ammons and Ashbery, and so on, in incoherent multiplicity. Each scholar makes up his or her own idea about the unity of American literature, and each idea is incompatible with all the others. Readings is right again when he says the interest in canon formation in recent literary scholarhsip in the United States arises from the fact that we do not have an inherited traditional canon and must create one by fiat, in another form of that future-anterior speech act characterizing United States culture generally. If you have a canon that can be taken for granted, as to a considerable degree they do in England, you do not need to worry about it or theorize about it.

V

The most important recent change in literary study in the United States is the development of cultural studies. Why did the massive shift to cultural studies from language-based theory begin to occur just when it did, that is, around 1980? The shift was no doubt overdetermined. Many factors accompanied it, for example the decisive effect of the Vietnam War and the civil rights movement. One crucial force, however, was the growing impact of new communication technologies. Of course changes in communication have been going on throughout the twentieth century, but they have much accelerated in recent years as we have entered the electronic age. The younger scholars who have turned so spontaneously and so massively to cultural studies are the first generation of university teachers and critics who were brought up with television and with new forms of commercialized popular music. Many of them as children and teenagers spent as much time watching television or listening to popular music as reading books. I do not say these are necessarily bad activities. They are just different. Reading books can also be bad for you, as Emma Bovary and Lord Jim show. The critics of this new generation have been to a considerable degree formed by a new visual and aural "culture" (but it is culture in a somewhat new sense of the word: the media part of a global economy of consumerism). This new culture is fast replacing the culture of the book. It is not surprising that young scholars should wish to study what has to a considerable degree made them what they are, in spite of their lingering participating in the culture of the book. Nevertheless, strong evidence of the weakening force of literature in the United States is the way so many young scholars trained in literary study, presumably once possessed of a vocation for it, should now feel so compelled to study popular culture, film, magazines, and the like that they more or less abandon their original vocation for literature.

The goals of all these new developments—cultural studies, women's studies, studies in various minority discourses, and so on—are laudable. Who could oppose giving a voice to the heretofore voiceless, to women and minorities, to gays and lesbians, to the economically disadvantaged? Who could oppose giving a place in the university to all the ethnic varieties that characterize both our national society (I speak of the United States and from my "subject position" here and now in 1997) and the new global society that is nearer every day? Who could oppose using such study to help create the worldwide democracy to come, that horizon of all our political and intellectual effort? Who could oppose the careful study of popular culture and of those media—television, video, cinema—that shape our minds and behavior more than books do these days? A fundamental part of work in cultural studies has been descriptive and archival. Works in different media and from different cultures, works by women and minorities, need to be identified, categorized, edited, republished, brought into the open, made available in the university and to the general public so they can be effective there. Putting these neglected works in the classroom, in the curriculum, in books, articles, conferences, and study groups is, however, only the beginning of the job. Knowledge is not enough. Archiving multiculturalism may even denature or negate the power such works have to make cultural change. The university has a formidable power of recuperation and neutralization. I shall suggest later how this recuperation might be resisted.

As the epochal cultural displacement from the age of the book to the age of hypertext has accelerated, however, we have been ushered ever more rapidly into a new and threatening living space. As Derrida has cogently argued in a recent seminar, this new electronic space, the space of television, cinema, telephone, videos, faxes, e-mail, and the Internet, has profoundly altered the economy of the self, of the home, of the workplace, and of the politics of the nation-state. These were traditionally ordered around the firm boundaries of an inside-outside dichotomy, whether they were the walls between the privacy of the home and the world outside or the borders between the nation-state and its neighbors. The new technologies invade the home and confound all these inside-outside divisions. On the one hand, no one is so alone as when watching television, talking on the telephone, or sitting before a computer screen reading e-mail or searching an Internet database. On the other hand, that private space has been invaded and permeated by a vast simultaneous crowd of verbal, aural, and visual images existing in cyberspace's simulacrum of presence. Those images cross national and ethnic boundaries. They come from all over the world with an equal spurious immediacy. The global village is not out there, but in here—a clear distinction between inside and out no longer holds. The new technologies bring the uncanny or *unheimlich* "other" into the privacy of the home. They are a frightening threat to traditional ideas of the self as properly living rooted in one dear particular culture-bound place, participating in a single national culture, and firmly protected from any alien otherness. They are threatening also to traditional ideas of political action as based in a single topographical location, a given nation-state with its firm boundaries and its ethnic and cultural unity. Derrida calls this set of assumptions the *ontopolitologique*. It is not surprising that there should be powerful reactions to this "new and powerful advance of technological prosthesis that, in a thousand different ways, ex-propriates, de-localizes, de-territorializes, *extirpates*, that is to say, in the etymological sense, therefore the radical sense of this word, uproots, therefore *dis-etymologizes*, dissociates the political from the topological, separates from itself what has always been the very concept of the political, meaning by that what links the political to the topical, to the city, to the territory, to the ethno-national frontier."[14]

One reaction to this uprooting, dislocation, and blurring of borders discussed by Derrida is the violent return to nationalisms, to ethnic purities, and to fanatical militarized religions that are leading to such horrible bloodshed around the world. Though nothing could be more different from ethnic cleansing in Rwanda or Bosnia than a program in cultural studies, the development of such studies may be another very different reaction to the threat new communications technologies pose. Cultural studies can function as a way to contain and tame the threat of that invasive otherness the new technologies bring across the thresholds of our homes and workplaces.

This containing and taming takes a double contradictory form. On the one hand it reestablishes firm boundaries between one nation and another, one ethnic group and another, one gender or sexual orientation and another. The tradition of dividing the disciplines along national, linguistic, generic, or ethnic lines in the university remains to a considerable degree intact, in spite of much talk of interdisciplinarity and crossing the boundaries. Often the traditional divisions are now simply expanded to include separate programs in women's studies, gay and lesbian studies, Native American studies, African American studies, Chicano/Chicana studies, Asian American studies, film studies or visual culture studies, and so on. All these "others" are given a place in the university, but they are fenced off in a firm reestablishment of the inside-outside dichotomy that the new technologies threaten. The "others" are kept safely outside. Interdisciplinarity still presupposes the separate integrity of the disciplines that are crossed, that interact.

On the other hand, the return, wherever it occurs, to a mimetic, representational, descriptive methodology turns that threatening otherness into something that in theory (for this is a theory too) can be easily understood, "translated" (a term often used for this), and appropriated. The universalizing idea of "culture" in cultural studies is a place of exchange turning the other back into the self, that is, into something like the dominant culture. Individual works are often seen as unproblematically representative of the culture they reflect. A few carefully chosen examples can stand for the whole culture and give us a means of understanding it and taking it in. This procedure depends on a referential or thematic way of interpretation that sees texts or other cultural artifacts as reflective of a transparently understandable context. It also depends on an uncritical acceptance of the extremely dubious trope of synecdoche, part for whole, just as does taking "deconstruction" to stand for the whole of theory. This transparently understandable context can be easily translated into the terms of the university discipline assigned to assimilate it. The assumption of translation without essential loss is the key presupposition here. Such forms of archival appropriation have been in place in the university since the Humboldtian research university was first established. They are part of the foundational heritage of the university that says everything has its reason, can be brought to light, known, understood, assimilated. This double contradictory gesture says at once that the other is really other and may be kept safely outside, and that the other is not really other and may be made a *heimlich* member of the family.

This double gesture is by no means universal in cultural studies. Theory of the sixties, seventies, and eighties has gone on being effective. This includes the deep understanding of the divisions within culture by Raymond Williams and others in Britain, as well as the understanding of ideology by Althusser and other continental Marxists.[15] But wherever the double gesture is made, whether explicitly under the aegis of what David Simpson calls the "revolt against theory" or just spontaneously, as a defensive reflex to perceived threat, it will disable the project of cultural studies. It will prevent cultural studies from reaching their goal of political and institutional change toward that democracy to come. The acceptance by the university of cultural studies has been suspiciously rapid and easy. This may be because those in charge unconsciously assume it to be nonthreatening, to be leaving the old institutional structures more or less intact. The rise of cultural studies has accompanied the technologizing and globalizing turn in the university, and where it is an antitheoretical return to mimetism, it is no more than the mirror image of that turn.

Why does an antitheoretical turn, whenever it exists, disable cultural studies? For one thing, it often accompanies a regression to just that conservative hegemonic ideology it would contest. The right and certain components of the left are mirror images. You cannot use the ideology of those you would displace to displace their ideology. Wherever cultural studies accept and deploy antitheoretical, unreflective, precritical notions of the self and its agency, of referentiality, of the transparent factuality of cultural artifacts, of the possibility of unproblematically narrativizing history or of describing cultural features, their work will likely be politically ineffective.

VI

Rather than accepting uncritically the traditional model of the university as the place where everything is assimilated and archived as one more part of what can be unproblematically known, we need to develop a new university of dissensus, of the copresence of irreconcilable and to some degree mutually opaque goods.[16] We should get as much understanding of other cultures as possible, but with an uneasy recognition that just as translation may be impossible though we keep doing it, so the otherness of other cultures, like the otherness of other persons, may be ultimately impossible to know, though we must keep trying to know them. Along with that "must," however, should go a disquieting recognition that knowledge too is a form of violence against other cultures. The call or demand made on us by other cultures is not just for understanding but, as Anthony Appiah has forcefully argued, for respect.[17] Respect is not a statement of knowledge, a constative assertion. It is a speech act, a pledge, an attestation: "Yes, I respect that. I respect its otherness. I want that otherness to persist."

A university of respect rather than of knowledge, one based on dissensus rather than the search for consensus, would certainly be a transformation of the traditional university based on the search for a universalized truth. The presupposition of all I have said is that the university is being transformed irreversibly by the end of the cold war, the globalization of capitalism, and the new communication technologies. Nostalgia for the old Humboldtian university or even the hope that we might turn it into a new unified multicultural university to replace the monocultural one will not be effective in reversing the changes. The responsibility of those who teach and do research in the new university without idea is to see as clearly as possible where we are (no easy task) and to figure out ways to make use of what is left. This remnant must be the instrument of our transformative praxis.

This will be extremely difficult, because nostalgia for the old university of consensus devoted to the promulgation of a single culture will not easily die, since the very idea of the university depends on it, and also because in the new transnational university it will be hard to keep the humanities from becoming vestigial, no more than an assembly of programs teaching the communication skills needed by educated technocrats in the service of transnational corporations. Such a university would be primarily devoted to the production, transfer, and exchange of information. Rather than forming citizens of one nation-state, humanities programs in such a university may come to be charged with producing people trained for service in a global economy and trained also as expert consumers of that economy's products.

How can we humanists effectively resist this, and in the name of what alternative goal? A new university of dissensus would correspond best to the actual social and intellectual context within which the university is now embedded, and would also best counter the technologizing trend. It is extremely difficult to imagine how such a university would or should be organized, how it would be administered, who would decide how funds should be allotted, and how its accomplishments in teaching and research would be measured. Nevertheless, only such a university will justly respond to the situation in which we find ourselves today, and only such a university might hope to resist the new totalizing forces that go so strongly toward making the university an instrument of globalization helping create a new universal technologized society of consumers. Only a university of dissensus could be the locus of work toward the democracy to come that is the horizon of our calling.

NOTES

1. The best discussion of this is by William Readings in *The University in Ruins* (Cambridge: Harvard University Press, 1996). I have learned much from this important work, the best of the many current books about the transformation of the Western university. Readings's death in a commuter plane crash in the fall of 1994 was a great loss to scholarship and criticism, as well as a great personal loss for me.

2. George Eliot, *Middlemarch* (Harmondsworth: Penguin Books, 1974), 375.

3. See J. Hillis Miller, "Teaching *Middlemarch*: Close Reading and Theory," *Approaches to Teaching Eliot's "Middlemarch"*, Kathleen Blake, ed. (New York: The Modern Language Association of America, 1990), 51–63.

4. Marcel Proust, *A la recherche du temps perdu*, Jean-Yves Tadié, éd. de la Pléiade (Paris: Gallimard, 1989), 4:350; *Remembrance of Things Past*, trans. C. K. Scott Moncrieff (New York: Vintage, 1982), 3:795. Further references will be to these texts.

5. All these features of fractals are discussed in Hans Lauwerier, *Fractals: Endlessly Repeated Geometrical Figures*, trans. Sophia Gill-Hoffstädt (Princeton: Princeton University Press, 1991). Hans Lauwerier was until his retirement professor of mathematics at the University of Amsterdam. I mention this to indicate that his book is based on professional knowledge of the mathematics of fractals.

6. *What Future for the State? Daedalus* 124(2)(Spring 1995). This issue has essays by social scientists with titles like "The New World Order, Incorporated: The Rise of Business and the Decline of the Nation-State" (Vivien A. Schmidt). According to Schmidt, the result of the "liberalized new world order" is "a strengthening of business, with transnational corporations less tied to nations and national interests, and a weakening of the nation-state overall, in particular of the voice of the people through legislatures and nonbusiness, societal interests" (76). It would be hard to exaggerate the change in the United States university being brought about by the shift in funding from government agencies to transnational corporations.

7. Richard O'Brien, "Global Financial Integration: The End of Geography," in *Royal Institute of International Affairs, Chatham House Papers* (London: Pinter, 1992), 7.

8. Wallace Stevens, *Opus Posthumous* (New York: Knopf, 1957), 165.

9. See, for example, Samuel Weber, *Institution and Interpretation* (Minneapolis: University of Minnesota Press, 1987); Bernard Bergonzi, *Exploding English: Criticism, Theory, Culture* (Oxford: Oxford University Press, 1990); Peter Elbow, *What Is English?* (New York: The Modern Language Association of America; Urbana: The National Council of Teachers of English, 1990); Jacques Derrida, *Du droit à la philosophie* (Paris: Galilée, 1990); Gerald Graff, *Professing Literature: An Institutional History* (Chicago: University of Chicago Press, 1987) and *Beyond the Culture Wars: How Teaching the Conflicts Can Revitalize American Education* (New York: Norton, 1992); Jaroslav Pelikan, *The Idea of the University: A Reexamination* (New Haven: Yale University Press, 1992); Alfonso Borrero Cabal, *The University as an Institution Today* (Paris and Ottawa: UNESCO and the International Development Research Center, 1993); Ronald A. T. Judy, *(Dis)Forming the American Canon: African-Arabic Slave Narratives and the Vernacular* (Minneapolis: University of Minnesota Press, 1993); Antony Easthope, *Literary into Cultural Studies* (London and New York: Routledge, 1991); Bruce Wilshire, *The Moral Collapse of the University: Professionalism, Purity, and Alienation* (Albany: SUNY Press, 1990). Most of these are discussed by Readings.

10. As Readings puts this in a comment on Ronald A. T. Judy's *(Dis)Forming the American Canon:* "I am concerned to introduce a transitional step into the passage from the modern German University of national culture to the bureaucratic University of excellence, one which positions the United States University as the University of a national culture that is contentless" (*The University in Ruins,* 201).

11. Franklin Court, *Institutionalization of English Studies* (Stanford: Stanford University Press, 1992); Robert Crawford, *Devolving English Literature* (Oxford: Clarendon Press, 1992). One chapter of Crawford's book is entitled, "The Scottish Invention of English Literature" (16–44).

12. New York: Columbia University Press, 1989.

13. F. O. Matthiessen, *American Renaissance: Art and Expression in the Age of Emerson and Whitman* (New York: Oxford University Press, 1941); Charles Feidelson, Jr., *Symbolism and American Literature* (Chicago: University of Chicago Press, 1953); R. W. B. Lewis, *The American Adam: Innocence, Tragedy, and Tradition in the Nineteenth Century* (Chicago: University of Chicago Press, 1955); Perry Miller, *The New England Mind* (Cambridge: Harvard University Press, 1953); Roy Harvey Pearce, *The Continuity of American Poetry* (Princeton: Princeton University Press, 1961); Sacvan Bercovitch, *The*

Puritan Origins of the American Self (New Haven: Yale Univeristy Press, 1975); Harold Bloom, *Figures of Capable Imagination* (New York: Seabury Press, 1976).

14. From an unpublished seminar, my translation. Here is the original French: "Une nouvelle et puissante avancée de la pro-thèse technologique qui, de mille façons, ex-proprie, dé-localise, dé-territorialise, *extirpe*, c'est-à-dire, au sens étymologique, donc radical de ce mot, déracine, donc *désétymologise*, dissocie le politique du topologique, sépare de lui-même ce qui a toujours été le concept même du politique, à savoir ce qui lie le politique au topique, à la cité, au territoire, à la frontière ethno-nationale."

15. At least they understand culture as it is exemplified by the United Kingdom, a class society very different in social structure from the United States. In the United States, race, gender, and ethnic particularity are much more important than class in the European sense in determining the hierarchy of power and privilege.

16. Some parts of this essay develop ideas proposed in a brief essay published in *The Times Literary Supplement* in the summer of 1994. A funny thing happened to that essay on the way to the printer. It was cut and elegantly revised by the *TLS* editor, Alan Jenkins. I was given the opportunity to read and approve this new version. At some later point, however, the word "dissensus," still present in the final version I approved, was changed to "dissent." The word "dissenter" was then used in the title invented by someone at the *TLS*: "Return Dissenter." This change made my essay say the exact opposite of what I intended it to say. "Dissent" names a resistance to some hegemonic orthodoxy, as the dissenters in England resisted the established Church of England, or as Matthew Arnold makes fun of what he calls the "dissidence of dissent." "Dissensus," on the other hand, presupposes a situation where no dominant orthodoxy exists from which to dissent, only decentered and nonhierarchical communities of "peripheral singularities," as Bill Readings called them. I do not suppose that the change from "dissensus" to "dissent" was the result of a conspiracy by the *TLS* to subvert what I was trying to say. Some copyeditor or perhaps even some computer program was probably offended by the word "dissensus" and replaced it with a word in the *TLS*'s vocabulary. The subversion of my meaning was a striking example of the massive power of ideological assumptions in the media as they work in the seemingly neutral form of a journalistic "house style." It is apparently just not possible, within the *TLS*'s style, to say what I was trying to say. Therefore, I say it in this present essay.

17. In an unpublished lecture given at a conference in New York City, March 4, 1994.

FOUR

The Function of the Literary in a Time of Cultural Studies

Sacvan Bercovitch

The signs of the times are that cultural studies is here to stay. I hope that as it grows and flourishes it will preserve the literary in what still remains literary and cultural studies. What is at stake here is not just an issue of aesthetics but, more important (for my present purpose), the prospects of open dialogue in the humanities. I realize that my appeal to the literary in this context will raise objections about disciplinary distinctions. So let me say at once that I don't believe we have yet found a vantage point beyond disciplinarity. To recognize that disciplines are artificial is not to transcend them. Indeed, it may reinforce our sense of limitations. For example, we know that literature meant something different in fifteenth-century Italy from what it does now, but we know it because of a discipline called history. Information comes from institutional channels, not from Beyond: this commonplace holds true not only for specialists in English but also for eclectic students of culture. Their "bricolage approach," too, is spun out of the webs of disciplinarity: a certain controversial method in sociology, Marxism; a certain embattled method in psychology, psychoanalysis; a certain disputed mode of philosophy, deconstruction; or most tellingly, those vacillating combinations of sectarian methodologies (Althusser's Marx plus Lacan's Freud plus . . .). For our time and place, metadisciplinarity is a form of nostalgia born of frustration with modern specialization.

I share that frustration, but I believe that the way out (if there is one) lies *through* our recognition of limitation. To that end, I want to focus on two elementary aspects of the quasi-discipline we literary critics have inherited. One is formalist, the other political. The formalist aspect has to do with fictionality, the as-if world we enter, as Coleridge said, through a willing suspension of disbelief, allowing for the temporary dissolution of common-sense barriers between fancy and hard fact, so that even events that are empirically impossible may become a means of conveying what's humanly probable. We might conceive of literature in this sense as a test of the cultural work of the imagination. The as-if text proves its worth by heightening our understanding of the world as we know it. But the challenge may also be turned in the other direction. We can extend the literary approach to mean a willing suspension of *belief*, and we can apply it as such—as a temporary, ludic *resistance* to received modes of explanation—to the disciplinary frameworks, the structures of belief, within which we learned those hard facts in the first place. So conceived, textual criticism would be a test of the imaginative reach of the human sciences.

This sort of interchange implies the second, political aspect of the literary. I refer to the cultural foundations of textuality. What makes a work of literature extraordinary is not that it leaves the ordinary behind, but just the opposite. Its deep meanings and abiding values, including its aesthetic values, derive from its embeddedness in the ordinary—which is to say, from precisely the sort of everyday issues raised by cultural studies. Thus literary criticism has a double task. It is responsible for its evidence to textual realities that are uniquely *here*, in a world of their own, and broadly out *there*, in history and society. This doubleness has issued as a variety of questionable conjunctions. I have in mind the chronically unhappy marriage called literary history; the interdisciplinary tradition that appropriates literary works for cognitive purposes (Faulkner sociologized, theologized, psychologized); and the recent linguistic turn, which tends, conversely, to appropriate cognitive projects for literary purposes (society as text, history as narrative, Freud as storyteller). I am not forgetting the remarkable achievements of each of these approaches. My point in stressing the difficulties they raise is to focus on the problematic position of the literary in our time of cultural studies.

With that problem in view, let me suggest a fourth, counterdisciplinary function for literary study. I call it counter- (as distinct from anti-) disciplinary because it is meant not to discredit disciplinarity, but to test or challenge it. The assumption behind the test is that the disciplines we've developed to study culture have genuine cognitive value. They offer important data about the world we live in, and in some cases they tell us what we can reliably take to be the truth. But of course it's truth up to a point, within certain boundaries. And the advantage of literary criticism is that it frees cultural critics from being bounded in that cognitive sense. It allows them to contextualize what we know disciplinarily about culture—the truths-up-to-a-point of the human sciences—in terms of make-believe literary facts. The purpose is not to transcend the world out there. Quite the contrary: it is to challenge our knowledge of it in ways that return us more concretely, with more searching cultural specificity, to our nontranscendent realities.

I conceive of that act of recontextualization as a test by negation. We might compare this to the scientist's commitment, before proposing a new theory, to try by all means to disprove it. The difference is that for the scientist this test by negation is a means of progress and control. In the literary case, negation is both means and ends. There is no new system to replace the old if the test succeeds; no old system to keep in place if the test fails. In the counterdisciplinary game I propose, such terms as failure and success have to do with the limitations of systems, old and new. What's gained is a clearer, deeper sense of those limitations, a form of knowledge that *sustains* tensions. This will not solve the problem of the disciplines, but it may help us make use of the problem itself in ways that further our understanding of culture.

My example is two different instances of the chess analogy, one in Faulkner's *Light in August*, the other in a series of remarks by Wittgenstein, the philosopher most amenable nowadays (along with Heidegger) to cultural studies. The two passages appear in the appendix to this essay; the differences between them are what we'd expect, disciplinarily: the play of the imagination versus the rigors of logic. Faulkner invokes a chess game only to move, surprisingly, to a religious image. At the start, a man is compared to a pawn—the analogy is timeless, absolute (capital-P Player and pawn)—and at the end a man is compared to the Savior of the Christian Gospels, God incarnate as Christ. The victim's blood rushes out and he seems "to soar into their memories forever and ever"—clearly an allusion to the resurrection. But the crux of the scene, its center of significance, is a vivid description of a southern lynching: a "choked cry," a slashed loincloth, the peaceful, unbearable eyes. That particular event is the proper interpretive frame, the literary context, for those "broader" universalist allusions. Chess and the cross are abstractions applicable to situations across time and place, but their applicability in this passage depends on a specific action in a specific place and time. By the rules of this game, Fate and Christ are explained by a local fiction. Each of these absolutes carries various general meanings, of course—philosophical, theological—but as these generalities clash and coalesce here, in the literalness of this text, their meanings assume a culturally distinct substance, grounded in a certain make-believe figure, Joe Christmas, in Jefferson, Mississippi.

Wittgenstein's passage works in the opposite way. Here the analogies function (as he says) like an "x" in logic. They are local instances designed to prove an ahistorical abstraction. And provocatively, both instances are make-believe. In the first case, someone decides: "Now I will make myself a queen with very frightening eyes, she will drive everyone off the board." A patent fiction, but it's surrounded by a series of abstractions that seem incontrovertible. The point is: chess works like syntax, and syntax is the way that language functions. We've got to play by the rules. That "we" includes anybody, anywhere. To emphasize the point, Wittgenstein concludes with another analogy, this time to a hypothetical chess-planet, Mars, where theory and practice merge so that you can win a war by proving "scientifically" that the king will be captured in three moves. Again, a patent fiction, and again it makes perfect sense. Those made-up specifics (an imaginary player inventing a chess queen; a science-fiction world governed by the laws of chess) are contextualized by the laws of language. The implications of the fictions themselves are an invitation to cultural studies—consider that queen with frightening eyes—but the point of it all, the disciplinary frame of those implications, is that this is the way language works, all human language, anywhere. Wittgenstein's analogy is a thought-experiment that makes the imagination a vehicle of logic. The impossibility of the queen with frightening eyes proves a conceptual truth. In this sense, his passage may stand for the discipline at large. When Descartes says, "I think, therefore I am," he requires me to erase the multitude of particulars that literature builds upon—for example, all the particulars that make me different from Descartes. To understand Heraclitus' theory of flux ("We never step into the same river twice") requires me to banish the specific questions that literature starts and ends with: "Which river?" "At what time of year?" "Who is 'we'?" This mode of explanation inheres in all disciplines. We might say that ahistoricism is a disciplinary prerequisite, expressing an abiding human limitation: the urge to say it all.

By contrast, Faulkner's analogy is an image-experiment that makes the logic of absolutes a vehicle of local description. It's a difference in the relation between ends and means. Whereas philosophy uses particulars to arrive at general abstractions—an example or two can signify the totality of all language, including that of mathematics—the literary text uses generalities and abstractions to convey a local event. Here it is the particularities that "explain," even when the question concerns God or Fate. The reason is not that writers eschew totalities and absolutes. They have been absolutists more often than not. Nor is it that literature is subversive. The concept of the subversive artist is one more made-up abstraction (a fairly recent one); writers have been just as complicit in the ways of the world as any other group of people. Rather, it's that fictional particulars (unlike particulars in logic) bear a volatile relation to abstractions. They challenge us to understand what we believe in its cultural specificity. Philosophy says, "I think, therefore I am." Literature says, "That's what *you* think."

The result is "The Problem of the Disciplines" cited in the appendix: "Whereof one cannot speak, thereof one must be silent." Wittgenstein's well-known dictum may be taken as professional common sense. We often talk about what we don't know. It can make for very animated conversation. But it's the sort of conversation that philosophy calls chatter. Disciplines tell us what we can articulate knowingly—what makes logical sense, what we can prove happened, what we can predict will happen. In this view, literature is the realm of cognitive silence. By and large, that's what philosophers have always told us, from Plato on; and what certain postmodern aesthetes have retold us in their own way. Poetry doesn't *do* anything, and literature doesn't *teach* anything beyond itself. In Roland Barthes' phrase, its truth value lies in an infinite playfulness directed against "the fascism of language" (i.e., cognitive language of all kinds).[1] Wittgenstein's remark about Kafka is typical: "Here's a man who takes a lot of trouble to tell us what's *not* troubling him."[2] That rigorous disciplinary judgment applies to Faulkner as well. Wittgenstein's image of trouble is a fly trapped in a bottle. The philosopher shows the fly the way out. So does the economist and the psychologist. Faulkner, like Kafka, tells us what it's like to be the trapped fly. Even as he invokes the transcendent (God, Fate), he traps it in contrary as-if dictions that keep recalling us to our bottled-in condition.

Suppose then that, reversing tradition—inverting the standard interdisciplinary relation between text and context—we reconceive Wittgenstein's "one" in a literary context. In order to do so, we have to change the impersonal, transcultural, ahistorical universal "one" of philosophy (the one who has nothing more to say) into a fictional character. And after all, *isn't* it a fiction? Wittgenstein invented it, just as he invented the chess-planet. What does that invented person's remark about keeping silent mean? To answer that, we have to ask for further specifics: Who is the speaker? Where and when was this spoken? And once we've thus ventured outside the parameters of disciplinary logic, we are free to ask for further specifications. We can point out, for example, that the aphorism comes at the end of a work, the *Tractatus-Logico-Philosophicus*, that claims to solve all the problems of philosophy—all of them, once and for all. What if the author meant to ridicule such claims? "Whereof one cannot speak, thereof one must be silent": could this be a satiric comment, intended to characterize an academic Don

Quixote driven mad by reading too much symbolic logic? Suppose that by "one" Wittgenstein were mocking the entire enterprise of philosophy. What if "Ludwig Wittgenstein," the apparent author of the *Tractatus*, is really a figure of ridicule, the Obsessive Systematizer, speaking on and on about that whereof anyone, especially philosophers, ought to be silent?

This is not perversity on my part. Narrative irony is a standard literary device. It becomes a dominant technique in modern literature, with its emphasis on subjectivity and point of view, but actually it's endemic to all literary works—a feature inherent in the as-if ground of literary studies—and as such it offers a direct contrast with disciplinarity in its use of evidence. Narrative irony specifies the abstractions in the text as the expression of a certain individual, in a certain time and place, and thereby opens those abstractions to questions of culture. The disciplinary approach, on the contrary, specifies in order to abstract. For example, we could not teach *Being and Time* as a mockery of Heideggerian thought or Gibbon's *Fall of the Roman Empire* as a parody of historiography. If we did, we would be teaching a course in literature. Of course, philosophers and historians have sometimes written in this literary way, just as writers have sometimes written philosophy and history, but to say that is to reaffirm disciplinary boundaries. And the same boundaries apply in the matter of interpretation. We could dismiss Blake's claim concerning *Paradise Lost*—that Milton was of the devil's party without knowing it—by recourse to Calvinist exegesis; but that would be a theological argument. And conversely: we could read Marx's *Capital* from an ironic narrative perspective as a hymn to the irresistible powers of capitalism, but that would be mainly of literary interest. Disciplinarily—e.g., for purposes of economic theory—that interpretation would not matter.

At the risk of stating the obvious, let me stress that I am not arguing against abstractions. Rather, I'm proposing that we can regard those abstractions—without denying their general explanatory power—with the kind of cultural specificity that we apply to Christ and Fate in Faulkner's text. We can insist that, considered from a literary perspective, those abstractions have a specific textual habitation and a name. That is, we can set them in open dialogue with the particulars they explain (or explain away) in terms of rational abstractions. Thus we can interpret particulars and abstractions reciprocally, within a context that is at once rational and dissonant, systemic and make-believe, generally applicable and distinctive to this special set of circumstances. It is a context within which we may contest disciplinary boundaries, without pretending to transcend them (as Barthes does), and without denying their cognitive value. According to a famous dictum in statistical science, a founding principle of the insurance industry, "Nothing is more uncertain than the life of a man; nothing is more certain than the life span of a thousand men."[3] Disciplines depend upon such abstractions. Literary study can challenge the certainties they offer by considering the abstractions themselves in the same culture-specific terms we would apply to the uncertain life of a man.

Do we need literary criticism for this task? Alas, we do. Experience has shown all too often the arrogance of power/knowledge on the part of disciplines. Once we set disciplines loose on culture, they tend *sui generis* toward absolutes, closure, and solutions. Disciplines are control freaks. They psychoanalyze history, they philosophize aesthetics, they stage ideas as examples in economic theory, they make teleologies out of everyday situations. They are incurable cognitive imperialists, even when they champion humility, even when they come bearing the gifts of process and tolerance. This has been true from Plato's monologic dialogues to Derrida's predetermined indeterminacies.

All disciplinary roads lead to Wittgenstein's chess analogy. Can you willfully reinvent the queen? The disciplinary answer is No, in thunder: absolutely not. It's no accident that chess has become a commonplace of modern disciplines. For the sociologist Georg Simmel, it's a paradigm of the way that people think and behave. For Ferdinand de Saussure, it's the single best image of the science of linguistics. Others use it to describe the laws of history, institutional structures, and the rules of cultural coherence. Most directly, chess has served philosophically as *the* model of disciplinary cognition. Wittgenstein tells us that it represents "the nature of all propositions," "the basic relation between words and the world." We describe the world, he declares, "as we would talk about the rules of chess."[4]

For purposes of literary and cultural studies, Faulkner has a better idea. He talks about the rules of chess as we might describe a particular part of the world. His analogy comes in a climactic scene in the novel. The protagonist, Joe Christmas, who embodies the southern race problem (is he black or white?), has murdered his benefactor, Joanna Burden, and set fire to her house. The hunt for the killer is a major plot-frame of the novel. Faulkner underlines its significance by allusions to *Paradise Lost* and *Oedipus Rex*. The lynch mob is led by Percy Grimm, a patriot-fanatic who's driven (we're told) by "a belief that the white race is superior to any and all other races and that the American uniform is superior to all men." As the chase draws to a close the townspeople gather in a kind of outraged festivity, almost a holiday mood. One aspect of *that* context may be gleaned from a newspaper description of July Fourth in a southern town: "the birth of the nation was celebrated in the most sacred and festive manner, with firecrackers, rockets, Negroes, and whiskey in all its forms."⁵ Faulkner's scene might be read as a commentary on that catalogue:

> [Grimm] was moving again almost before he had stopped, with that lean, swift, blind obedience to whatever Player moved him on the Board. . . . He seemed indefatigable, not flesh and blood, as if the Player who moved him for pawn likewise found him breath. . . .
>
> But the Player was not done yet. When the others reached the kitchen they saw . . . Grimm stooping over the body . . . and when they saw what Grimm was doing one of the men gave a choked cry and stumbled back into the wall and began to vomit. Then Grimm too sprang back. . . . "Now you'll let white women alone, even in hell," he said. But the man on the floor had not moved. He just lay there, with his eyes empty of everything save consciousness . . . [looking] up at them with peaceful and unfathomable and unbearable eyes. Then his face, body, all, seemed to collapse . . . and from the slashed garments about his hips and loins the pent black blood seemed to rush like a released breath. It seemed to rush out of his pale body like the rush of sparks from a rising rocket; upon that black blast the man seemed to rise soaring into their memories forever and ever.

Imagine this passage as a move in a chess game. An abstract player, like a god in a Greek tragedy—like the Fate that drives Oedipus to Thebes—moves a white piece into position to capture what appears to be its black counterpart. The capture itself, however, turns into a surprising reversal. Metaphorically, it's the black pawn that wins, or seems to; it captures our imagination by emerging as the crucified Jesus, a triumphant black king.

Now, this transformation calls the logic of chess as we know it into question, but—and this is crucial to literary function—it does not dissolve or even blur the analogy itself. It may actually be said to enforce the truism that the analogy implies (life is a game of chess) since the passage as a whole expands the scope of the game to include religion, race, politics, and sexuality. And yet the game, so expanded, depends on a set of make-believe particulars. What's the relation of Oedipus to Percy Grimm and Joe Christmas? Is this relevant to the castration that follows, and does castration point us toward racist concepts of black manhood (as in Grimm's cry about white women)? Does Faulkner's pun on "rising rocket" connect sexual and national layers of meaning? What bearing does all this have on the intertextual allusions to *Paradise Lost* and *Oedipus Rex*, the Fall and self-knowledge? Such queries are raised by the entire narrative, and to answer them leads us necessarily to disciplinary sources and rational explanations. The search for fictional significance is a matter of coherent configurations, like a strategy in chess. We bring pawn, queen, and king together into a certain logical juxta-position, and we proceed to play out the interpretation according to the rules of the game.

From a literary perspective, this entire systematic, rational procedure is disciplined by the fictions of *Light in August*. And as we've seen, *this* "disci-pline"—our literary concern with the fictional particular—entails a double set of concerns, political and formalist, worldly and as-if. In the first case, we are required to interpret the fictions through their cultural connections. Faulkner's Christ figure means (among other things) a tradition of southern lynching, a sexual mythology of blackness, a patriotic ritual, and a history of class antagonism against blacks on the part of poor whites like Percy Grimm. To explicate the scene without reference to issues of sex, race, gender, and American violence would be to drain the passage of its *aesthetic* force (ambi-guity, complexity, defamiliarization, chiasmus, etc.). Formalist explication itself requires us here to draw on disciplines called history, sociology, etc. But we need not authorize these as *textual* explanations. Instead, we can see them in the as-if light of the text. They are abstractions whose meaning depends on the facts of *this* fiction. Our task as literary critics is to make sense of those disciplinary insights in terms of certain literary-cultural specifics. To do so, let me suggest, would be to address a troubling issue for literary critics engaged in cultural studies: What can we contribute in our dialogue with the human sciences? For example, what can we say about matters that concern (say) sociology that sociologists can't say as well, or better? Answer: a liter-ary-cultural perspective can open up sociology as a cognitive system by investing its abstractions with the malleability, the ungroundedness of liter-ary evidence. For this analytic occasion, suspending sociology's beliefs, we take the fictive for our measure of truth. The insights we gain thereby about race, sexuality, class, and national rituals function as a mode of inquiry. We prove disciplinary norms (in the primal double sense of "prove," as affirma-tion and as doubt) by the as-if terms of fiction.

The challenge is as demanding in its way as the leap of faith. The norms involved are part of our cultural inheritance. We entrust our lives to them. They represent the certainties by which we act, our categories of value and thought. And these certainties, be it noted, are not only logically "necessary" but humanly desirable, necessary to our sense of well-being. We *want* philosophers to give us Answers (or at least the Right Questions). We want economists to figure things out once and for all. How could we *not* value the achievements of the culture through which, after all is said and done—after we've recognized the tentative nature of its truths and exposed its deficiencies and traps—we define ourselves, make decisions, and formulate alternatives? And yet, against all this, there's the as-if truth of the literary. Now, for this moment, in this interpretive interval, we are invited to suspend normative cultural frames of reference. To play *this* game, we have to recognize that the truth is—we don't know. We are dealing by definition with truth beyond the point of organized knowledge but within the scope of culture. For now, these un-disciplined specifics provide our framework for cultural analysis.

Imagine a version of chess created in that counterdisciplinary spirit: for example, a game that (by a willing suspension of belief) could accommodate Wittgenstein's queen with frightening eyes. We're asked to explain the chess rules through a newfangled figure that suddenly drives everyone off the board. What sort of game could permit that and still be chess, as we played it yesterday, or as someone played it, say, 500 years ago, at the end of the fifteenth century?

In order to reply, we would have to imagine two quite different ways to play chess. One of these is the game we know. We follow the rules by which a chess piece is an x in logic, a particular that stands for an abstraction. We could think of it as a kind of Weberian Ideal Type, a cultural representation that, cognitively, transcends the varieties of cultural experience. The queen on this board stands for *the* queen ahistorically. That's a pure example of the sort of database that disciplines work with: case histories, statistics, hard facts that support regulatory generalizations. That dream you had last night supports the Oedipal theory, ahistorically. These economic statistics prove the general rule of class struggle. As Wittgenstein remarks:

> Every syntax . . . [is] a system of rules. . . . Chess does not consist in my pushing wooden figures around a board. If I say "Now I will make myself a queen with very frightening eyes, she will drive everyone off the board" you will laugh . . . [because] the totality of the game determines the [piece's] logical place. A pawn is . . . like the "x" in logic. . . . [And so too, by extension, any particular chess strategy] must be considered a scientific question, [similar to the question of] whether the king could be mated . . . in three moves.

"Totality," "the game determines": the picture at which (by contrast) we are asked to laugh—a player suddenly, willfully, reconceiving the queen—implies the impotence of radical innovation, the absurdity of "my pushing" against the object's "logical place," my impudence in talking about that of which we cannot speak.

Of course that's not what Wittgenstein means to say, here or elsewhere in his later thought. And it's the later Wittgenstein I mean to invoke, the resolutely anti-abstractionist, anti-absolutist author of *Philosophical Investigations*. That's precisely why I chose him for my exemplary antagonist. I might more comfortably have settled on a systematizer like Hegel, who believed that philosophy is the thoughts of God before creation; or a social scientist like Durkheim, for whom "only the universal is rational" and only the rational counts ("the particulars and the concrete baffle understanding," he explains; they belong exclusively to "poets and literary people who describe things as they seem to be without any rational method").[6] But my point is: *even* Wittgenstein shares this approach—as does the great modern tradition he represents of the antisystemic in philosophy, from Kierkegaard and Nietzsche through Heidegger. Disciplinarily, the antisystemic is also a form of systematicity. It is antisystemic in relation to other approaches in philosophy; but in relation to literature and literary study it remains bound to the cognitive principles implicit in Wittgenstein's x in logic. A Wittgensteinian literary critic will make the literary a text-proof of (his or her) Wittgenstein; we can virtually predict the result of any such analysis.

I believe that Wittgenstein expresses the frustrations of philosophy qua philosophy, the discipline that requires us to know logically, cognitively, what we're talking about. They are the frustrations of a professional thinker who is a philosopher, like it or not, and accordingly saddled with the restrictions of disciplinarity. I've found that these are more or less the same restrictions that confine cultural critics who come with any systemic answer or configuration of answers, implicit or explicit, to problems of culture. Their answers make sense, to be sure, and like Wittgenstein's analogy they persuade us insofar as they correspond to the rules of the game as we play it. But that's only one way to describe the game of chess.

The other way is inscribed in Faulkner's questionable analogy. And the first thing to say about it is that it does not contradict Wittgenstein. On the contrary, it compels inquiry by its groundedness in accepted generalizations, and it derives its aesthetic meanings from the familiar game of chess. Nonetheless, it defies systemic inquiry. For example, it requires us to analyze Fate as an American legionnaire, Percy Grimm, in an act of terror marked by "black blood" and lit up by a festive "rush of sparks." What does Fate mean in these fictive terms? How could such an analysis proceed?

To begin with, we would be dealing in layers, not levels, of meaning. Levels imply an up-to-date, state-of-the-discipline answer. They demand closure, at least for the time being, like the answer to the last house on the block. Other houses may eventually spring up, but until they do, *that* last house is the right answer. And it's a valuable answer. It allows us to get *some-*

where, rather than running in hermeneutic circles. Nonetheless, the right answer forms a hermeneutic circle of its own. The last-house-on-the-block answer is always the same. Once *the* house has been identified, we can always predict—wherever we're coming from, however we frame the question, whatever the occasion—where we'll arrive at the end. The last house on the block is sexuality for Freud, class for Marx, Christ for Christians, pragmatism for pragmatists, power for Foucauldians, and Wittgenstein for Wittgensteinians. And so far as *they* are concerned it was fundamentally the same at the end of the fifteenth century as it is now.

By contrast, the layers I speak of are reversible, interchangeable. Faulkner introduces the chess analogy in a highly specialized way (player and pawn) to explain the lynching of Joe Christmas. But in the course of working out the fiction—as Faulkner plays out that as-if situation—he develops the analogy into a multilayered configuration (sex-Christ-Fate-race), any layer of which could serve as the deep one, depending on which perspective you prefer (psychology, theology, philosophy, sociology). Thus, considered as a whole, this literary configuration suggests that levels of meaning are not hierarchies (as in scriptural exegesis or in social science). They are made up, even if we find them to be true in any given situation, or under certain conditions. They are as-if meanings *as well as* true or false meanings, and as a result they are inherently subject to interchangeability. They can complement each other, expand or circumscribe each other, question or contradict each other. And the more particulars they force us to account for in the process, the better. Any analysis of meaning here must presuppose the *limitations* of human knowledge. It must confront the possibilities *within culture* that lie beyond the point of received truth. Disciplines also acknowledge those limitations, of course; they always remind us how far we have yet to go. But they do so in order to tell us how far we've come, and to urge us forward. The literary voice comes to us from the other side of the divide—the side that, although demonstrably *in* this world, is not (yet) cognitively *of* it.

This counterdisciplinary perspective entails a counterconventional use of the language of interpretation. I've indicated this by my distinction between levels and layers of meaning. Literary depth, as I understand it, involves common questions rather than revelatory answers. It is a depth measured by the capacity of cultural specifics in the text to resist disciplinary appropriation. Let me add to that the distinction between positive vis-à-vis negative universals—we might call them disciplinary vis-à-vis literary universals. By negative or literary universals I mean limitations: our universal human limitations of will, reason, imagination, and endurance. These are the universals that bind the cultural specifics of the literary text. And by positive or disciplinary universals I mean the particular solutions we devise to overcome those limitations, or at least to make do with them. These are the abstractions common to the human sciences. As solutions, they differ from one society to another, one century to the next: *a* theory of justice, *a* standard of excellence, *an* explanation for violence. Cognitively, they lead upward from fact to concept, from the representative particular to the general solution. And as I said, literature builds upon those positive universals— it thrives on concepts and solutions—but as literary critics we have the license to recontextualize these as expressions of negative universals. We can see them—Christ, Fate, Dialectical Materialism, Oedipal Sexuality—as clusters of cultural specifics, grounded in the volatile materials of textuality. That is to say, we can interpret them from the same perspective we use in understanding what the lynching of Joe Christmas "really" means.

The sort of information this provides does not constitute knowledge in any disciplinary sense. It does not offer control, not even on the secondary level that Aristotle posited in defining the aesthetic as the realm of the probable, since what I'm suggesting calls that very concept into question. (What is the probable in any given text but a cultural specific?) Certainly it does not offer us instruments of progress. Marxists think they know more about history than empiricists or idealists. Psychoanalysts are certain that pre-modern theories of the dream are as outmoded as the Ptolemaic system. Wittgensteinians think that they can reason better than Platonists, not just differently but more clearly. But no Faulknerian will claim that *Light in August* teaches us more about society, psychology, or philosophy than Milton does, or Sophocles, and certainly not more about literature.

What we have, then, are two models of analysis, two ways of playing chess—one systemic, the other countersystemic. The literary model as I conceive it is different, not superior. I believe in the disciplinary quest for truth. We *should* want to find answers (the best way to organize society, the highest moral principles). The language games we play would become less human, less than human, if we gave up on positive universals. It would be scandalous to revise the past without believing in some sense in historical truth, or to institute social change without believing in some sense in progress. When I suggested just now that the probable in any given text is a cultural specific—a certain notion of greatness, a particular ideal of manhood—I assumed the viability of the concept itself of the probable (not only to disciplinary discourse but also to aesthetic appreciation). My point is the challenge, the test by negation. It's the job of cognitive disciplines to try to get us closer to answers, however distant *the* answer remains. And the job of literary study is to keep the game going. Literary particulars offer a context for an inquiry into the probabilities we live with. That inquiry can teach us more about ourselves, perhaps more about others, certainly more about the dynamics between language and culture. Indeed, we might say that negation in this context has a dimension of progress in its own right. Counterdisciplinarity, as I conceive it, can contribute to the overall project of cultural studies by insisting *through* negation that we are always already more than our culture tells us we are, just as a language is more than a discipline and just as a literary text is more than the sum of the explanations, solutions, probabilities, and abstractions that it accumulates as it travels across time and space.

Suppose we tried to reconstruct the game of chess in these counterdisciplinary terms. What would a game look like? Answer one: it would look like Faulkner's text. Answer two: it would look like a lot of literary texts. Answer three: it would look a lot like the world we live in. Answer four: it would look just like *the* game of chess. We think of any given chess match (Fischer versus Spassky, Kasparov versus Deep Blue) as the epitome of the arbitrary (a game) as the systemic (universal law). But in the long view a chess match, any match, is a story of continual transition, involving the zigzag histories of cultures, a shifting configuration of the most unlikely reciprocities between rules governing different areas of life, the ancient, multilingual, transnational "game of games." The origins of chess remain a matter of dispute, but we know that in Malaya the rules changed with successive religious influences (Hindu, Shintoist, Islamic); that in India, China, and the Middle East chess moves were directly linked to large-scale war games; and that the original Near Eastern and Arabic names for chess (*chatrang, shantranj*) reflect variations in political hierarchy, as do early Korean forms of the game. We know further that, during the Renaissance, chess was played at tournaments with human "pieces" on enormous fields; that the meanings of chess pieces have fluctuated with the fates of empires; and that fluctuation has brought with it constant crisscrossings of institutional, conceptual, and even technological structures—in our day—for instance, the radical changes introduced by the Fischer timeclock. A contemporary match could be contextualized through the overlappings of feudal Spanish knight and castebound Indian pawn with our space-age timer at a courtly Renaissance tournament.[7]

Think of what it would mean to describe a chess match in this context! It would be like explaining the castration of Joe Christmas through allusions to Fate and the crucifixion, to *Oedipus Rex* and *Paradise Lost*, to southern history, national holidays, and race-class-gender. We would have to account for the most unlikely transhistorical correspondences, transpositions, transgressions, inversions. The point of analysis would be to explain why we are *not* bound to systems, including those we play by. Why (to recall Faulkner's Oedipal-Miltonic chess game) did the wisdom of the Greeks fail to solve our moral problems? Why did the triumph of Christianity turn into the world of Joe Christmas? And conversely, why, as *Light in August* also testifies, did Christianity and the wisdom of the Greeks prevail in spite of those de facto failures? Why, in spite of all we've learned, do we still invoke Fate? How does chess, with its antique, mixed-up hierarchy, persist in our democratic world? And how can we account, except by negation, for the metamorphoses that constitute the mix—as for example in medieval Rome, when the Persian vizier or counselor was replaced by the queen; or several centuries later, when the queen assumed what we now consider to be her lawful place on the board?

That last moment is significant enough to stand as a paradigm for chess in general. It inaugurated the rules of modern chess, the game as we now play it. Evidently, half a millennium ago, in the last quarter of the fifteenth century, somewhere in Spain, Portugal, or Italy, the game of chess changed qualitatively. The significant developments centered on speed of contact and scope of personal initiative. The main innovation lay in the expanded powers of the queen, which, from being the weakest player, weaker than the pawn, suddenly became the strongest single unit on the board. By the 1490s—the decade when America was instated as a global player—chess had begun anew. According to experts, the game then developed a coherent new system with a complete theory of its own, widely known as the theory of the Mad Queen, *eschés de la dame enragée, ala rabiosa.* Chess historians have made the predictable Renaissance correspondences: expanded mobility, the new individualism, the invention of the printing press, and the great queens of empire, from Isabella of Spain to Elizabeth of England. And indeed Isabella herself is directly implicated: the first published treatise on the New Chess was dedicated to her in 1496 by the author, the courtier-poet Luis de Lucena, who had it bound together with a group of Petrarchan sonnets and entitled it all *The Game of Love.*

Lucena's Mad Queen is an emblem of literary context. She is a fit opponent for the queen with frightening eyes, emblem of the disciplinary taboo: "Thou shalt not violate the rules of the game." Wittgenstein's queen is imaginary, as-if, but she enforces actual restrictions; Lucena's Mad Queen is an actual historical figure, but she proves that systemic logic can be malleable, susceptible to agency and cultural change. And in doing so, she brings together the games of technology, imperialism, and social hierarchy, of courtly love and the sonnet. Each of these games invites an x-in-logic procedure, but taken together, as an overlapping configuration of different game rules—the conflicting rules of what Wittgenstein would call a family of games—they require explanations that are countersystemic. Such explanations are based on the silences that underlie our systems of knowledge. And they work cognitively by opening up the possibilities available to analysis under the rules. *Under,* as in subject to the rules, but also within them, at once undergirding the rules and undermining them; *under* as in underlie, involving possibilities that in some sense *these* absolutes really do speak the truth—possibilities too of an unsettling kind, prospects that have been declared out of bounds, or that have not yet been explored—variations, transformations, or innovations that may affect the rules themselves, and so alter the nature of the game. *Under,* as in the volatile layers of literary depth.

Now, let me translate all this into the terms of literary and cultural studies.

1. At any given time, culture is relatively coherent, a system of disparate but interlinked areas of life (religious, economic, moral, etc.), each of which might be compared to the game of chess. Literary analysis can help mediate among them.

2. Culture is a countersystemic cluster of interlinked but disparate areas of life, the rules of which, considered together, resemble *the* game of chess. The best single model of the game for our time and place is a literary text.

3. The literary text simultaneously engages, embraces, and disclaims the rules that frame the rhetorics of culture, and it does so in precisely the area, language, that bears the most responsibility for the ways we understand the world. We can extend our counterdisciplinary outlook, accordingly, to the rhetorics from which it came, from which it's made, and through which it appeals.

4. Literature is a testament to the power of cultural systems; but literary analysis requires us to see cultural systems as testaments to the power of textual transvaluation, and to recognize that the abstractions on which those systems build may in time become specific points of departure, perhaps points from which to reconceive the game at large. So reconceived, the game of culture, while systemic at any given moment, remains universally subject to intervention— as when the thousand-year-old doctrine of the king's divine right became a key player in the language game of American individualism: Jefferson's "kingly commons," Whitman's "divine average," Faulkner's pawn-become-king, the black and/or white king with unbearable eyes.

I take that last, surprising, willful, overdetermined, and arbitrary figure to represent the function of the literary in our time of cultural studies. It opens up a language game that requires us to play for keeps (win, lose, or draw) in a counterdisciplinary match that we expect will leave us, wherever we end, in the midst of things, professionally and humanly.

APPENDIX

A. *The Problem of the Disciplines*

> Whereof one cannot speak, thereof one must be silent (Wovon man nicht sprechen kann, darüber müß man schweigen).
>
> —LUDWIG WITTGENSTEIN, *Tractatus Logico-Philosophicus*, trans. C. K. Ogden
> (London: Routledge, 1989), 189.

B. *The Literary Text*

> [Grimm] was moving again almost before he had stopped, with that lean, swift, blind obedience to whatever Player moved him on the board. He seemed indefatigable, not flesh and blood, as if the Player who moved him for pawn likewise found him breath. . . .
>
> But the Player was not done yet. When the others reached the kitchen they saw Grimm stooping over the body . . . and when they saw what Grimm was doing one of the men gave a choked cry and stumbled back into the wall and began to vomit. Then Grimm too sprang back. "Now you'll let white women alone, even in hell," he said. But the man on the floor had not moved. He just lay there, with his eyes empty of everything save consciousness . . . [looking] up at them with peaceful and unfathomable and unbearable eyes. Then his face, body, all, seemed to collapse . . . and from the slashed garments about his hips and loins the pent black blood seemed to rush like a released breath. It seemed to rush out of his pale body like the rush of sparks from a rising rocket; upon that black blast the man seemed to rise soaring into their memories forever and ever.
>
> —WILLIAM FAULKNER, *Light in August* (New York: Random House, 1932), 439–40.

C. *The Disciplinary Text*

> Every syntax can be regarded as a system of rules for a game. I have been reflecting on what . . . [it] can mean [to say] . . . that a formalist

regards the axioms of mathematics as similar to the rules of chess. I would like to say: not on the axioms of mathematics, but the whole syntax is arbitrary.

I was asked in Cambridge whether I think that mathematics concerns ink marks on paper [as does literature]. I reply: in just the same sense in which chess concerns wooden figures. Chess, I mean, does not consist in my pushing wooden figures around a board. If I say, "Now I will make myself a queen with very frightening eyes, she will drive everyone off the board," you will laugh. It does not matter what a pawn looks like. What is rather the case is that the totality of rules of the game determines the logical place of a pawn. A pawn is a variable, like the "x" in logic. . . .

If you ask me: where lies the difference between chess and the syntax of a language, I reply: solely in their application. . . . If there were men on Mars who made war like the chess pieces, then the generals would use the rules of chess for prediction. It would then be a scientific question whether the king could be mated by a certain deployment of pieces in three moves, and so on.

—WITTGENSTEIN AND THE VIENNA CIRCLE: CONVERSATIONS RECORDED BY
FRIEDRICH WAISMANN, ed. Brian McGuiness, trans. Joachim Schulte and Brian
McGuiness (Oxford: Oxford University Press, 1979), 103–4.

NOTES

1. Roland Barthes, "Inaugural Lecture, Collège de France," in Susan Sontag, ed., *A Barthes Reader* (New York: Hill and Wang, 1982), 461–62. This paper is a revised version of a talk I gave at the Critical Theory Institute of the University of California, Irvine. My thanks to John Carlos Rowe and the members of the Institute for their hospitality and their intellectual generosity.

2. Quote in Ray Monk, *Ludwig Wittgenstein: The Duty of Genius* (New York: Viking Penguin, 1990), 498.

3. Elizur White, 1856, quoted in Susan L. Mizruchi, *The Science of Sacrifice: American Literature and Modern Social Theory* (Princeton: Princeton University Press, 1998).

4. Ludwig Wittgenstein, *Philosophical Investigations*, trans. G. E. M. Anscombe (New York: Macmillan, 1953), 46e–47e (no. 108).

5. Quoted in Stephen James's forthcoming doctoral dissertation (Harvard University) on July Fourth rituals.

6. Quoted in Mizruchi, *Science of Sacrifice*.

7. Richard Eales, *Chess: The History of the Game* (New York: Oxford University Press, 1985), 18–38. My references to chess history are drawn from a variety of sources, the best of which remains H. J. R. Murray, *A History of Chess* (Oxford: Oxford University Press, 1913).

FIVE

Discipline and Distraction:
Psycho, Visual Culture, and Postmodern Cinema

Linda Williams

Whatever the pictorial turn is . . . it is not a return to naïve mimetic theories of representation, or a renewed metaphysics of pictorial presence: it is, rather, a postlinguistic, postsemiotic rediscovery of the picture as a complex interplay between visuality, apparatus, discourse, bodies, and figurality. It is the realization that spectatorship (the look, the gaze, the glance, the practices of observation, surveillance, and visual pleasure) may be as deep a problem as various forms of *reading* (decipherment, decoding, interpretation, etc.) and that visual experience or "visual literacy" might not be fully explicable on the model of textuality. Most important, it is the realization that while the problem of pictorial representation has always been with us, it presses inescapably now, and with unprecedented force, on every level of culture, from the most refined philosophical speculations to the most vulgar productions of the mass media.

—W. J. T. MITCHELL

If you've designed a picture correctly, in terms of its emotional impact, the Japanese audience would scream at the same time as the Indian audience.

—ALFRED HITCHCOCK

You might think that the discipline of film studies would be one of the first to welcome the idea of a pictorial turn—that it might even be ideally suited to envision what Mitchell in the passage quoted above calls a "global critique of visual culture." In fact, however, because film studies achieved its first academic legitimacy through appropriations of linguistic models of textuality, and because its highly influential feminist strain has achieved its greatest recognition via Laura Mulvey's well-known attack on "visual pleasure," it has not embraced this "postlinguistic, postsemiotic rediscovery of the picture as a complex interplay between visuality, apparatus, discourse, bodies, and figurality" as thoroughly as it might. Though I admit to not being exactly sure what this new turn really means, I agree that something about the way viewers take in and process the visual, something about the way bodies negotiate the proliferating images of contemporary visual culture, was not adequately addressed in the "linguistic turn" and needs to be addressed now.

The following study of the place of Alfred Hitchcock's *Psycho* (1960) in the discipline of film studies is one way of addressing this question. I am interested in how W. J. T. Mitchell's notion of a "pictorial turn" relates to the discipline of film studies and to the periodization of American cinema. My focus is on the critical and spectatorial reception of a film that has been crucial to the constitution of new ways of seeing, and feeling, films—ways that are simultaneously more distracted and more disciplined than the so-called classical cinema. Released in the summer of 1960—a date that has been taken by some, though certainly not by all, to mark the end of the classical Hollywood style and mode of production and the beginning of a much more amorphously defined postclassical, postmodern cinema—*Psycho* has nevertheless not previously been viewed as a quintessentially postmodern film.[1] I will explore some of the reasons for this in a later section. For the moment let me try to defend the invocation of the term "postmodern" in cinema.

To do so is to open up a thorny area of debate. The term is imprecise and is enormously complicated by the way the medium of cinema has, since its inception, been equated with modernity. Fredric Jameson sees postmodernism in cinema as a relatively recent occurrence determined by the "cultural logic of late capitalism" manifested in a schizophrenic, decentered subjectivity that can be seen in popular cinema in the pervasive mode of nostalgia and pastiche that flattens all time (1991), or, more recently, in the prevalence of paranoid conspiracy thrillers in which communication technologies are often central metaphors (1992).

Anne Friedberg, on the other hand, has argued the need to first sort out cinema's problematic relation to the modern, as well as its relation to the various cinematic avant gardes, before leaping to embrace the "p" word (1993). For Friedberg the very apparatus of the cinema makes the stylistic categories of modernism and postmodernism inappropriate, since it constructs a "virtual, mobilized gaze" through a photographically represented "elsewhere and elsewhen" that is already postmodern. Thus for Friedberg there is no precise moment of temporal rupture between the modern and the postmodern, but only a subtle transformation produced by the increasing centrality of the image-producing and reproducing apparatuses (170).

I agree with Friedberg that the basic elements of the so-called postmodern condition consist in the "instrumentalized acceleration of spatial and temporal fluidities" that have always operated in cinema (179). In this sense all cinema *is*, as Friedberg puts it, "proto-postmodern." I also agree with her that a mere thematics of nostalgia does not adequately define a postmodern film. However, the temptation remains to locate specific films or genres that emphatically perform the kind of acceleration of fluidities Friedberg mentions. My own particular temptation is to locate within the history of cinematic reception a moment in which audience responses to postmodern gender and sexual fluidity, schizophrenia, and irony began not only to become central *attractions* of "going to the movies" but to call for new spectatorial *disciplines* capable of enhancing these attractions.

I therefore argue that Alfred Hitchcock's *Psycho* (1960) marks a moment in popular film reception when the more stable qualities of the "classical Hollywood cinema"—defined as a cinema of strong narrative logic and causality, psychological motivation, character-driven events, spectatorial absorption into a diegesis, and identification with characters (Bordwell et al. 1985)—began to be replaced by postmodern styles and themes in a mode of reception that I shall characterize as simultaneously more distracted *and* more disciplined than that of the so-called classical cinema. I will argue, ultimately, that it is this peculiar combination of heightened distraction with heightened discipline that marks the postmodern reception of cinema.

In the above citation, W. J. T. Mitchell argues that "the picture"—by which he means still and moving analogical and digital images of all kinds—has come to represent our most pressing postmodern problem: "The picture now has a status somewhere between what Thomas Kuhn called a 'paradigm' and an 'anomaly,' emerging as a central topic of discussion in the human sciences in the way that language once did: that is, as a kind of model or figure for other things (including figuration itself) and as an unsolved problem, perhaps even the object of its own 'science,' what Erwin Panofsky called an 'iconology' " (2). Mitchell isolates "the pictorial turn" not simply as the existence of an unprecedentedly vast image culture—including film, video, cybernetic technology, and electronic reproduction—but also as the emergence of visuality as a key theoretical problem of postmodernism. If we consult, however, any one of a number of recent theorists of the visual, we immediately encounter a problem: as Martin Jay has recently noted, the antihumanist, counterenlightenment tendencies of twentieth-century French thought have been inextricably wedded to a "denigration of vision." Bluntly put, theorists of vision are themselves deeply suspicious of the visual.

Martin Jay's magisterial, intellectual history of the role of vision in contemporary French theory, *Downcast Eyes: The Denigration of Vision in Twentieth Century French Thought*, traces the complex historical strands of a "French suspicion of vision" that has indelibly marked current attempts to theorize visual culture. Jay argues that despite (or perhaps because of) the once-honored place of the visual in classical French culture, the late nineteenth century saw a crisis of the visual. The works of Georges Bataille and the Surrealists provide some of the most dramatic examples of this denigration of vision in the early twentieth century. Throughout Surrealism, but most emphatically in Bataille's *History of the Eye* and Buñuel and Dali's *Un chien andalou*, the eye is dethroned from its Cartesian position as organ of "pure and noble vision" and made a target of mutilation and scorn. Jay contrasts, for example, the serene dissection of the cow's eye in Descartes' *Dioptrique*, the founding document of the Cartesian perspectivalist tradition, to the insidious slicing of the woman's eye in Buñuel and Dali's film (260–61).

Jay traces this ocularphobic tradition through phenomenology's sadomasochistic dialectic of "the look," Lacan and Althusser's constructions of the deluded specular subject of ideology, Foucault's disciplinary gaze of surveillance, Debord's spectacle, Barthes and Metz's analyses of the "eye's technological extensions" (435) in photography and cinema, Derrida and Irigaray's critique of "phallog*ocular*centrism," and finally Levinas and Lyotard's promotion of an "ethics of blindness" in the postmodern sublime. Jay shows that the interrogation of vision and visuality is profound and pervasive in French theory. Jay especially helps explain the often vexed place of the visual in the discipline of film studies.[2] Although it is a simplification to say that vision has been "denigrated" in French theory, those of us who have been engaged in the study of French film theory ever since the "linguistic turn" brought academic respectability to what had previously been viewed as an uncritical fandom cannot help but recognize a partial truth in Jay's story. For it is true that vision has been consistently characterized as delusion in much French film theory, especially in Baudry and Metz. It is also true that the critique of vision easily slides into a denigration of the visual in general. From this perspective Jay's book offers unusual insight into the extraordinary appeal of French theory with respect to film study proper.

For example, Jay cites a moment, late in the tradition he traces, when Fredric Jameson invokes the full authority of the French antiocularcentric tradition in the opening words of his *Signatures of the Visible*: "The visible is *essentially* pornographic, which is to say that it has its end in rapt, mindless fascination. . . . Pornographic films are thus only the potentiation of films in general, which ask us to stare at the world as though it were a naked body" (1).³

"Rapt, mindless fascination" is certainly an apt formulation of what provokes current anxieties about the nature of contemporary mass visual culture and the dangers of visual capture. We must question, however, the actual usefulness of such a characterization of spectatorial submission to the visual image of film. The problem with such a formulation is that it sets up an opposition between the sensual pleasures of vision and the abstraction of critical thought—as if thought could never take place in and through a body. Accusing spectators of participating in an excess of both the visual and the corporeal, it reduces this excess to an "essential" pornography that simply vilifies viewing itself. Vision, especially vision that engages the body in visceral response, becomes stigmatized either as an abusive form of power or as a contrary, but equally stigmatized, passivity.

The problem we face in understanding contemporary forms of visual culture is how to take account of them without demonizing or denigrating this culture *for* its visuality. In the case of film studies in particular this often comes down to not demonizing the power of moving images to move the bodies of spectators. Jay's conclusion that "ocular-*ec*centricity," rather than blindness, should be the antidote to privileging any one visual order or scopic regime is at least the beginning of a way out of this dilemma. The idea that there are many scopic regimes that a history of visuality might begin to chart strikes me as a sensible starting point for a nondemonizing approach to postmodern visuality. Jay writes, "When 'the' story of the eye is understood as a polyphonic—or rather, polyscopic—narrative, we are in less danger of being trapped in an evil empire of the gaze, fixated in a single mirror stage of development, or frozen by the medusan, ontologizing look of the other. Permanently 'downcast eyes' are no solution to these and other dangers in visual experience" (592). The following essay on *Psycho* explores the impact of a film that has been too much discussed within an "antiocular" tradition and too little discussed in terms of specific regimes of spectatorial pleasure.

Psycho's Story of an Eye

Alfred Hitchcock's *Psycho* opens on a famous "bird's eye" view of the Phoenix skyline; after surveying the city laterally, the camera moves forward toward a half-open window blind, then through the window to allow us to become voyeurs of the aftermath of illicit sex in a sleazy hotel. Marion Crane and her lover Sam are half naked after a lunch-hour tryst. Never before in the history of mainstream American film had an erotic scene been played horizontally on a bed (Rebello 86). Never before had a film so blatantly enlisted voyeuristic pleasures. Marion begins the scene supine, in bra and slip; Sam, with his shirt off, stands over her. Soon he joins her on the bed; they kiss and express frustration at having to meet like this.

Marion later steals forty thousand dollars in order not to have to meet in cheap hotels. When she gets lost en route to Sam, she meets Norman Bates, who seems like herself caught in a "private trap." After a cathartic conversation with Norman in the parlor of the motel, Marion decides to return the money. Norman peers through a peephole as she prepares for her shower. In extreme close-up we see a gigantic (male) eye gazing at a partly disrobed (female) body. Yet the twist of *Psycho* will turn out to be that this "male gaze" unleashes not a conventional, masculine heterosexual desire (or assault) but a new being: the schizo-psychotic Norman-Mother who will act to foil Norman's heterosexual desire.

The sudden, unexplained violence of the attack in the shower came as a great shock to audiences who had been set up by the first third of the film to expect the slightly tawdry love story of Marion and Sam. The shower-murder's destabilizing effect on audiences is perfectly enacted by the following two shots. The same roving, voyeuristic camera eye that began the film appears to want to pick up the pieces of a narrative trajectory. But where should it go? What should it now see? The inquisitive, forward-propelled movement that inaugurated the story is now impossible; the camera can only look at the bloody water washing down the drain. Tracking "down the drain" graphically enacts what has just happened to all narrative expectation with the murder of the film's main character and star. From the darkness of the drain, echoing the counterclockwise spiral of the swirling water, vision reemerges in a reverse pull out of the dead, staring eye of Marion.

This baroque camera movement down the drain and back out of a dead, unseeing eye enacts a spectatorial disorientation that is one of the most striking features of watching *Psycho*. In a moment this abyss will be filled by a new focus on Norman, who will enter to clean up the mess and protect "Mother." But from this point on, the audience cannot comfortably settle into a conventional narrative trajectory. Instead, viewers begin to anticipate "Mother's" next attack and to register the rhythms of anticipation, shock, and release.

The above are familiar observations about *Psycho*'s rupture with narrative convention and "classical" narrative expectation. Anyone who has gone to the movies in the last twenty years—a period in which the influence of

Hitchcock in general and *Psycho* in particular has become increasingly apparent—cannot help but notice how a new "roller coaster" sensibility—a sensibility that is grounded in the pleasurable anticipation of the next gut-spilling, gut-wrenching moment—has gained ascendance in popular moving-image culture. Consider, for example, the collections of films that have often (rather loosely) been called thrillers: erotic thrillers as different as *Blue Velvet* (1986), *Fatal Attraction* (1987), and *Basic Instinct* (1992); older-style paranoid political thrillers such as *The Parallax View* (1974) and *All the President's Men* (1976) or the more recent political thrillers *JFK* (1991) and *The Pelican Brief* (1993); action thrillers, whether of the slightly more realistic Harrison Ford variety or the more stylized Hong Kong-influenced variety; older-style gross-out horror such as *The Texas Chain Saw Massacre* (1974) or *Halloween* (1978) and the hundreds of sequels of these and many other titles, the newer-style mainstream horror thrillers (with similar "psycho killer" monsters) such as *The Silence of the Lambs* [1991]); or, finally, the paranoid political thriller turned gender-destabilized romance such as *The Crying Game* (1992).[4] Although *Psycho* is not the direct antecedent of all these films, it does mark the important beginning of an era in which viewers began going to the movies to be thrilled and moved in very visceral ways.

Often the more sensational aspects of such "thrillers" are attributed to the entwined bogeymen of American mass visual culture, "sexandviolence," as if the mere escalation of realism in the representation of one or both of these attractions could explain the phenomenon of an increasingly "vulgar" mass visual culture. However, the much-discussed "graphic" representations of sex and violence in these films are rarely the result of an aesthetic of realism and much more often a matter of calculated genre effects. Hitchcock's boast, cited in the epigraph, that if you design a picture correctly, in terms of its emotional impact, you can get the Japanese and the Indian audiences to scream at the same moment belongs to such a spirit of generic emotional engineering through visual effects. If there is a common denominator in the films mentioned above, it is this new sense of going for a ride whose destination is less important than the vertiginous sensations felt along the way.

The New "Cinema of Attractions"

Scholars of early cinema have recently shown the importance of visual sensation in this period. As these scholars have learned to appreciate the sensational pleasures of this prenarrative, preclassical cinema, they have often noted affinities between this cinema and the contemporary return to sensation in special effects, extreme violence, and sexual display. While narrative is not abandoned in this newly sensationalized cinema, it often takes a back seat to a succession of visual and auditory "attractions." Tom Gunning's two remarkable essays on early cinema spectatorship describe a series of exhibitionistic events, actions, and displays of all sorts whose appeal did not depend on spectatorial absorption into diegetic illusion but on more "direct" visual attractions and on an "aesthetics of astonishment" that orchestrates these attractions. In Lumière and Méliès the attraction was the display of the cinematographe itself; in Edwin S. Porter it was an eclectic mix of exhibitionistic display—as in *The Gay Shoe Clerk*'s display of the woman shopper's ankle, or the display of theatrical tableaux. In the popular Hales Tours, the attraction was a simulated ride on a train, the illusion of being in motion, complete with ticket-taker conductor and the sound effects of brakes (Gunning 1986, 1990).

The early "cinema of attractions" is based on the film's dual ability visually to "show" something new or sensational and to "attract" viewers to this show. Gunning explains how most early cinema before Griffith placed a premium on calling attention to the ability of the apparatus to offer attractions over its ability to absorb spectators into a diegetic world. The term "attraction" is borrowed from Sergei Eisenstein, whose theory of the "montage of attractions" stressed the "sensual or psychological impact" of images on spectators through their ability to disrupt spectatorial absorption into "illusory depictions" (1988:35). It was, in fact, the destabilizing shock effect of the fairground roller coaster that Eisenstein had most in mind when he coined the term.[5] And it is very much such a quality that is the primary attraction of the new cinema described above.

The point of invoking the term "attractions" is not to argue that contemporary postclassical American cinema has reverted to the *same* attractions of early cinema. While there is certainly an affinity between the two, this new regime entails entirely different spectatorial disciplines and engages viewers in entirely different social experiences. Film historian Thomas Schatz has attempted to specify the institutional, economic, technological, and generic changes that constitute the attractions of what he likes to call "the New Hollywood." Schatz isolates common features of "high-cost, high-tech, high-speed thrillers," which in his predominantly negative account were most dramatically ushered in by the 1973 blockbuster *Jaws* and followed by the *Star Wars, Close Encounters, Raiders of the Lost Ark, E. T., Exorcist,* and *Godfather* megahits. Though Schatz himself would have no truck with such theoretical grand narratives as the rupture of the modern by the postmodern, his description of the appeal of these films nevertheless exemplifies both

Jameson's "cultural logic of late capitalism" and Friedberg's more modest description of the gradually increasing centrality of the image-producing and -reproducing apparatuses. For example, Schatz characterizes these "calculated blockbusters" as genre pastiches that are "visceral, kinetic, and fast-paced, increasingly reliant on special effects, increasingly 'fantastic' . . . and increasingly targeted at younger audiences" (23). He also shows how such films are designed more as concepts than conventional narratives and sold by corporate giants to worldwide, in some cases subliterate, global markets, often with future development into theme park rides in mind (29).

What is especially interesting in Schatz's description is the attention to the new packaging of thrills and the connection of these thrills not simply to the fairground of Eisenstein's attractions but to the postmodern theme park of Baudrillardian simulacra. For the crucial point about all the films Schatz mentions is not simply that some of them actually *are* theme park rides (e.g., Universal's "E.T." and Disneyland's "Star Tours"), but that many films now set out, as a first order of business, to simulate the bodily thrills and visceral pleasures of such rides. Since Schatz wrote his essay, the highest-grossing film of all time has become a movie about a dinosaur theme park run amok. The fact that this film has itself become a theme park ride only confirms the observation that the destabilized ride, the ride that seems to career most wildly out of control, is the one we increasingly want to take.

Perhaps the best way to understand this specific appeal to the roller-coaster sensibilities of contemporary life is to compare a traditional roller coaster—say, the rickety wood and steel affair on Santa Cruz's boardwalk, part of the fun of which is riding high above the boardwalk, beach, and ocean—with the roller coaster-style rides at Disneyland. The latter borrow from cinema in one of two ways: either they simulate a diegetic world through cinematic mise-en-scène—but still literally move the body through actual space—like the "Matterhorn," or they are elaborate updates of early cinema's Hales Tours, "moving" the audience through virtual, electronically generated space, like Tomorrowland's motion-simulation "Star Tours." This ride, which literally goes nowhere, feels just as harrowing as an actual roller coaster, even more so when the added narrative informs us that the robot pilot has malfunctioned, causing us to nearly collide with a number of objects. The narrative information that we are out of control enhances the virtual sensation of wild careening.

In both forms of ride, the roller coaster has become more like the movies; and movies, in turn, have become more like roller coasters. In this convergence of pleasures the contemporary, postclassical cinema has reconnected in important ways with the "attractions" of amusement parks. But these attractions have themselves been thematized and narrativized through their connection with the entire history of movies; even the "Matterhorn" is based on a now-forgotten 1959 movie, *Third Man on the Mountain*. It would be a mistake, therefore, to think of these new forms of attractions as simply reverting (or regressing) to the spectatorial sensations of early cinema. Rather, we need to see them as scopic regimes demanding new kinds of spectatorial discipline.

That discipline was already being cultivated in one form by the long lines beginning to form in the late fifties at the newly built Disneyland. Just as the newly thematized roller coasters like the "Matterhorn" and the later motion-simulation roller coasters like "Star Tours" base their thrills on destabilizing movement through real or simulated narrativized space, so a film like *Psycho* introduced, long before the blockbusters Schatz describes as defining the New Hollywood, what might be called a roller-coaster concept to the phenomenon of film viewing. For *Psycho* the ride began, like the rides at Disneyland, with the line and the anticipation of terror. It continued in the film proper with an unprecedented experience of disorientation, destabilization, and terror. When the forward-moving, purposeful, voyeuristic camera eye "washes" down the drain after the murder of Marion and emerges in reverse twisting out of her dead eye, audiences could, for the first time in mainstream motion-picture history, take pleasure in losing the kind of control, mastery, and forward momentum of "classical" narrative.

Billy Crystal's joke at the 1993 Academy Awards ceremony that *The Crying Game* proved that "white men *can* jump" offers a good example of the kind of pleasurable destabilization that I am trying to identify. The shocking attraction of this film is the appearance of a masculine mark of gender where none was expected. This gender-shock would not have been possible without the remarkable ability of audiences and critics to keep the secret of a key protagonist's gender. Gender shock is, of course, what *Psycho* also gave to its audience. The "shock" of the surprise depends on the discipline of the kept secret. *Psycho* is the film that first linked an erotic display of sexual attractions to a display of sexualized violence. But its attractions were not deployed within a stable heterosexual framework or within the hegemony of an exclusive masculine subjectivity. This new twist on some very "basic instincts" is at the heart of postmodern gender and sexuality in popular cinema.

The Place of *Psycho* in Film Studies

In a general way we all know that *Psycho*'s surprise assault in the shower on both its main character and its audience altered the viewing—not to men-

tion the bathing—habits of the nation. Yet even though spectator-position-
ing has been endlessly discussed in scholarly analyses of the film, the much
more mundane phenomenon of audience response has been treated as mere
trivia.[6] One reason for this lack of scholarly attention to *Psycho*'s impact on
popular audiences is the early appropriation of the film's import to a modernist, avant-garde aesthetic with no interest in assessing popular appeal and
influence. Faced with *Psycho*'s difference from classical norms, critics and
scholars seem to have assumed that the film must be a form of modernist
rupture.

David Bordwell's survey in 1989 of the rhetoric of *Psycho* criticism is a
good place to begin to trace this modernist appropriation of the film. Bordwell's account of the interpretations of *Psycho* traces a remarkable process of
legitimization whereby a film initially seen as a minor, low budget, black-
and-white Hitchcock "thriller" not up to the "master" 's usual standards was
five years later the subject of an extremely influential chapter of a major
auteur study, ten years later a classic worthy of close analysis, and fifteen
years later an example of a subversive work of modernism. All subsequent
interpretations, including recent ones by Rothman (1982), Jameson (1990),
and Žižek (1992), assume the centrality of the film to cinema studies as constituted and legitimized by reigning psychoanalytic paradigms of film theory
in the seventies. Yet as Bordwell shows, what is missing from such interpretations is a quality mentioned by Hitchcock himself and cited in an epigraph
to Robin Wood's influential auteur study: "fun." "You have to remember
that *Psycho* is a film made with quite a sense of amusement on my part. To
me it's a *fun* picture. The processes through which we take the audience, you
see, it's rather like taking them through the haunted house at the fairground"
(Bordwell 229; Wood 106).

With *Psycho*'s entrance into the canon of the twenty or so most frequently taught and critically revered films, this fairground appeal to sensational fun fell by the wayside. The more exalted Hitchcock's critical reputation became, the less he, or anyone else, learned about the secrets of this fun.
As he once noted, "My films went from being failures to masterpieces without ever being successes." So interested was Hitchcock in understanding the
powerful effect *Psycho* had on audiences that he proposed that the Stanford
Research Institute study its popularity. But when he found out they wanted
$75,000 to do the research, he told them he wasn't *that* curious (Spoto
456–57).

One reason so much academic film criticism has passed over the question of the film's "attractions" has to do with psychoanalytic and feminist
critical paradigms that have believed audiences' visual pleasure anathema to

"good"—whether feminist, modernist, or avant-garde—cinema. A good example is Kaja Silverman who, in *The Subject of Semiotics* (1983), claims that *Psycho* is an important film worthy of careful analysis because it disrupts classical narrative closure: "*Psycho* obliges the viewing subject to make abrupt shifts in identification. . . . Thus the viewing subject finds itself inscribed into the cinematic discourse at one juncture as victim and at the next juncture as victimizer" (206).

What interests me in this description of a spectator identifying first with the victim, then, without knowing it, with the victimizer is the absence of pleasure, or fun, taken in either position. The characterization of the viewer as castrated and thwarted presents the experience of viewing the film as a form of punishment. Silverman—and most critics who wrote about the film in this mode—is saying that the film is about painful castration and perversely thwarted desires.[7] Spectators who first identify with the neurotic desires of Marion are subsequently caught up in the perverse and psychotic desires of Norman and then, presumably, punished for such errant identification by a narrative that does not follow the "classical" (realist) narrative trajectory of resolution and reassurance.

Silverman introduces here the seeds of a sadomasochistic dynamic that she and others have fruitfully developed in later work.[8] But she cannot develop it here, in relation to *Psycho's* viewing pleasure, because her analysis is still wedded to a Mulveyan formula that sees all viewers seeking to escape an unpleasurable threat of castration. Since such escape is presumably thwarted by *Psycho*, the film seems to Silverman to disrupt classical narrative. However, this disruption is, in effect, prevented from offering popular and suspect pleasures by its supposed enactment of castration: "When the stabbing begins, there is a cinematic cut with almost every thrust of the knife. The implied equation is too striking to ignore: the cinematic machine is lethal; it too murders and dissects" (211).

We see here a clear observation of the assaultive nature of the film, but only as a form of punishment, not, as I show later, as a pleasurable visual attraction audiences were becoming disciplined to enjoy. *Psycho* is good for us, Silverman seems to say, because it punishes us for having been sucked into it. This punishment is conceived as a modernist disruption of normative masculine visual pleasure aligned with classical narrative. Silverman thus offers a particularly striking example of Martin Jay's antiocularism. Her high modernist tradition of psychoanalytic criticism is uninterested in the film's popular appeal—or in any sense of a culture of fun accruing to it—and has a clear interest in denying such appeal. This modernist *Psycho* is critical and negative. It is grounded in a film theory to which the notion of endlessly

deferred, unsatisfiable *desire* is central and to which the notion of visual pleasure and fun is anathema.[9]

If today we can begin to recognize *Psycho* as fun, it is partly because the
popular contemporary slasher film has taught us this lesson through generic
repetitions of what was once so strikingly original in *Psycho*. But it is also
because genre study has sometimes been the one place in film studies where
repeatable audience pleasures, as opposed to thwarted or punitive desires,
have been scrutinized. Genre study is also where some of the major antiocular truisms of contemporary film theory have been most thoroughly reex-
amined in terms of the social experiences of spectators. It is thus not surprising that the study of the horror genre has given us, however indirectly,
an implicit appreciation of *Psycho*'s pivotal place in the transition to a postmodern visual culture.

Approached as a horror film, *Psycho* is often regarded as a turning point
in the history of the genre: the moment when horror moved, in Andrew
Tudor's words, "from collective fears about threatening forces somewhere
'out there' " to a "sexuality, repression and psychosis" that is frighteningly
close to home and potential in us all (46–47). Carol J. Clover's study of contemporary horror film, *Men, Women, and Chain Saws*, has also commented
on the enormous influence of a tale "of sex and parents" inaugurated by *Psycho* (49). In her chapter on the contemporary "slasher film," Clover notices
how powerfully a masculine viewer casts his emotional lot with a "female-
victim-hero."[10] This "final girl," survivor of gruesome slice-and-dice may-
hem, is, in her knife- or chain saw-wielding triumph at the end, anything
but passive and not very feminine. Where traditional views of the horror
genre have too simply polarized gender as active male monster and passive
female victim, Clover's analysis of the low exploitative subgenre of the
slasher film discovers that a vicarious "abject terror, gendered feminine" is
crucial to the genre, and that this terror is merely the starting point of a
roller-coaster ride that careens wildly between the gendered poles of feminine abjection and masculine mastery.

In a sense, Clover develops Silverman's insight that identification in *Psycho* shifts between victim and victimizer, though mostly in relation to the
contemporary horror tradition spawned by this film, and as masochistic
pleasure, not punishment. In order to understand sadomasochistic pleasures
that are perhaps more basic to contemporary film viewing than any modernist rupture, Clover argues that all forms of contemporary horror involve
the thrill of being assaulted—of "opening up" to penetrating images. Using
horror's own metacommentary on itself to fill in what she calls the "blind
spots" of (antiocular) theories of spectatorship by Metz and Mulvey, Clover

asserts the importance of "gazes" that do not master their objects of vision but are reactive and introjective (225–26).

Psycho's relation to the slasher genre and its peculiar gendered pleasure might seem obvious. Yet it is only in retrospect that we can place it "in" the slasher subgenre, or perhaps only if we wish to include its sequels of the 1980s—*Psycho II*, *III*, and *IV*—as part of its text. Although the basic conventions of gender-confused psycho "killer," "terrible place," "phallic weapon," and "multiple victims" are already in place with *Psycho*, the convention of the powerful and triumphant "final girl" is only incipient with the survival (though not yet the self-rescue) of Marion's sister Lilah. Since this "girl's" reversal from abject victim to triumphant victor is crucial to the energy of the genre, it is possible to say that *Psycho* does not fully "fit" the psycho-killer genre.

What, then, is *Psycho*? Or, more precisely, what was *Psycho* on first viewing and what has it become since? Through subsequent viewings it has become the familiar antecedent for familial "slice-and-dice" horror. But audiences who first went to see it did not go to see a slasher horror film; they went to see a *Hitchcock* thriller with a twist—about which there was a great deal of excitement and quite a bit of mystery. The crucial significance of *Psycho*, measurable today in terms of its influence on the slasher film but measurable in its own time in terms of its new attractions challenging certain production code taboos against depictions of both sex and violence, is not that it showed more sex or more violence than other films—which, literally speaking, it didn't—but rather, as Clover notes, that it sexualized the motive, and the action, of violence (24).

Just how we understand this sexualization of violence seems to be the key issue in assessing the impact, the influence, and the postmodernity of *Psycho*'s particular roller-coaster ride of attractions. The shower sequence is one of the most analyzed sequences in American film. As Barbara Creed notes, many critics, including Fredric Jameson, have pointed to it as the most horrifying moment in all of cinema (Creed 148; Jameson 1992:35). Certainly part of its fame derives from the technical brilliance of the way it is cut. Many a film teacher, myself included, has taught the importance of editing by punning on its powerful effects of cutting—of both flesh and film.

It was almost a reflex of poststructuralist psychoanalytic criticism to "read" the shower sequence as an act of symbolic castration carried out on the presumably already "castrated" body of a woman with whom spectators have identified. Marion's body—insisted on by some form of undress in two scenes prior to the shower-murder—unleashes Norman's desire for her, which in turn unleashes "Mrs. Bates," the mother who kills to protect her son from the sexual aggressions of "loose" women. As I myself once put it, in a condemnatory outburst: "The woman is both victim and monster. . . . Norman, the matricide and killer of several other women, is judged the victim of the very mother he has killed" (1984:93–94). The female monster unleashed by the female victim seemed to permit the simultaneous vilification and victimization of women. Yet as Carol Clover has correctly pointed out, such a feminist critique does justice neither to the obvious bisexuality of the slasher killers spawned by Norman nor to the newfound strength and resourcefulness of the female victims spawned by Marion and her sister (21–64).

In a recent book on horror cinema, Barbara Creed argues that what has been missing from psychoanalytically based studies of horror films is an appreciation of the disturbing power of the "monstrous feminine." This power challenges the prevalent view, especially in discussions of horror cinema, that femininity constitutes passivity. Creed goes on to argue in a chapter on *Psycho* that the really important story of this film is precisely that of the castrating mother. While it has become conventional to interpret the phallic mother as endowed with a fantasy phallus whose function is to disavow the male fear of castration—and thus the "actual" "lack" in the mother's body—Creed insists that *Psycho* offers an image not of a phallic mother disavowing lack, but of a castrating mother whose power is presumably located in her difference from the male.[11]

Creed has a point about the Kristevan powers of (abject, female) horror. However, because she points to the monstrous feminine as an archetype, she fails to account for the remarkable emergence of this monstrosity in the wake of the influence of *Psycho*, or for the historical importance of *Psycho* itself. For the really striking fact about this film is not its illustration of a previously unacknowledged archetype, but that archetype's influential emergence in 1960. This is not to say that there have not been female monsters before *Psycho* or that conventional male monsters of classic horror are not often sexually indeterminate.[12] It is to say, however, that *Psycho's* array of dislocations—between normal and psychotic; between masculine and feminine; between eros and fear; even between the familiar Hitchcockian suspense and a new, frankly gender-based horror—are what made it the important precursor of the thrill-producing visual attractions Schatz discusses as crucial to the New Hollywood. Thus Hitchcock's decision to make the traditional monster of horror cinema a son who dresses up as his own mummified mother was a decision not so much to give violent power to "the monstrous feminine," but, much more dramatically, to destabilize masculine and feminine altogether.

"He's a transvestite!" says the district attorney in a famously inadequate attempt to explain the root cause of Norman's disturbance. The line has been criticized, along with the psychiatrist's lengthy speech about how Norman became his mother, as Hitchcock's jab at the inadequacies of clinical explanation. Certainly Norman is not a mere transvestite—i.e., a person whose sexual pleasure involves dressing up as a member of the opposite sex—but rather a much more deeply disturbed individual whose whole personality has at times, as the psychiatrist puts it, "become the mother." Yet in the scene that supposedly shows us that Norman has finally "become the mother," what we really see is Norman, now without wig and dress, sitting alone in a holding area reflecting, in the most feminine of the many voices given Mrs. Bates, on the evil of "her" son.

In other words, while ostensibly illustrating that Norman now "is" the mother, the film provides a visual and auditory variation on Norman's earlier sexual indeterminacy. The shock of this scene is the combination of young male body and older female voice: visual evidence of male, aural evidence of female. It is thus not the recognition of one identity overcome by another that fascinates so much as the tension between masculine and feminine poles. The film's penultimate image drives this home. Briefly emerging as if from under Norman's face is the grinning mouth of Mrs. Bates's corpse. Again the shock is that of indeterminacy: both Norman *and* mother. Thus the psychiatrist's point that Norman is entirely mother is not visually or aurally proven. Instead, these variations of drag become overtly thematized as ironic, and almost camp, forms of play with audience expectations regarding the fixity of gender.[13] Norman is not a transvestite, but transvestism is a major "attraction" for audiences of these scenes.

A similar point can be made for the earlier climax of *Psycho* during Norman-Mrs. Bates's thwarted attack on Lilah in the fruit cellar. Here again the "attraction" is neither the appearance of Mrs. Bates as woman nor the revelation, when "her" wig falls off in the struggle, that "she" *is* her son. At the precise moment that Norman's wig begins to slip off in his struggle with Sam—when we see a masculine head emerging from under the old-lady wig—the audience glimpsed, for the first time in a movie theater, a truly shocking absence of gender stability. Gender of the monster is revealed in this film in very much the terms Judith Butler offers: as an imitation without an origin, a corporeal style of performance, a construction (138–39).

There can be no doubt, however, that one primary "attraction" of the film's horror is its spectacular mutilation of a woman's naked body. Abject terror, as Clover puts it, is "gendered feminine" (51). There is also no doubt that the introduction of certain psychoanalytic conventions on screen conspire to vilify the mother and her sexuality as causes of Norman's derangement. These are certain misogynist features of a film that, for a variety of reasons, struck a responsive chord with American audiences in a way that Michael Powell's similar, but more truly modernist, "laying bare" of the device of voyeurism in *Peeping Tom* (also 1960) did not.[14] Over the next twenty years the horror genre would begin to establish a formula for reproducing and refining the various sexual and gendered elements of this experience in ways that would not lessen the attraction of the violence against women, but would empower the "final girl" to fight back and invite spectators to identify alternately with her powerless victimization and her subsequent empowered struggle against it.

Psycho thus needs to be seen not as an exceptional and transgressive experience working against the classical norms of visual pleasure, but rather as an important turning point in the pleasurable destabilizing of sexual identity in American film history: it is the moment when the experience of going to the movies began to be constituted as providing a certain generally transgressive sexualized thrill of promiscuous abandonment to indeterminate, "other" identities. To undergo this abandonment, however, audiences had to be *disciplined*, not in Silverman's sense of being punished, but in Foucault's sense of voluntarily submitting to a regime.

Disciplining Fear: "The Care and Handling of *Psycho*"

From the very first screenings of the film, audience reactions, in the form of gasps, screams, yells, and even running up and down the aisles, were unprecedented. Although Hitchcock later claimed to have calculated all this, saying he could hear the screams when planning the shower montage, screenwriter Joseph Stephano claims, "He was lying. . . . We had no idea. We thought people would gasp or be silent, but screaming? Never" (Rebello 117). No contemporary review of the film ignored the fact that audiences were screaming as never before. Here are some typical reviews:

> Scream! Its a good way to let off steam in this Alfred Hitchcock shockeroo . . . so scream, shiver and shake and have yourself a ball.
>
> *(L.A. Examiner,* August 11, 1960*)*

> So well is the picture made . . . that it can lead audiences to do something they hardly ever do any more—cry out to the characters, in hopes of dissuading them from going to the doom that has been cleverly established as awaiting them.   *(Callenbach 48)*

And on the negative side:

> Director Hitchcock bears down too heavily in this one, and the deli-
> cate illusion of reality necessary for a creak-and-shriek movie becomes,
> instead, a spectacle of stomach-churning horror.
>
> *(Time,* June 27, 1960, 51*)*

> *Psycho* is being advertised as more a shocker than a thriller, and that is
> right—I am shocked, in the sense that I am offended and disgusted.
> . . . The clinical details of psychopathology are not material for trivial
> entertainment; when they are used so they are an offense against taste
> and an assault upon the sensibilities of the audience . . . it makes you
> feel unclean.   *(Hatch 39)*

Having unleashed such powerful reactions, the problem now was how
to handle them. According to Anthony Perkins, the entire scene in the hard-
ware store following the shower-murder—the mopping up and disposal of
Marion's body in the swamp—was inaudible due to leftover howls from the
previous scene. Hitchcock even asked Paramount Studios head Lew Wasser-
man to allow him to remix the sound to allow for the audience's vocal reaction. Permission was denied (Rebello 163).

Hitchcock's unprecedented "special policy" of admitting no one to the
theater after the film had begun was certainly a successful publicity stunt, but
it also transformed the previously casual act of going to the movies into a
much more *disciplined* activity of arriving on time and waiting in an orderly
line. As Peter Bogdonovich (1963) has noted, it is because of *Psycho* that audiences now go to movies at the beginning. One popular critic wrote in a Sun-
day *Arts and Leisure* section about the new policy: "At any other entertainment from ice shows to baseball games, the bulk of the patrons arrive before
the performance begins. Not so at the movies, which have followed the policy of grabbing customers in any time they arrive, no matter how it may
impair the story for those who come in midway" (*View* 1). This reviewer then
takes it upon himself to advocate the exhibition policy so important to *Psycho's* success and impact on audiences: that no one be admitted late to the
film. Hitchcock defended this policy in an article published in the *Motion
Picture Herald,* saying that the idea came to him one afternoon in the cutting
room: "I suddenly startled my fellow-workers with a noisy vow that my front-
wards-backwards-sidewards-and-inside-out labors on 'Psycho' would not be
in vain—that everyone else in the world would have to enjoy the fruits of my
labor to the full by seeing the picture from beginning to end. This was the
way the picture was conceived—and this was how it had to be seen" (17–18).

This "policy," unheard of at the time, necessitated important changes in the public's moviegoing habits: audiences had to be trained to learn the times of each show; if they were late they had to wait for the next screening; and once they bought their tickets, they had to be induced to stand patiently in ticketholder lines. The theater managers' new buzzwords were to "fill and spill" theaters efficiently at precise intervals, thus affording more screenings. The unprecedented discipline required to "fill and spill" was in paradoxical contrast with the equally unprecedented thrills of the show itself.

Here is how another columnist described the discipline and thrill of seeing the film over a month after its release:

> There was a long line of people at the show—they will only seat you at the beginning and I don't think they let you out while it's going on.
> . . . A loudspeaker was carrying a sound track made by Mr. Hitchcock. He said it was absolutely necessary—he gave it the British pronunciation like "nessary." He said you absolutely could not go in at the beginning. The loudspeaker then let out a couple of female shrieks that would turn your blood to ice. And the ticket taker began letting us all in. A few months ago, I was reading the London review of this picture. The British critics rapped it. "Contrived," they said. "Not up to the Hitchcock standards." I do not know what standards they were talking about. But I must say that Hitchcock . . . did not seem to be that kind of person at all. Hitchcock turned us all on. Of all the shrieking and screaming! We were all limp. And, after drying my palms on the mink coat next to me, we went out to have hamburgers. And let the next line of people go in and die. Well, if you are reading the trade papers, you must know that "Psycho" is making a mint of money. This means we are in for a whole series of such pictures.   *(Delaplane)*

How shall we construe this new disciplining of audiences to wait in line? Michel Foucault (1978) writes that "discipline produces subjected and practiced bodies, 'docile' bodies" (138). He means that what we experience as autonomy is actually a more subtle form of power. Obviously, the bodies of the *Psycho* audience were docile. Indeed, the fun of the film was dependent upon the ability of these bodies to wait patiently in line in order to catch the thrills described above. No one coerced them to arrive on time and wait in line. They did it for fun. This fun derives partly from the exhilaration of a group submitting itself, as a group, to a thrilling sensation of fear and release from fear. In this highly ritualized masochistic submission to a familiar "master," blood turns to ice, shrieking and screaming are understood frankly as a "turn on," followed by climax, detumescence, and the final recovery and renewal of (literal and metaphorical) appetite.

The passage also offers a rich mix of allusions to gender, class, and nationality: the mink coat next to the columnist is clear indication both that these pleasures were not for men only and that a wide variety of the public participated. Hamburger counters mink; snooty English "standards" are foils to America's favorite fantasy of the leveling democratic entertainment of "the movies." What we see here is a conception of the audience as a group with a common solidarity—that of submitting to an experience of mixed arousal and fear and of recognizing those reactions in one another and perhaps even performing them for one another.[15]

This audience, surveilled and policed with unprecedented rigor outside the theater, responding with unprecedented vocalized terror inside the theater, is certainly disciplined in the negative sense of Foucault's term. But it is also an audience with a newfound sense of itself as bonded around the revelation of certain terrifying visual secrets. The shock of learning these secrets produces a camaraderie, a pleasure of the group that was, I think, quite new to motion pictures. A certain community was created around *Psycho*'s secret that gender is often not what it seems. The shock of learning this secret helped produce an ironic sadomasochistic discipline of master and slave with Hitchcock playing the sadistic master and audiences playing the submissive victims.

An important tool in disciplining the *Psycho* audience were three promotional trailers, two quite short ones and one six-minute affair that has become a classic. All hinted at, but unlike most "coming attractions" trailers refrained from showing too much of, the film's secret. In the most famous of these, Hitchcock acts as a kind of house-of-horrors tour guide at the Universal International Studios set of the Bates Motel and adjacent house (now the Universal Studios Theme Park featuring the *Psycho* house and motel). Each trailer stressed the importance of special discipline: either "please don't tell the ending, it's the only one we have"—or the importance of arriving on time. But there was also another trailer, not seen by the general public but even more crucial in inculcating discipline in the audience. Called "The Care and Handling of *Psycho*," this was not a preview of the film but a filmed "press book" teaching theater managers how to properly exhibit the film and police the audience.[16]

The black-and-white trailer begins with a scene outside the DeMille Theater in New York, where *Psycho* began a limited engagement before being released nationwide. To the accompaniment of Bernard Herrmann's driving violin score, we see crowds in line for the film. A man in a tuxedo is a theater manager, the narrator urgently informs us, in charge of implementing the new policy, which the trailer then explains. The sly voice of Alfred Hitchcock is heard over a loudspeaker explaining to the waiting audience that: "This queuing up is good for you, it will make you appreciate the seats inside. It will also make you appreciate *Psycho.*" The mixture of polite inducement backed up by the presence of Pinkerton guards and a life-size lobby card cutout of Hitchcock pointing to his watch add up to a rather theatrical, sadomasochistic display of coercion. We hear Hitchcock induce the audience to keep the "tiny, little horrifying secrets" of the story while insisting on the democracy of the policy that will not even make exceptions for the Queen of England or the manager's brother.

Perhaps the most striking thing about this trailer is that it worked: audiences not only learned to arrive on time, but also eagerly joined the visible crowds on the sidewalks waiting to see the film. When shaken spectators left the theater they were grilled by those waiting in line, but only answered that you had to see it for yourself (Rebello 161). By exploiting his popular TV persona as the man who loves to frighten and the man audiences love to be frightened by, Hitchcock achieved the kind of rapt audience attention, prompt arrival and departure, that would have been the envy of a symphony orchestra. Yet he achieved this attention with the casual, general audience more used to the distractions of amusement parks than the discipline of high culture.

On July 17, 1955, Disneyland had already opened its doors to large numbers of visitors taking in the total visual attraction of a variety of film-oriented "fantasy lands." In August of 1964, Universal Studios began offering tram-ride tours of its movie sets and would eventually expand to a more movie-related and thrill-inducing competitor to Disneyland, including the *Psycho* set and a presentation of how certain scenes from the film were shot.[17] Clearly, the sort of discipline that Hitchcock was teaching was more like that of the crowds at these theme parks than any kind of simple audience taming. Lawrence Levine has written compellingly about the taming of American audiences during the latter part of the nineteenth century. He argues that while American theater audiences had in the first half of the nineteenth century been a highly participatory and unruly lot, spitting tobacco, talking back to actors, arriving late, leaving early, stamping feet, and applauding promiscuously, they were gradually tamed by the arbiters of culture to "submit to creators and become mere instruments of their will, mere auditors of the productions of the artist" (183). Levine tells, for example, of an orchestra conductor in Cincinnati in 1873 who ordered the doors to be closed when he began to play, admitting no one until the first part was finished. When he was resisted, his argument was: "When you play Offenbach or Yankee Doodle, you can keep your doors open. When I play Handel . . . they must be shut. Those who appreciate music will be here on time" (188). Levine argues that this late nineteenth-century American audience lost a sense of itself as an active force, a "public," and became instead a passive "mute receptor" of the will of the artist through this discipline. New divisions between high and low meant that it was more and more difficult to find audiences who could serve as microcosms of society, who felt like participants in a general culture, and who could articulate their opinions and feelings vocally (195).

With Hitchcock's policy trailer we certainly see some elements of Levine's tamed audience: Pinkerton guards, loudspeakers, "docile bodies" waiting patiently in line, not to mention Hitchcock's disembodied voice insisting that seeing the film from the beginning is "required." Certainly Hitchcock asserts "the will of the artist" over the audience. However, this will is in the service of producing visceral thrills and earsplitting screams that are a far cry from the politely suppressed coughs of the concert hall. It seems that the efficiency and discipline demonstrated outside the theater needs to be viewed in tandem with the unprecedented patterns of fear and release unleashed inside. Hitchcock's discipline, like that of the emerging theme parks, was not based on the stratification of audiences into high and low nor, as would later occur in the ratings system, on the stratification of different age groups or the acquisition of the same kind of passivity and silence that Levine traces in late nineteenth-century America. In Hitchcock's assumption of the persona of the sadist who expects his submissive audience to trust him to provide a devious form of pleasure, we see a new bargain struck between filmmaker and audience. If you want me to make you scream in a new way and about these new sexually destabilized secrets, the impresario seems to say, then you must line up patiently to receive this thrill.

Hitchcock is, of course, only doing what he often did in his trailers: teasing the audience with their paradoxical love of fear, shock, surprise, and suspense—all emotions that he can rely upon audiences to know he will manipulate for maximum pleasure. His famous cameos in the early parts of most of his films are another way of teasing the audience, though also of disciplining them to pay close attention. Like the patient crowds standing in line at Disneyland, or the crowds that would eventually stand in line to see the *Psycho* house and motel at Universal Studios, these disciplined audiences were a far cry from both seventies' film theory's notion of distanced, voyeuristic mastery and Levine's passive, mute receptors.[18]

Psycho is popularly remembered as the film that violated spectatorial identification with a main character by an unprecedented killing off of that character in the first third of the film. But in order for audiences to experience the full force of that violation, Hitchcock required the kind of rapt entrance into the spell of a unified space and time that classical theories of spectatorship assume but that the classical Hollywood cinema, with its distracted viewers wandering into theaters at any old time, had perhaps only rarely delivered. *Psycho* thus needs to be viewed as a film in which disciplined audiences arrived on time in order to be attentively absorbed into the filmic world and narrative, and in which distracted "attractions" of the amusement-park variety are equally important. The more rapt viewers' initial attention, the more acute the shock when the rug was pulled out from under them.

Lawrence Levine's analysis of the nineteenth-century taming of the audience argues for a singular process of repressing unruly body functions. Theaters, opera houses, large movie houses were, for him, agents in teaching audiences to adjust to new social imperatives, training them to keep strict control of emotional and physical processes. Levine may be right that bodily repression was necessary to concert- and theatergoers. But the (mostly unwritten) history of cinema reception will require more than a concept of bodily repression to understand the various disciplines of filmgoing that have taken place in this century.[19] It will certainly require a more Foucauldian concept of discipline as productive of certain precise bodily regimes of pleasure rather than as merely repressing the physical. For, as we have seen, *Psycho* simultaneously elicits more bodily reaction along with greater bodily discipline.[20]

The lesson of the "care and handling" of *Psycho* is thus how first Hitchcock and then Hollywood learned the ways that greater spectatorial discipline could pay off in the distracted attractions of postclassical cinema. *Psycho* needs to be seen as a historical marker of a moment when popular American movies, facing the threat of television, in competition and cooperation with new kinds of amusement parks, began to invent new scopic regimes of visual and visceral "attractions." In this moment visual culture can be seen getting a tighter grip on the visual pleasures of film spectators through the reinstitution of a postmodern cinema of attractions.

Figure 1, a photograph of a Taiwanese audience in thrall to a projection of what is purported to be Alfred Hitchcock's *Psycho*, might be taken as a dramatic example of a large, international audience caught up in the roller-coaster ride of horror that is this film. This picture, taken with infrared film in Taipei and published in the trade publication *Paramount World* (July–August 1960), could be taken as evidence of Hitchcock's successful emotional engineering, proof that, as he put it, "If you designed a picture correctly, in terms of its emotional impact, the Japanese audience would

Figure 1

scream at the same time as the Indian audience" (Houston 448). Here is a
spectacle of spectatorship itself—of spectators in thrall to what W. J. T.
Mitchell calls the most "vulgar productions of the mass media." But as this
chapter has tried to show, the spectacle of spectatorship cannot be reduced
to a single, or a simple, image. And it is not really clear that Hitchcock was
ever correct in assuming an identity of audience response. Note, for example, how much more crowded together this Taiwanese audience is compared
to the London audience pictured in the subsequent photos. To reduce spectatorial audience reactions to, in this case, a singular response of fear is to fail
see the different regimes and disciplines that may be observed by different
viewers.

One way of picturing the variety of these regimes and this perhaps
unique moment of discipline and distraction that was *Psycho* is to consider
an entire series of publicity photos of audiences watching *Psycho* in the same
trade publication. These photos were taken at the Plaza Theatre, London
during the film's first run in Britain. Figure 2 shows a fragment of a very
intense-looking audience, jaws set, watching hard except for two people with
averted eyes. We can note here the somewhat defensive postures indicating
moments of anticipation—arms crossed; one person holding ears, suggesting the importance sound has in cueing the anticipation of terror. Figure 3
shows closer details of what may be the same audience. Here we begin to

Figure 2

note significant gender differences. While the men look intently, the women cringe, refusing to look at the screen, as I had once suggested women do at horror films (1984). In fact, figure 4 shows just how dramatically male viewers seem to assert their masculinity by looking (note the "cool" man who both looks and strokes his tie).

Let's suppose, for the sake of argument, that these scared women in the audience are looking at one of the following: the "scary woman" at the moment of attack ("Mrs. Bates," figure 5) or a terrified woman being attacked (Marion, figure 6). What is the best way to describe the specifically gendered reactions of these women spectators to terror? Consider the experience of watching the first attack on Marion in the shower. At this point in the film all viewers can be assumed to be somewhat identified with Marion and to be relatively, though not completely, unprepared for the attack—after all, the film is called *Psycho*. They are taken by surprise by this first, irrational irruption of violence, mystified by the lack of a distinct view of the attacker, shocked by the eerie sound and rhythms of screaming violins blending with screaming victim, and energized by the rapid cutting of the scene. This much is true for all spectators. Why then do women appear so much more moved, often to the point of smiling, grabbing ears, averting and covering eyes? The question, it seems, is whether female viewers can be said to more closely identify with Marion, especially at the height of her fear and pain, than males. Do we identify more, and thus find ourselves more terrorized,

Figure 3

Figure 4

Figure 5

Figure 6

because we are insufficiently distanced from the image in general and from this tortured image of our like in particular?

Men, in contrast, may identify with Marion but forcefully limit their correspondence to her. Since terror is itself, as Clover so aptly notes, "gendered feminine," the more controlled masculine reaction immediately distances itself from the scared woman on the screen. It more quickly gets a grip on itself (as does the man with his tie) and checks its expression. Yet at the same time that it exercises this control, this masculine reaction fully *opens up* to the image to, as Clover puts it, "take it in the eye" (202). If, as she argues, all forms of contemporary horror involve the masochistic and feminine thrill of "opening up" to, of being "assaulted" by, penetrating images, we might say that the men can be seen to open up more because they feel they "correspond" less to the gender of the primary victims (and to the femininity of fear itself).

For the woman viewer, however, this "taking it in the eye" pleasures initially less than it does the man. Because women, for all sorts of social, physiological, and psychoanalytic reasons, already perceive themselves as more vulnerable to penetration, as corresponding more to the assaulted, wide-eyed, and opened-up female victim all too readily penetrated by knife or penis, women's response is more likely to *close down*, at least initially, to such images. This is to say that the mix of pleasure and pain common to all horror viewing and aligned with a feminine subject position is negotiated differently by men than by women. Thus all viewers experience a degree of pain that is felt as feminizing. But in their greater vulnerability, some women viewers react by acting to filter out some of the painful images. In my earlier essay on *Psycho*, I took the woman's refusal to look at the screen as a sensible resistance to pain. Now I'm more inclined to suggest that, as with the general audiences who were disciplined to arrive on time, a much more complex and disciplined negotiation of pleasure is taking place, and that this negotiation takes place over time, as we watch first this film and then its host of imitators—something these instantaneous photos cannot register. By involuntarily averting our eyes, for example, we women viewers partially rupture our connection with the female victim. In the process, we may also establish a new connection with the other women in the audience whose screams we hear. This new connection then itself becomes a source of highly ritualized feminine pleasure. We enjoy being scared *with one another*—a camaraderie that allows us to measure our difference from Marion. Notice, for example, the smile on the half-hidden mouth of the woman in figure 7.

Figure 7

Thus, while our first reactive, introjective experience of fear may elicit almost involuntary screams and the "closing-down" response of not looking, we don't stop feeling the film because we stop looking. In fact, our reliance on musical cues may even induce us to feel more at this juncture. What are the violins saying about the danger of looking again? What is my girlfriend's posture telling me about how I might respond? Eventually, however, through the familiarity afforded by the film's repeated attacks, we begin to discipline ourselves to the experience of this reactive, introjective gaze. At this point women may discipline themselves to keep their eyes more open. Of course, these pictures do not really tell what audiences felt, and like all still images these are frozen moments, a few hundredths of seconds out of a 109-minute film. They could also have been faked. Nevertheless they dramatize, in acute body language, some general points about the changing distractions and disciplines of film spectatorship inaugurated by *Psycho*.

The first point is that, however much we speak about the disembodied and virtual nature of cinematic, and all postmodern, forms of spectatorship, there are still real bodies in the theater, bodies that acutely feel what they see and that even when visually "assaulted" experience various mixes of vulnerability and pleasure. These people *are* on a kind of roller coaster. They are both disciplined and distracted. "Rapt, mindless fascination" is an inadequate formulation of the engagement with these moving images.

A second point is that this discipline may involve the audience in a new level of performativity. While learning to enjoy the roller-coaster ride of a new kind of thrill, the audience may begin to perceive its own performances of fear as part of the show. As we also saw in the extended description of seeing *Psycho* by the columnist, these performances—screaming, hiding eyes, clutching the self as well as neighbors—may be important to the pleasures audiences take, as a group, in the film. Such spectatorial performances are certainly not new with *Psycho*. However, the self-consciously ironic manipulations of "the master" eliciting these performances from audiences in a film that is itself about the performance of masculinity and femininity represents a new level of gender play and destabilization. Though this destabilization may have shaken those of us who saw the film on initial release out of some conventional expectations about gender, I would not argue that the experience was necessarily good or bad. It simply was a founding moment of the greater awareness of the performativity of gender roles increasingly ushered in by a postmodern, postclassical reception of cinema.

A final point is that the discipline involved here—both inside and outside the theater—takes place over time. Spectators who clutched themselves, covered eyes or ears, and recoiled in fear at the shower-murder may have been responding involuntarily, the first time, to an unexpected assault. But by the film's second assault this audience was already beginning to play the game of anticipation and to repeat its response in increasingly performed and gender-based gestures and cries. By the time the game of slasher-assault became an actual genre in the mid- and late seventies, this disciplined and distracted, this attentive, performing audience gave way to the equivalent of the kids who raise their hands in roller-coaster rides and call out: "Look Ma, no hands!"

Film critics and historians need to investigate the histories of these particular pictorial turns. To find the experience of the popular, fun *Psycho* beneath the layers of ocularphobic high modernist critique is to denigrate neither the film's intelligence nor the intelligence of the audiences who have enjoyed it. It is, rather, to recognize how important the visual and visceral experiences of narrativized roller coasters have become and how assiduously audiences have applied themselves to the disciplines of distraction.

NOTES

A very short, journalistic version of this essay appeared in *Sight and Sound* (December 1994). Thanks to Agnieszka Soltysik for much of the research concerning the reception of *Psycho*, to Nita Rollins for the significance of roller coasters, to Michael Friend of the Margaret Herrick Library for all sorts of advice and information, including access to "The Care and Handling of *Psycho*." Thanks also to members of the University of California, Irvine's Critical Theory Institute, and to many other U.C., Irvine colleagues, for helpful suggestions.

   1. Bordwell, et al. actually date the end of their study of the classical Hollywood era of cinema in 1960. This date would be quite convenient for the argument I propose about the postmodernity of *Psycho* if they actually claimed that 1960 represented a real change in the Hollywood style of filmmaking. However, they argue that while the mode of production has changed, moving from the studio system to a package-unit system relying on the enormous profits of occasional blockbusters to drive economic expansion into related acquisitions in the leisure field, the Hollywood style has not changed that much (360–77). On the contrary, I think it has, and that *Psycho* is a good example of the nature of this change.

   2. In an introduction to an anthology of essays on cinema spectatorship (1994), I refer to this vexed place of the visual in an abbreviated fashion as "gaze theory." Gaze theory is an overly simplified account of cinematic spectatorial vision promulgated by film theorists of the seventies and eighties as a unitary way of seeing grounded in Renaissance perspective and the *camera obscura* model of vision often believed to be embedded within the technical apparatus of cinema itself. For an excellent discussion of the strengths and the limitations of this tradition within feminist and apparatical film theory see Mayne (1993).

3. I would add that such claims regarding the "essential" pornography of the visual image—especially in the *moving* images of film and video—are hardly new with Jameson. Theorists as diverse as André Bazin (1967–1971), Stephen Marcus (1964), Stanley Cavell (1979), Yann Lardeau (1978), Teresa de Lauretis (1984), and Jean Baudrillard (1988) have all made some form of the same invidious comparison.

4. Jameson discusses the paranoid political thriller genre in *The Geopolitical Aesthetic* (1992).

5. Gunning writes, for example, "the relations between films and the emergence of the great amusement parks, such as Coney Island, at the turn of the century provide rich ground for rethinking the roots of early cinema" (in Elsaesser, 58). A similarly rich ground for rethinking postmodern cinema might be the relation between cinema and the theme parks of the second half of the century.

6. A case in point is the division between scholarly, critical studies and the kind of "making of" or popular reception books which, though anecdotal, are often more in tune with the popular impact of works. See for example Stephen Rebello's excellent *Alfred Hitchcock and the Making of "Psycho"* (1990).

7. I include myself (1994) in the aggregate of feminist critics who have either taken the film to task for its misogyny or, like Silverman, redeemed the film by virtue of its excessively punitive qualities. However, I prefer to cite, and critique, Silverman because I believe *The Subject of Semiotics* to have had a profound influence on thinking about Hitchcock, modernist cinema, and gaze theory. See also Modleski (1988:14–15).

8. See Silverman (1992), Studlar (1988), Clover (1992).

9. One measure of the high seriousness of this tradition could be seen in Robin Wood's straight-faced interpretation of Mrs. Bates's famous line about the fruit cellar— "Do you think I'm fruity?"—as offering the "hidden sexual springs of his behavior," followed by a simple explication of the line as "the source of fruition and fertility become rotten" with not a word about the gay implications of Norman's fruitiness.

10. Clover does not consider the female viewer as a significant component of the audience of slasher films.

11. Creed does not make this point about difference specifically in relation to *Psycho*, but she does make it generally with respect to the monstrous feminine, adapting it from my own (1984) formulation of the woman's power-in-difference in horror films when women victims look at the monster and seem to see a monstrosity that mirrors their own difference from a phallic "norm."

12. Rhona Berenstein's study of classic horror film, for example, extends Clover's insights into an earlier realm of horror often considered the province of the sadistic "male gaze" to argue that viewing pleasures were a more complicated form of role play than even Clover's masochistic pleasure of being assaulted can account for. In a genre in which monsters are masked and unmasked, heroes are feminized and doubled with monsters, and heroines are both victimized and aligned with the monster's potency, viewer pleasure cannot be accounted for by simple binaries of masculine/feminine, Oedipal/pre-Oedipal, homo/hetero. Berenstein thus argues not for a subversion of a monolithic male gaze through a challenge to pleasure, but for an account of viewing pleasures that entails a play of shifting gender and sexual identifications. Audiences themselves, Berenstein argues, become performers of gender roles in the game of attraction-repulsion played out in the genre.

13. See Butler (1990), Berenstein (1993), Garber (1992).

14. Both films are about knife-wielding psycho killers. Both begin with illicit sex—sex in a hotel room in *Psycho*, the initially filmed assignation-murder of a prostitute in *Peeping Tom*; both then travel down a circuitous garden path to sexually motivated murder. Both films were more "graphic" in their displays of sex and violence than previous narratives. In both, we are led to identify with the impulses of murdering peeping Toms who are presented as sympathetic young men beleaguered by oppressive parents—Norman by his dead mother, Mark by his dead filmmaker father.

The films differ, however, in one very important respect: Hitchcock initially fools us, in effect, about the perversions in which we are enlisted. Powell "plays fair" and lets us know immediately that the nice boy who is so damaged by his private family romance is in fact a psycho killer who murders women while filming them and then projects what amounts to a snuff film for his private pleasure. Hitchcock, on the other hand, plays deviously and doesn't let on that the nice young man who seems to be protecting his mother is really a sexually confused psychotic condemned to murder anyone who interferes with his psychotic relation to his mother-himself. Thus Powell's construction of the audience's relation to Mark, who is actually a moral being who destroys himself rather than destroy the "good" woman who breaks into his psychotic repetition compulsions, is ironically more threatening to moral and psychological certainty than Hitchcock's construction of the audience's relation to Norman. For Norman has no moral awareness of his deeds at all, because they are done "by" Norman-as-mother. Thus *Peeping Tom* took the critical heat for being truly perverse while *Psycho* acquired the reputation of the self-reflexive critique of perversion. The strong negative reaction to *Peeping Tom*, coupled with its poor box office receipts, virtually ended Powell's career, while the initially negative critical reaction to *Psycho* did it no harm at all.

15. In 1971, film critic William Pechter (1971) pinpointed this camaraderie of the audience in his own description of how it felt to watch *Psycho*: "The atmosphere . . . was deeply charged with apprehension. Something awful is always about to happen. One could sense that the audience was constantly aware of this; indeed, it had the solidarity of a convention assembled on the common understanding of some unspoken *entente terrible*; it was, in the fullest sense, an audience; not merely the random gathering of discrete individuals attendant at most plays and movies" (181).

16. I thank Michael Friend and the Margaret Herrick Library for allowing me to screen this fascinating trailer.

17. The recent Universal Studios "rides"—with the possible exception of the fanciful flight on E.T.'s bicycle, or the more jolting experiences of catastrophic earthquake (*Earthquake*) and fire (*Backdraft*)—seem to operate in the more sensationalizing, blockbuster, Hitchcock tradition of catastrophe and terror to move audiences quite seriously. In April of 1992, the guide on the tram-ride portion of the tour showed how thoroughly the Hitchcockian model of assault on the body had been absorbed: "At Universal Studios we not only like to show you the movies, we like you to feel them too." For an excellent discussion of the "hypercinematic" nature of the Disney experience see Scott Bukatman (1991).

18. It is worth noting that Hitchcock's next project was to have been a film set against the background of Disneyland with Jimmy Stewart as a blind pianist whose sight is restored in an operation and who goes to Disneyland in celebration. While there he

discovers that the eyes he has been given are those of a murdered man. He thus begins to hunt down "his" killer. After the manifest perversions of *Psycho*, the then child- and family-centered Disney claimed that not only would he not permit Hitchcock to shoot in his park, he would not permit his own children to see *Psycho* (Spoto 471).

Hitchcock was greatly disappointed. Yet he may have had at least partial revenge. In a filmed address made some time later to a British film society, we can see Hitchcock inventing the rudiments of what would one day become the Universal Studios Tour. Called the Westcliffe Address—basically a filmed speech overlaid with documentary shots of the Universal Studios backlots featuring, of course, as the movie-centered amusement park now does, the *Psycho* house as one of its main attractions—the speech is fascinating for its anticipation of the Hollywood rival to Disneyland that would take a more catastrophic, Hitchcockian, assaultive approach to its attractions. As we have already seen, what Hitchcock anticipated, not only in this address but in *Psycho* itself, was the process whereby amusement parks would become more like movies and movies would become more like the new amusement parks. The Westcliffe Address is in the archives of the Margaret Herrick Library.

19. Janet Staiger offers an impressive theorization and practice of cinematic reception study in her recent *Interpreting Films* (1992).

20. Berenstein (1993) argues that such performances were a common feature of classic horror cinema. She cites the publicity stunt of a woman planted in the audience of each screening of *Mark of the Vampire* as an extreme example. The woman's task was to scream and faint at predetermined moments, so that ushers would remove her from the theater and whisk her away in a waiting ambulance.

WORKS CITED

Bazin, André. *What Is Cinema?* Trans. Hugh Gray. 2 vols. Berkeley: University of California Press, 1967–1971.

Baudrillard, Jean. *Selected Writings.* Mark Poster, ed. Stanford: Stanford University Press, 1988.

Bellour, Raymond. "Psychosis, Neurosis, Perversion." *Camera Obscura: A Journal of Feminism and Film Theory* 3–4 (1979): 105–32.

Berenstein, Rhona. "Spectatorship as Drag: The Act of Viewing and Classic Horror Cinema." In Linda Williams, ed., *Viewing Positions: Ways of Seeing Film.* Rutgers University Press, forthcoming.

——. *Attack of the Leading Ladies: Gender and Performance in Classic Horror Cinema.* New York: Columbia University Press, 1996.

Bordwell, David. *Making Meaning: Inference and Rhetoric in the Interpretation of Cinema.* Cambridge: Harvard University Press, 1989.

Bukatman, Scott. "There's Always Tomorrowland: Disney and the Hypercinematic Experience." *October* 57 (1991): 55–78.

Butler, Judith. *Gender Trouble: Feminism and the Subversion of Identity.* New York: Routledge, 1990.

Callenbach, Ernest. *Film Quarterly* XIV(1)(Fall 1960): 47–49.

Cavell, Stanley. *The World Viewed.* Cambridge: Harvard University Press, 1979.

Clover, Carol. *Men, Women and Chain Saws: Gender in the Modern Horror Film.* Princeton: Princeton University Press, 1992.

Delaplane, Stan. August 12, 1960. *Los Angeles Examiner.*

DeLauretis, Teresa. *Alice Doesn't: Feminism, Semiotics, Cinema.* Bloomington: Indiana University Press, 1984.

Douchet, Jean. "Hitch and His Public." In Jim Hillier, ed., *Cahiers du cinema: The 1960s: New Wave, New Cinema, Reevaluating Hollywood.* Cambridge: Harvard University Press, 1986.

Durgnat, Raymond. "Inside Norman Bates." In *Films and Feelings.* Cambridge: MIT Press, 1967.

Foucault, Michel. *Discipline and Punish: The Birth of the Prison.* Trans. Alan Sheridan. New York: Vintage, 1978.

Garber, Marjorie. *Vested Interests: Cross-Dressing and Cultural Anxiety.* New York: Routledge, 1992.

Gunning, Tom. "The Cinema of Attractions: Early Film, Its Spectator and the Avant-Garde." *Wide Angle* 8 (3–4): 63–70. Reprint in Thomas Elsaesser and Adam Barker, eds., *Early Cinema: Space, Frame, Narrative.* London: BFI, 1990, 56–62.

Hatch, Robert. *The Nation,* July 2, 1960, 39.

Hitchcock, Alfred. *Motion Picture Herald,* August 8, 1960, 17–18.

Houston, Penelope. "Alfred Hitchcock: I." In Richard Roud, ed., *Cinema: A Critical Dictionary,* vol. 1. Norwich: Martin Secker and Warburg Limited, 1980.

Jameson, Fredric. "Postmodernism, or, The Cultural Logic of Late Capitalism." *New Left Review* 146 (July–August 1984): 59–92.

——. *Signatures of the Visible.* New York: Routledge, 1990.

——. *The Geopolitical Aesthetic: Cinema and Space in the World System.* Bloomington: Indiana University Press, 1992.

Kapsis, Robert. *Hitchcock: The Making of a Reputation.* Chicago: University of Chicago Press, 1992.

Klinger, Barbara. "The Institutionalization of Female Sexuality." In *A Hitchcock Reader.* Ames: Iowa State University Press, 1982, 332–39.

Lardeau, Yann. "Le sexe froid (du porno au dela)." *Cahiers du cinema* 2899 (June 1978): 49, 52, 61.

Levine, Lawrence. *Highbrow/Lowbrow: The Emergence of Cultural Hierarchy in America.* Cambridge: Harvard University Press, 1988.

Mayne, Judith. *Spectatorship and Cinema.* New York: Routledge, 1993.

Mitchell, W. J. T. "The Pictorial Turn." *Art Forum* 30(3)(March 1992): 89–94.

Modleski, Tania. *The Women Who Knew Too Much: Hitchcock and Feminist Theory.* New York and London: Methuen, 1988.

Paramount World (July–August 1960).

Pechter, William S. *Twenty-four Times a Second.* New York: Harper and Row, 1971.

Perkins, V. F. "The World and Its Image." *Film as Film.* Harmondsworth: Penguin, 1972.

Poague, Leland and Marshall Deutelbaum, eds. *A Hitchcock Reader.* Ames: Iowa State University Press, 1986.

Rebello, Stephen. *Alfred Hitchcock and the Making of "Psycho".* New York: Harper-Collins, 1990.

Rothman, William. *The Murderous Gaze.* Cambridge: Harvard University Press, 1982.

Silverman, Kaja. *The Subject of Semiotics.* New York: Oxford University Press, 1983.

——. *Male Subjectivity at the Margins.* New York: Routledge, 1992.

Spoto, Donald. *The Dark Side of Genius: The Life of Alfred Hitchcock.* New York: Ballantine, 1983.

Staiger, Janet. *Interpreting Films: Studies in the Historical Reception of American Cinema.* Princeton: Princeton University Press, 1992.

Tudor, Andrew. *Monsters and Mad Scientists: A Cultural History of the Horror Movie.* Oxford: Basil Blackwell, 1989.

Williams, Linda. "When the Woman Looks." In Mary Ann Doane, Patricia Mellencamp, and Linda Williams, eds., *Re-Vision: Essays in Feminist Film Criticism.* The American Film Institute Monograph Series, vol. 3. Frederick, Md.: University Publications of America, 1984.

——, ed. *Viewing Positions: Ways of Seeing Film.* New Brunswick: Rutgers University Press, 1994.

Wood, Robin. *Hitchcock's Films.* New York: Paperback Library, 1965.

Žižek, Slavoj, ed. *Everything You Always Wanted to Know About Lacan but Were Afraid to Ask Hitchcock.* New York: Verso, 1992.

SIX

Fashion and the Racial Construction of Gender

Leslie Rabine

In the debates about the merits of cultural criticism in relation to text-based disciplines, no area of culture gets a more dubious reception than fashion. Inescapably frivolous, lowbrow, consumerist, feminized, wasteful, useless, and pleasurable, fashion appears to have no redeeming quality that could link it to the more sublimated, manly, contemplative pleasures of great literature, art, or philosophy. Ironically, the same kinds of moral disapproval directed at fashion itself since the newly empowered bourgeoisie consigned it to women now greet its critical study—or such has been my experience. It's as if the extravagant, excessive, immodest, seductive powers of fashion would uncontainably flood the intellectual field. This may be the case.

Although I suspect that the disapproval stems in part from a fear that the critical study of fashion makes too explicit the unadmitted pleasures, desires, and narcissisms linking any scholarship to its object of study, that is not the argument this essay will follow. It examines the inseparable mixture of frivolous pleasure and serious work not in scholarly practice but in the practice of fashion. The very defects of mass-consumer fashion from the point of view of high culture, intellectual asceticism, and moral rectitude make it an ideal instrument for the production of subjects, identities, and ideologies. It is ideal as the conflictual arena in which subjects are produced both through their subjection to corporate ideology and through their own ambiguously emancipatory self-fashioning.

As the symbolic medium connecting bodies to their social world, fashion transforms them into readable texts. In this guise, it constitutes an unstable, multivalent language. By turns marker of social status, disguise, and masquerade, fashion reveals, conceals, and, most important, creates its wearer's identity. The messages of fashionable clothing, like textual language, invariably exceed the intentions of its wearer-author. She is spoken by fashion's larger system of signification as much as she conveys her own meanings, with the result that fashionably clothed bodies are crisscrossed with conflicting meanings. And like the semiotic displacements of textual language, the ever-shifting borders between fabric and skin in fashionable dress draw upon an irresolvable play whereby clothing represents what it seeks to hide, draws obsessive attention to what it covers, and thus produces the body as object of desire.

These layers of discourse and desire in the text of fashion are concentrated and complicated by the text of the fashion magazine, which acts as a microcosm of corporate cultural logic. Here the fetishistic gaze solicited by the fashionably clothed body is intensified by the fashion photograph that demands fantastic identification. This fantasy mirror of photography is contextualized in its sociohistorical world, as the photos are surrounded by articles and commentary on political and cultural events. The whole complex of imaginary self-image and sociohistoric context is framed by the powerful machinery of corporate publicity and ownership, which commodifies and transforms into its own ideology every utterance and gaze that enters its space.

Given the pervasive power of fashion in constructing the racial, gender, class, and sexual identities of women, especially young, vulnerable women, critical theorists would be seriously remiss if we did not direct to it the countervailing power of our analytic tools and make that power available to wearers of fashion. This essay proposes to so analyze the racialized construction of white and African American feminine identities through the processes of identification deployed by *Essence* and *Mirabella* magazines.

But to propose that critical analysis serve the interests of people subjected to race-gender oppression raises yet another controversy in the debates between cultural studies and classical disciplines. If a first debate questions mass culture as a proper object of study, the second asks what theoretical concepts we should bring to bear upon our studies. From the perspective of critical theories based on European philosophy and literature, it may seem problematic that I organize this essay around the critical concept of the "culture of dissemblance," taken from the work of black feminist historian Darlene Clark Hine. Its centrality here might be all the more debatable for the fact that this concept has a very problematic status within black feminist theory itself. Hine defines it as follows:

Black women, as a rule, developed and adhered to a cult of secrecy, a culture of dissemblance, to protect the sanctity of inner aspects of their lives. The dynamics of dissemblance involved creating the appearance of disclosure, or openness about themselves and their feelings, while actually remaining an enigma. Only with secrecy, thus achieving a self-imposed invisibility, could ordinary black women accrue the psychic space and harness the resources needed to hold their own in the often one-sided and mismatched resistance struggle.   *(915)*

In the nineteenth century, black women created a culture that, says Hine, "shielded the truth of their inner lives and selves from their oppressors" (912) in order "to resist the misappropriation and to maintain the integrity of their own sexuality" (913) as well as "to become agents of social change" (915).

As a tool for analyzing postmodern culture, Hine's theory might seem strangely outmoded. An inner/outer dichotomy is the framework around which cluster the homologous pairs of truth/appearance, secrecy/revelation, and real self/social self—all of which suggest an inner essential core to black women's identity. But both Elsa Barkley Brown and Paula Giddings find that it explains Anita Hill's initial silence as a victim of sexual harassment (Brown 306; Giddings 92:456). On the other hand, Giddings praises Hill for having finally stepped outside the culture of dissemblance. Evelynn Hammonds also finds limited the power of such dissemblance to enable women as agents of social change. Both Giddings and Hammonds argue that beyond a certain limit, dissemblance inhibits black women from articulating and redefining their own sexuality as well as from transforming social institutions.

The culture of dissemblance and its inhibiting effects implicate white women at least as much as black women. Therefore, in studying how fashion in a black women's magazine epitomizes the operations of a politically ambiguous cultural form that is both continuing and crumbling, this essay also investigates the way that dominant fashion and white women's critical writing about it reproduce the imperative for a black feminine culture of dissemblance. A passage from Elizabeth Wilson's "Fashion and the Postmodern Body" illustrates this reproductive move by white cultural critics, myself included, who write about race:

> Perhaps style becomes a substitute for identity, perhaps its fluidity (in theory it can be changed at will) offers an alternative to the stagnant fixity of "old-fashioned" ideas of personality and core identity, perhaps on the contrary it is used to fix identity more firmly. Either way, we may still understand dress as one tool in the creation of identities. For

example, in New York in 1990 Afro-Americans were looking to Africa
in search of their roots and an alternative means of cultural expression.
. . . In fact, at least since the 1960s, black women and men *have* used
style to express collective identities, in opposition to the dominant culture.   *(9)*

African American fashion appears here as an "example," but an example
of what? Instead of serving to explore the question that begins the passage—
whether postmodern style fluidifies or fixes identity—the choice of African
American style as example seems to lead Wilson to evade the very question
she sets out to settle. Once the subject of African American adoption of
African style is introduced, the issue of whether its use in the black community attempts to fix an essentialized, idealized identity looms large and
demands examination. Rather than examining the challenges that it poses to
ethnically biased postmodern theories of flux and fluidity, Wilson arrives at
an impasse in her questioning, and lets her argument fall apart.

The "fixity" that stubbornly gets reproduced in her writing is the oppositional racial system we have inherited. Wilson's discussion demonstrates on
a performative level that even "postmodernism as fragmentation" inherits
race, gender, and sexuality as dualistic systems whose terms cannot function
separately from each other (7). It suggests that a postmodern, fluid, white,
feminine identity depends for its production upon the image of a fixed black
feminine identity. It is this possibility that the following study of fashion
explores.

"The Secret Is Out"

Among the many elements of Hine's concept that intriguingly illuminate a
study of postmodern fashion is her discussion of black women's ability "to
craft the veil of secrecy" (915) and their fear for "those who . . . tore the pro-
tective cloaks from their inner selves" (916). Her rhetoric hints at a relation
between resistance to oppression and the more literal veils and cloaks of fashion.

The July 1992 issue of *Essence* featured a photoessay on lingerie dressing
bearing the Hinian (or apparently post-Hinian) title "The Secret Is Out:
Romantic Lingerie Tiptoes out of the Boudoir and into the Spotlight." The
1990s fashion of lingerie dressing has the double advantage of embodying a
whole series of fantasy fashion and identity exchanges between white and
African American women while at the same time evoking on many levels the

inside/outside symbolism of Hine's "culture of dissemblance." Deborah Gregory, the author of the photoessay, has been writing on the politics of fashion since the magazine's inception. Her 1992 piece brings into focus not only contemporary changes in the racial construction of gender, but also, on a more personal level, my own love/hate relationship with glamorous fashion in consumerist society. The complex politics of style in *Essence* magnifies the contradiction between the transformative, fascinating power of beautiful clothing and its inseparability from the oppressive power of corporate capitalism.

"The Secret Is Out" brings together two histories: that of the development of a black feminine aesthetic in *Essence* since it began publishing in 1970, and that of the development of sexy dressing in mass-culture clothing style during the decade leading up to 1992. An overview of each of these histories will explain the import of "The Secret Is Out."

Essence as Cultural Institution

By far the major mass-circulation magazine for black women with a readership of 5.2 million, and the most politically progressive among the African American-targeted magazines, *Essence* began publishing about ten years before the proliferation of marketing-niche magazines packaging America's minority cultures for mainstream-style consumption. In this pioneering position, it has from its start been riven by an ever-more-intense ambiguity between providing its readership a forum for emancipatory politics and serving as the vehicle for their commodification and corporate censorship.

This ambiguity involves the "culture of dissemblance" because *Essence* figures itself rhetorically to its readers by means of such dissemblance. It represents itself as a private space, protected from the white gaze, where black women and black men can safely discuss issues that are "taboo in public discourse" (Giddings 92:456). On the other hand, that space is already thoroughly imbued with the white gaze of corporate control that manifests itself in the advertising. These ads resemble what Sinclair calls "institutional advertising," whose "point is to induce a favorable attitude towards an industry or corporation" (Sinclair 2), but go a step further; as such, they make explicit the underlying message of all advertising. In spite of this corporate ownership of the private space, I still had the feeling of reading *Essence* as an ethnographic intruder, peeking into a community designed to protect its participants from such interlopers.

Many of the taboo issues discussed in that community concern gender and sexual conflicts among African Americans, and *Essence* has published forums on intracommunity rape, sexism in rap and hiphop music, and lesbian, gay, and straight sexualities. One subject that brought the culture of dissemblance to a painful crisis was the Anita Hill/Clarence Thomas hearings. *Essence* explored the crisis in three different issues, while the venerable black magazine *Ebony*, which had played a strong role supporting civil rights struggles in the fifties and sixties, maintained a prudent silence, as if the whole event had not occurred.

Essence published not only an interview with Hill and an article about her, but also a forum featuring twenty black intellectuals (Jan. 1992). This forum was organized around a question articulating the inside/outside split: "Should blacks speak out against other blacks?" (58), or in other words, should they lift the veil of secrecy to white institutions? Comments from contributors like: "Our dirty little secret is finally out in the public" (George E. Curry, 59) or "Black people have matured . . . to the point that we can air our dirty linen in public just like white people do" (Joyce Ladner, 92) implied that the pages of *Essence* were not usually for the general "public."

The inclusion of men and male voices behind the veil of privacy in *Essence* would seem to contradict Hine's theory, since according to her, the culture of dissemblance was formed to protect black women's inner lives not only from white sexual abuse but also from abuse by black men. But *Essence* figures its readerly space as a haven so powerful that it can transform the men who enter it into women's empathetic partners.

Yet this powerfully figured and protected inner space of *Essence* is not invaded but rather produced by the corporate publishers and sponsors who control and censor it. Although overt censorship may no longer be used to ensure the fit of editorial content to advertisements, this was not the case at the beginning of *Essence*'s publication history. The first issue of *Essence* was a dummy issue never actually published. Its first editor, Ruth N. Ross, introduced the magazine with a spirited, militant statement of purpose:

> With the jolting shifts of the black Movement and the swelling wave of black consciousness around the world, we black women, particularly and at long last, come into our own. For we are the women who have been placed on the lowest rung of the western world's ladder of beauty. For we who have lived with humiliating and detested images of ourselves imposed upon us by other people, for we who have borne the double burden of both femaleness and blackness, for us the impassioned cry "Black is Beautiful" lifts us up, for the first time, high onto a pedestal and into the spotlight of *Essence* magazine: the magazine that

will speak in our name, provide us with a platform from which our voice may be heard.

The first published issue, identical to this mock-up in most respects, contains a different version of the editorial, signed not by editor Ross but by the publisher, The Hollingsworth Group:

> With the swelling of black consciousness around the world, you, the black woman, are at long last coming into your own. The impassioned cry "Black is Beautiful" lifts you up for the first time onto a pedestal and into the spotlight of *Essence* magazine—the magazine that will speak in your name and in your voice.

The editor's signature appears only under a statement of gratitude to the publisher.

In spite of this censorship of "negative" (i.e., critical) writing, *Essence* did manage to vigorously debate and transform the racist politics of beauty. As a glossy women's magazine, *Essence* had to be in large part about fashion and beauty. Born during the Black Power movement, it could not avoid the way in which a white beauty imperative, accumulating a long history of Western slave culture and economics, invests the arena of skin, hair, and makeup with political struggle.

But an issue that goes even more deeply to the heart of the racist construction of black woman as dehumanized Other is that of body shape and size. Ahistorical myths of essentialized "white" and "black" races, with their equally mythical "body types," have produced stereotypes of the black female body as excessive. In this cultural climate, *Essence* is the only mass-circulation fashion magazine that has consistently tried to transform the dominant feminine body aesthetic. White fashion magazines have not come to terms with this issue.

Several black feminist theorists and historians have documented the transformation of black women's bodies into screens for white mythical projections of their promiscuity, sexual voraciousness, and animality. These in turn have been used to justify the institutionalization of rape and sexual abuse against them since the time of slavery (Brown 304–6; Collins 178; Crenshaw 411; Giddings 84:46–49, 82–88; White 27–61). bell hooks writes:

> Representations of black female bodies in contemporary popular culture rarely subvert or critique images of black female sexuality which were part of the cultural apparatus of 19th-century racism and which still shape perceptions today. . . . Black presence in early North American society allowed whites to sexualize their world by project-

ing onto black bodies a narrative of sexualization disassociated from
whiteness.   *(62)*

The protected private space figured in *Essence* allows it to subvert the
stereotyped image of black female sexuality in certain startling ways. It
thereby also subverts the feminine image of fashion in general. *Essence* is the
only fashion magazine to break the taboo against showing a wide range of
body shapes and sizes in fashion editorial layouts. While this in itself may
not seem very revolutionary, using images of large women in fashion layouts
is one of the very few, if not indeed the only, taboo that does remain unbro-
ken in fashion magazines of the postmodern era.

An early attempt by *Essence* to confer upon large bodies the same kind
of pleasurable frivolity reserved for the aesthetic standard appears in a 1975
fashion layout entitled "The Return of the Voluptuous Woman." It begins:
"Starshine on: As a people we are more aware of our bodies—possess a super
body-consciousness. A heightened sense of our nubility. At last the spotlight
falls on, men's eyes wander to, the VOLUPTUOUS woman" (May 1975:54).
In what was also to become a common practice in *Essence*, the fashion essay
featured women who were not professional models. The fashions themselves
deviate emphatically from the body-hiding drapes habitually shown for large
women in fashion catalogues. The copy calls attention to the glamour and
the bareness of the dresses, and the sexuality they signify: "An actress and a
very mobile lady, Florene is aware of her body . . . and how to show it. In a
size 12, she wears a body-revealing, very plunging aqua polyester gown."

The fashion copy and the photos in "The Return of the Voluptuous
Woman," with their exaggerated emphasis on exhibition for male eyes, seem
to contradict both the "culture of dissemblance" and feminist theories of the
male gaze. But this contradiction marks the magazine's attempt, in some
ways limited and in some ways startling, to change the feminine image and
its field of vision.

The "male gaze," a concept from 1970s feminist film theory, points to
the phallocentric bias inherent in Western visual culture at the level of structure. The male gaze is not the look of a particular, visible man, but the eye
of the camera, and beyond that, the unseen, nonpersonified structuring
principle of the field of vision. It produces man as the subject and woman as
the object of vision, desire, pleasure, and sexuality. Fashion critics, borrow-
ing the concept of the male gaze to analyze fashion photography, found that
they had to change it. Fashion magazines do not simply assimilate the male
gaze, but make it over for the visual pleasure of women (Fuss, Rabine, Silverman, Young 206–7). In the fashion magazine, woman is both subject and

object of the gaze. The image is both identificatory mirror and object of desire for the viewing subject (Fuss 213).

But the images of large women in *Essence* transform the visual field more dramatically. However dated the rhetoric of "The Return of the Voluptuous Woman," the fantasy it inscribes opens up the visual field of feminine pleasure. The implied viewing subject of mainstream fashion photography desires to be the ideal image as determined by normative conventions of the Euroamerican feminine aesthetic. By contrast, the image in "The Return of the Voluptuous Woman" is to the implied viewer a mirror reflection of a highly idealized version of herself that defies convention in an unprecedented way. To validate this unconventional mass-media fantasy, the photography must then take the step of transforming the male gaze as guardian of visual convention. "The Return of the Voluptuous Woman" *embodies* the disembodied gaze by including in its photographs images of men looking with admiration. In order to remake it in the image of feminine viewers as a gaze captivated by the sexual attraction and power of large women, the photos also incorporate that remade gaze into their own fantasy space. The male gaze is figured as no longer the structuring principle of the visual field but just one of its visible, and therefore controllable, elements. Although the male gaze does continue in its disembodied form to govern the visual field, it is now doubled. Its embodied, personified double, reduced to a visible object, changes the components of the dominant field and transforms their relation. The inner space behind the culture of dissemblance turns out to be a transformed visual field. It does not simply protect black women, but re-creates the abusive "outside" where they are spectacles for the fantasies, pleasures, and/or rejections of white and black male gazes. In this space readers assume the power to control the gaze and thereby reclaim their sexual and visual pleasure.

This refigured space can transform more complexly the Western visual field because of another historically inherited oppositional structure. According to Iris Marion Young,

> Women take pleasure in clothes, not just in wearing clothes, but also
> in looking at clothes and looking at images of women in clothes,
> because they encourage fantasies of transport and transformation. We
> experience our clothes, if Hollander is right, in the context of the
> images of clothes from magazines, film, TV that draw us into situa-
> tions and personalities that we can play at. *(206)*

In 1975, black women did not have such film, magazine, and TV images readily available to them. Excluded from the pantheon of images of beauty, their fantasies of transport had to be based on self-made images. But this exclusion flows out of black women's (and men's) position within oppositional eighteenth- and nineteenth-century aesthetic philosophies, based on a bipolarity of beautiful/ugly. Black people, as Sander Gilman has documented, occupied paradigmatically the term in opposition to beauty. In Hegel's aesthetic they were deemed incapable both of reflecting beauty and of producing it: "They never achieve a sense of human personality—their spirit sleeps, remains sunk in itself, makes no advances and thus parallels the compact, undifferentiated mass of the African continent" (qtd. in Gilman 94). In Hegel's dialectic, Africans are outside of history: "What we properly understand by Africa, is the Unhistorical, Undeveloped Spirit, still involved in the conditions of mere nature" (qtd. in Gilman 96). Associated with the negative term of the aesthetic dialectic, Africans are thus excluded from its terms of beauty. In the postmodern period the negative term of the dialectic is no longer so negative in the moral or aesthetic sense, but it continues to operate structurally in the mainstream feminine aesthetic. Although feminine standards of beauty have admitted ethnic looks, they still retain from this old metaphysical opposition between the beautiful and the ugly a definition of beauty in terms of body size.

Even though *Essence* is a mass-cultural magazine, it shows that constructions of black femininity, having inherited the position of the secondary, negative term, bring with them, as they gain admission to Western notions of history and individuality, the multiplicity and heterogeneity consigned to that term. Addressed to women historically situated as other in a restricted aesthetic, *Essence*, even as a mass-market institution, develops an alternative feminine aesthetic, including a wide range of previously forbidden versions of feminine identities.

Since 1975, many more film, magazine, and TV images of black women have become available to the readers of *Essence*, but these images generally fit the conventional ideas for feminine beauty. The magazine, in the meantime, has not only increased its display of large models in fashion editorials but has also ceased to call attention to their largeness or make it an issue. They are simply included in the *Essence* canon of beauty as a matter of course.

Other fashion magazines did not show any large models until 1993, and then only in a Guess Jeans ad, where the display of a large model was calculated to provoke a shocked reaction but also to hide most of her body. Large models are more and more frequently included in feature articles explicitly about the issues of weight and large models in fashion, but not in fashion editorial layouts (*Glamour*, Mar. 1992; Jan. 1993; Jan. 1995; *Allure*, Jan. 1993). Photographs either crop the models below the neck, or pose them to hide their bodies. Magazines like *Big Beautiful Woman* and *Dimensions* create a counteraesthetic as narrow as the thin dictate they oppose. They also make size the explicit point of their photos.

Essence, by contrast, naturalizes large bodies in fashion by including large models in photo layouts together with thin models. In "The Secret Is Out," on the fashion of lingerie dressing for the street, the nonchalant, naturalizing inclusion of large bodies takes an especially daring turn. The issue's table of contents features a full-length photo of Delilah Nelson, a large, very voluptuous model. Wearing a delicate white lace catsuit, she presents a startling challenge to the eye disciplined to the fashion-magazine standard. Her conventional fashion pose and placement on the page, along with her easygoing stance and relaxed smile, casually denies the fact that such images remain strictly forbidden in the advertisements that frame the private space of *Essence*. In the essay itself, Nelson is joined by three other models, two conventionally thin, the fourth larger than she. Their presence in the photoessay brings together two historic developments—that of the different feminine aesthetic in *Essence* and that of sexy dressing in mainstream fashion.

Sexy Dressing and Women's Rights in the 1990s

Lingerie dressing was the culmination and turning point of the sexy dressing style that began in 1986, with skirts going above the knee in shaped Lycra dresses that *Vogue* called "body-hugging." This new style signaled a change in clothing as a semiotic system. In addition to signifying women's traditional value as objects for the male gaze, fashion also signified women's own power (whether fictional or real) as newly constituted subjects of sexuality, economics, and self-representation. Fashionable white middle-class women had a new status as signifiers of social value.

Since the establishment of bourgeois fashion in nineteenth-century Europe, clothing had played a major role in producing the symbolic categories of class-based gender (Baudelaire, Flügel, Kuchta, Veblen). Clothing for bourgeois women was both decorative and decorous, while for men it was somber and severe. Critics and historians of clothing have seen this polarized clothing symbolism as instrumental in constructing the opposition between man as subject and woman as his object. In economic terms, the bourgeois woman's dress figured her as the possession of an individual man and the mark of his wealth. The clothing that coded the proletarian was more garish and daring, associated with prostitutes. It signified its wearer as the unprotected possession of any and all male predators.

The sexy fashions of the late 1980s and early 1990s blur both the sub-ject/object dichotomy of gender and the respectable woman/whore dichotomy of class. Like cross-dressing and drag, which also had a lot of play in mainstream fashion magazines in the early nineties, sexy fashions upset the boundaries of gender opposition. But the two modes of dress do so dif-ferently. In a seeming contradiction, the gender-blurring women's fashions of the 1990s are *more* "feminine" than the fashions of the early 1980s that they replace. They use the delicate materials traditionally associated with femininity—lace, silk, ribbons. They also emphasize those parts of the body traditionally associated with women's display for male pleasure. While cross-dressing plays with the visible differences through which men and women perform their gender identities (Berlant and Freeman, Case, Garber, Butler 93), contemporary sexy styles destabilize the conceptual categories on which the gender system depends. For one thing, they undo the set of oppositional homologies that identify man with the subject and woman with the object. Secondly, they undo the oppositional signs of class that used to indicate whether women depended economically on men as wives or prostitutes. In so doing they signify that women have gone beyond economic dependency on men. The wearer, of course, may not actually enjoy the independence that her clothing encodes. The power of these fashions lies in their ability to transform underlying symbolic structures, not in an ability to transform directly and immediately individual wearers' lives.

Because fashion's power operates on the level of code and symbol, lin-gerie dressing represents the culmination of sexy dressing. Lingerie does not expose more of the body than the Lycra tank-dress, but it is coded with con-notations of intimacy, privacy, nudity, and self-revelation (Craik 12, Ewing, Hollander, Steele 116, 119). Although the lingerie dress can actually cover more of the body and adapt itself to a greater range of body shapes and sizes than the body-hugging minidress, it is more daring. Symbolically, it desta-bilizes not only the subject/object and bourgeoise/prostitute dichotomies, but more fundamentally the inside/outside dichotomy. And doubly so: underwear is worn inside other clothing as a kind of second skin; it is also displayed only inside the home, and usually only in sexual intimacy. Lingerie dressing violates both of these "insides," as it is worn as outerwear out on the street.

Does "The Secret Is Out" then mark the end of the culture of dissem-blance? The evidence suggests that the answer is both yes and no. On the one hand, Deborah Gregory leans heavily on the rhetorical possibilities of shak-ing up the inside/outside dichotomy. This is striking in view of the fact that other fashion writers have barely mentioned this aspect of lingerie dressing, focusing instead on the liberal rhetoric of choice and right. Fashion reporter Suzy Menkes is typical. In an article on corset-dressing she writes: "A woman now believes that if she chooses to enhance her curves, that is her right; and if a man misinterprets that signal as a come-on, that is his problem" (*Mirabella*, Feb. 1995:130). "The Secret Is Out," by contrast, plays rapturously on the meanings of in and out. The image of the catsuited model is accompanied by the caption: "This season, lingerie is no longer just an inside story." In the essay itself, Gregory embroiders on the theme: "Look what has tiptoed out of the boudoir: luscious bits of lingerie . . . they are just too romantic to hide this summer. Whether you dress these poetic pieces up or down, rest assured you'll hit the streets as pretty as you wanna be!" (74). In the first spread the models interact as they model white lace lingerie: "The inside story is bursting out from under wraps; with the irresistible innocence of white. Pure and simple, the delicate extras you'll want right now include second-skin teddies, satiny slips, contour-sleek girdles and racy lacy leggings" (75).

On the other hand, an angry letter to the editor from a reader named Todra does not reject daring expressions of sexual pleasure, but firmly places them back in the public/private, inside/outside opposition. Given the title "Keep It in the Closet!" the letter reads:

> Telling African American women to wear their underwear outside only adds to women's problems today. Don't we have enough problems with men's lack of respect for our minds and our bodies? In the midst of AIDS, the Clarence Thomas and Mike Tyson cases and everyday disregard for our right to say no, should a contemporary African American woman wear her underwear outside? We've been stereotyped as lusty and loose for too long. Ladies, save the lingerie for private showings!   *(Sept. 1992:135–36)*

The letter responds to the symbolic fabric of lingerie. For Todra, the metaphorical nakedness of lingerie worn outside signifies neither pleasure nor power nor freedom from stereotypes, but the white and/or male stereotypes of black women's promiscuity that have historically been used to justify rape and sexual mistreatment. Contrary to signifying pleasure, the image of innerwear worn outside in *Essence* destroys for her the illusion of being inside a space framed by the black female gaze and protected for black women's sexual expression. Instead of evoking her pleasurable identification, the essay pushes her "outside" under the imagined gaze of hostile men and a stereotyping white society.

Todra's letter particularly impressed me, because in reading "The Secret

Is Out" I had not thought to bring to it the lens of the culture of dissemblance. Readerly codes inherited from a different position in the history of the racial construction of gender led me to a different kind of identification process with the images. My own fascination with them stemmed from their fantastic promise of transforming the venerable Western tradition that defines femininity as masquerade (Kofman, Lacan, Lemoine-Luccioni, Riviere). Todra's letter raises the issues that Hine elaborates, along with all they imply about the historical construction of gender and sexuality—white as well as black, male as well as female—through racial and sexual stereotypes of black women. Many black feminist historians and theorists have elaborated that history. It requires not only a reinterpretation of lingerie dressing, but a retelling of its origin. As with many other products of American culture, the style did not originate with a few white designers, but grows out of North America's history of race.

Insofar as sexy dressing signifies traditionally a bourgeois/proletarian divide, it signifies in dominant American culture a white/black divide. bell hooks analyzes the way in which the mass-media imagination associates blatantly sexy street style with the historically derogatory stereotype of black women:

> Unmasked by a virtuous white public, [Vanessa Williams] assumed (according to their standards) the right erotic place set aside for black women in the popular imagination. The American public that had so brutally critiqued Williams and rejected her had no difficulty accepting and applauding her when she accepted the image of fallen woman. Again, as in the case of Tina Turner, Williams [sic] bid for continued success necessitated her acceptance of conventional racist/sexist representations of black female sexuality. *(75)*

Wahneema Lubiano points out that this stereotyped image of black women determined not only the media treatment of rock singers, but also that of Anita Hill:

> Susan Douglas noted that Hill looked and acted prim, even prudish (*In These Times*, November 6–12, 1991, p. 18), behavior seen as deviant because it wasn't exuberant, earthy, physically expressive. It went against the grain of media, especially television, portraits of black women. This is a media criticism, of course, that countless African American feminists and cultural commentators have made for decades. *(341)*

Where the 1990s mode of sexy dressing signifies a woman's newfound freedom to control her own image, sexy dressing for black women has a double meaning. It also invokes a traditional image, one that the women do not control, that is imposed rather than freely chosen and that expresses the fantasies of an exploiting other rather than the women's own.

More to the point here, that image was developed in nineteenth-century America to construct a white/black sexual and gender binary. According to Nell Irvin Painter, "The sexually promiscuous black girl . . . represents the mirror image of the white woman on the pedestal. Together, white and black women stand for woman as madonna and as whore" (207). The image of black women as both the antithesis of the feminine, defined as essentially white, and the exaggeration of sexuality served the construction and naturalization of white masculine identity (Giddings 92:450–51).

Where middle-class white women, as the historically naturalized embodiments of virtue, can don garments semiotized as wanton to create ambiguous self-images, black women are in a different symbolic context. As hooks says in her critique of Madonna's appropriation of black feminine imagery:

> Since we are coded always as "fallen" women in the racist cultural iconography we can never, as can Madonna, publicly "work" the image of ourselves as innocent female daring to be bad. . . . The vast majority of black women in the United States, more concerned with projecting images of respectability than with the idea of female sexual agency and transgression, do not often feel we have the "freedom" to act in rebellious ways in regards to sexuality without being punished. *(160)*

Lingerie dressing has a heightened ambiguity in that its cultural meaning has been interlaced with a new political meaning. However fictive the clothing's political meanings of feminine freedom and power may be, the ability to wear these sartorial signifiers and express those meanings has become in itself a real right. Thus while middle-class white women can use sexy dressing to create undecidable cultural meanings because for them its new political meaning is unambiguous, black women must instead contend with an ambiguous political meaning. Sexy dressing appears as both a new-found right to which the demands of equality require access and an imposed burden, inherited from history. In fact, the ability of middle-class white women to create in this way their ambiguous images depends, as hooks points out, on a continuing association of danger and daring with an outcast dark body constructed as opposite.

Race and Gender in *Mirabella*

An example of fashion using black women as Other in the interests of a postmodern white feminine undecidability appears in a July 1994 photoessay in the mainstream fashion magazine *Mirabella*. Called "Georgia on My Mind," the essay purports to show "outstanding designs from the fall collections on great-looking women" (101). Given the recent integration of black models into fashion's commodified multiculturalism, this essay is all the more striking in that it photographs African American women as black. The *Mirabella* essay uses many of the fashion photography conventions unique to *Essence*, and is revealing for what it includes and excludes from those conventions. The women photographed are for the most part not professional models, but students and workers recruited in Savannah, Georgia. Many of them are large, overweight by magazine standards. Their faces do not conform to mass-media standards of beauty.

But unlike *Essence*, the *Mirabella* photoessay dresses only the thin women in slip-dresses and body-hugging evening gowns while it bundles the large women in heavy overcoats and suits. And unlike the intimate space of black women's visual pleasure in *Essence*, the space of "Georgia on My Mind" segregates its subjects from the surrounding fashion layouts into a kind of *National Geographic* exoticism for a white feminine gaze. The use of black-and-white film separates the photos from the other fashion layouts, while at the same time creating a distancing, exotic effect and also signaling "Georgia on My Mind" as a novelty piece.

Why this treatment of black feminine imagery? The blurbs accompanying the photographer's and stylist's credits at the beginning of the magazine give a clue. Polly Hamilton, the stylist for the fashion portfolio, is quoted as saying, "Women are all different. We're not all cut from one pattern, and no particular shape is better than another" (14). Kurt Markus, the photographer, is quoted similarly: "There's nothing invented about the beauty of the women we chose. I find that the concept of beauty as defined by fashion is so limited that it has no application to real life" (14). The point of the photoessay, achieved through the representation of blackness, is corporeal diversity. Hamilton and Markus here sound themes that *Essence* resolved in the seventies in spite of its commodified frame. In the nineties, mainstream fashion magazines have taken up these themes with intense concern, but without being able to attain resolution.

Glamour and *Allure* publish articles disapproving the narrow dictates of slenderness. Grace Mirabella's opening editorials repeatedly sound the theme of fashion's failure to incorporate diversity: "So when will we rethink how women are presented in advertisements, on television or in magazines? When will we show them in all their glorious diversity?" (Nov. 1994:32). Yet in spite of all this talk, no magazine can visually represent a diversity of ages and sizes among its regular professional models in fashion editorial layouts. An *Allure* article entitled "Fashion's Freshman Class" (Sept. 1994:164–71) emphasizes obsessively their "great diversity," the way they break the rules about modeling requirements that "were simply too limiting." But photographed under the heading "The latest models vary in size, age, and attitude. Just like real women," the women all look remarkably alike in size and shape.

The *Allure* article illustrates a growing contradiction in fashion magazines between the *said* and the *seen*. Fashion magazines now have a personality split between a feminist discourse on the body and images that depend on traditional unconscious structures of white Western imaginary identification (Fuss). Here is yet another opposition operating in mass culture, and black women are used in the *Mirabella* fashion essay to heal that opposition.

The use of white women as large-size professional models in fashion layouts would presumably interfere with the processes of identification between spectator and fantasy mirror provided by the fashion image. The very unreality of the standard models in the photographs makes them the reflection of imaginary identity. Models more realistically resembling the reader could not supply pleasurable, fantastic ideals. By contrast, the more "real" images of black women in "Georgia on My Mind" can reconcile the contradiction for subjects who desire to identify with themselves "as they really are" (*Mirabella* 7, 94; Markus 14), while their unconscious imaginary identity continues to be structured by the conventional feminine image. This is because the images of black women have, through the commodified ethnic diversity incorporated into mass culture, come to be accepted as "like us," yet not "us." The idealized photographic image of "real" black women can therefore function as a mirror for a white woman's fantasy self while still assuring the white feminine spectator that she is not really seeing herself reflected. She can identify and at the same time not identify.

Black feminine image conventions embody corporeal difference, variety, heterogeneity. In *Mirabella*, their image can therefore respond to a postmodern white feminine desire to embody difference without disturbing the narrow, homogeneous dictates of feminine beauty. In this way, a postmodern concern for multiplicity, diversity, and plurality in mass-culture magazines relies on maintaining the oppositional white/black structure of femininity and at the same time masks the opposition. By fixing heterogeneity in a black feminine body both othered and integrated, the *Mirabella* essay enables a white feminine identity of postmodern fluidity.

"Georgia on My Mind" illustrates one way in which postmodern culture can take advantage of black women's position as the negative term of a historically inherited aesthetic dialectic. That negative term may have been resignified as "positive" in value, but in logical structure it continues to be the driving force in a dialectics of feminine aesthetics. It continues, albeit in vastly changed ways, to reproduce the imperative for a black feminine culture of dissemblance and to heighten black women's political ambiguity.

WORKS CITED

Baudelaire, Charles. "Le Peintre de la vie moderne." In *Oeuvres complètes.* Y. G. Le Dantec and Claude Pichois, eds. Paris: Pliade, 1961, 1152–1197.

Berlant, Lauren and Elizabeth Freeman. "Queer Nationality." *boundary2* 19(1)(1992): 149–80.

Brown, Elsa Barkley. " 'What Has Happened Here': The Politics of Difference in Women's History and Feminist Politics." *Feminist Studies* 2 (1992): 295–312.

Butler, Judith. *Bodies That Matter: On the Discursive Limits of "Sex."* New York: Routledge, 1993.

Case, Sue-Ellen. "Toward a Butch-Femme Aesthetic." In Henry Abelove, Michele Aina Barale, and David M. Halperin, eds., *The Lesbian and Gay Studies Reader.* New York: Routledge, 1993.

Collins, Patricia Hill. *Black Feminist Thought: Knowledge, Consciousness and the Politics of Empowerment.* Boston: Unwin Hyman, 1990.

Craik, Jennifer. *The Face of Fashion: Cultural Studies in Fashion.* New York: Routledge, 1994.

Crenshaw, Kimberle. "Whose Story Is It, Anyway? Feminist and Antiracist Appropriations of Anita Hill." In Wahneema Lubiano and Toni Morrison, eds., *RACE-ing JUSTICE, En-GENDERing POWER: Essays on Anita Hill, Clarence Thomas, and the Construction of Social Reality.* New York: Pantheon, 1992: 402–10.

Ewing, Elizabeth. *Dress and Undress: A History of Women's Underwear.* London: Batsford, 1978.

Flügel, J. C. *The Psychology of Clothes.* London: Hogarth Press and The Institute of Psycho-Analysis, 1930.

Fuss, Diana. "Fashion and the Homospectatorial Look." In Shari Benstock and Suzanne Ferris, eds., *On Fashion.* New Brunswick, N.J.: Rutgers University Press, 1994, 211–32.

Garber, Marjorie. *Vested Interests: Cross-dressing and Cultural Anxiety.* New York: Routledge, 1992.

Giddings, Paula. *When and Where I Enter: The Impact of Black Women on Race and Sex in America.* New York: William Morrow, 1984.

——. "The Last Taboo." In Wahneema Lubiano and Toni Morrison, eds., *RACE-ing*

JUSTICE, En-GENDERing POWER: Essays on Anita Hill, Clarence Thomas, and the Construction of Social Reality. New York: Pantheon, 1992, 402–40.

Gilman, Sander. *On Blackness Without Blacks: Essays on the Image of the Black in Germany.* Boston: G. K. Hall, 1982.

Hammonds, Evelynn. "Black (W)holes and the Geometry of Black Female Sexuality." *Differences* VI(2–3)(Summer–Fall 1994): 126–45.

Hine, Darlene Clark. "Rape and the Inner Lives of Black Women in the Middle West: Preliminary Thoughts on the Culture of Dissemblance." *Signs 4* (1989): 912–20.

Hollander, Anne. *Seeing Through Clothes.* New York: Avon, 1975.

hooks, bell. *Black Looks: Race and Representation.* Boston: South End Press, 1992.

Kofman, Sarah. *The Enigma of Woman: Woman in Freud's Writings.* Trans. Catherine Porter. Ithaca: Cornell University Press, 1985.

Kuchta, David. "The Three-Piece Suit and the Politics of Masculinity." Unpublished paper.

Lacan, Jacques. "The Meaning of the Phallus." In Juliet Mitchell and Jacqueline Rose, eds., *Feminine Sexuality: Jacques Lacan and the Scole freudienne.* New York: Norton, 1982, 74–85.

Lemoine-Luccioni, Eugénie. *La Robe: Essai psychanaltique sur le vêtement.* Paris: Editions du Seuil, 1980.

Lubiano, Wahneema. "Black Ladies, Welfare Queens, and State Minstrels: Ideological War by Narrative Means." In Wahneema Lubiano and Toni Morrison, eds., *RACE-ing JUSTICE, En-GENDERing POWER: Essays on Anita Hill, Clarence Thomas, and the Construction of Social Reality.* New York: Pantheon, 1992, 290–322.

Marable, Manning. *How Capitalism Underdeveloped Black America: Problems in Race, Political Economy and Society.* Boston: South End Press, 1983.

——. *Race, Reform, and Rebellion: The Second Reconstruction in Black America, 1945–1990.* Jackson: Mississippi University Press, 1991.

Painter, Nell Irvin. "Hill, Thomas, and the Use of Racial Stereotype." In Wahneema Lubiano and Toni Morrison, eds., *RACE-ing JUSTICE, En-GENDERing POWER: Essays on Anita Hill, Clarence Thomas, and the Construction of Social Reality.* New York: Pantheon, 1992, 200–14.

Rabine, Leslie W. "A Woman's Two Bodies: Fashion Magazines, Consumerism, and Feminism." In Shari Benstock and Suzanne Ferris, eds., *On Fashion.* New Brunswick, N.J.: Rutgers University Press, 1994, 59–75.

Riviere, Joan. "Womanliness as Masquerade." In Victor Burgin, James Donald, and Cora Kaplan, eds., *Formations of Fantasy.* London: Methuen, 1986, 35–44.

Silverman, Kaja. "Fragments of a Fashionable Discourse." In Shari Benstock and Suzanne Ferris, eds., *On Fashion.* New Brunswick, N.J.: Rutgers University Press, 1994, 183–96.

Steele, Valerie. "Clothing and Sexuality." In C. Kidwell and V. Steele, eds., *Men and Women: Dressing the Part.* Washington, D.C.: Smithsonian Institution Press, 1989: 42–63.

Veblen, Thorstein. *The Theory of the Leisure Class.* 1899; reprint, London: Allen and Unwin, 1957.

White, Deborah Gray. *Ain't I A Woman? Female Slaves in the Plantation South.* New York: Norton, 1985.

Wilson, Elizabeth. "Fashion and the Postmodern Body." In Juliet Ash and Elizabeth Wilson, eds., *Chic Thrills: A Fashion Reader.* Berkeley: University of California Press, 1993, 3–16.

Young, Iris Marion. "Women Recovering Our Clothes." In Shari Benstock and Suzanne Ferris, eds., *On Fashion.* New Brunswick, N.J.: Rutgers University Press, 1994, 197–210.

MASS-CIRCULATION MAGAZINES AND NEWSPAPERS CONSULTED

Allure
Big Beautiful Woman
Dimensions
Ebony
Essence
Glamour
Los Angeles Times
Mirabella
Vogue

SEVEN

Accenting Hybridity:
Postcolonial Cultural Studies, a Boasian
Anthropologist, and I

James Boon

In 1988, I began offering a diversely disciplinary seminar: "Anthropology 413: Cultures and Critical Translation." The course involved "discourse" in several senses, including this one:

> According to Benveniste, the locutor of a historical enunciation is excluded from the story he tells: all subjectivity and . . . autobiographical references are banished . . . thus constitut[ing] the mode of enunciating the truth. The term "discourse," on the other hand, designates any enunciation that integrates in its structure . . . locutor . . . listener . . . desire . . . to influence.

Thus Julia Kristeva's *Langage: l'inconnu*, translated into the American academic marketplace in 1989, after her more recognizably feminist and Lacanian works took hold.[1]

Paradoxically, Kristeva's very definition sounds as if it "enunciates" the truth; she seems to gloss "discourse" by presuming to cancel its marks. But isn't this as it should be? What theorist adequate to rhetoric's turns and tropes would claim to absolve her discourse of antidiscourse, of desired oscillation with an imagined escape into the "anonymous structure of *la langue*"? Certainly not Kristeva, whose polyphony of approaches spans Bakhtin and such high-modernist linguists as Jakobson.[2]

Attuned to such paradoxes of discourse, Anthro 413 also pondered Greek, Hebraic, and Islamic "theories" of translation practices, along with Sanskritic and Mayan ones (all *in* translation, I'm afraid). We bridged diverse aesthetics of translation: Symbolist synaesthetics, Tantric ritualistics, and other glyphs. We juxtaposed rival politics of translation: Protestantism's Scripture unleashed into vernaculars everywhere, versus Islam's Koran deemed conveyable only as Arabic—opposite ideologies of translation, both historically rather global. We ranged from Evans-Pritchard translating "primitive" theologies magisterially, to Dennis Tedlock translating *Popol Vuh* recensions performatively into dialogic scrips redolent of spokenness (no offense intended to *écriture*). The seminar, then, got panoramic and serious.[3]

The seminar also stayed fractured and playful. We poached from Heidegger, for sure; but also from Wilhelm von Humboldt; from Walter Benjamin, and Derrida on Benjamin; plus Steiner on Benjamin, and Steiner against Derrida, and Derrida against Richard Wolin; and Hélène Cixous's curious little letter to the *New York Review of Books*, where she upheld absolutist academic French to police mistranslations of Derrida![4]

Up for grabs were venerable impasses in rhetoric-against-logic: Does language *re*fer or *de*fer? How might one translate "translate"? Is anything lingual—tonguish—always slipping? We noted the un-newness of language games by reading nonsense-sense in Lewis Carroll and Wittgenstein. We also read Gertrude Stein, via Neil Schmitz's tribute to the genius and gaiety of Gert, plus the twinning and twang of Twain, in Schmitz's wonderful *Of Huck and Alice* (read it like speech, *F'uckin' Alice*; killing the joke, explain *Alice*'s doubling: *Through the Looking Glass*, and *B. Toklas*). Neil Schmitz's inclusiveness extends to Krazy Kat.[5]

Anthro 413 retailed lingos, argots, and "vernacularity" (my coinage). One of the seminar's slogans became "language with an 's' at both ends"— or *SlanguageS*, a kind of pseudo-*topos*. Students savored the slangy in David Dabbydeen's creole-critical essay against Miltonic English, reprinted in *The State of the Language*, a godsend volume that ties arcana of semiotics, speech acts, and such to contemporary matters that matter: race, AIDS, gender, power, postmodernity, the press, money, anticolonialism, marginality, alternative musics. (This book helped the MTV set get on board, or jump ship.) Stretching toward "slangs" via Dabbydeen et al., we also stretched toward *langues*, via Saussure's semiology (and his *mots sous mots*), and via Edward Sapir (see below).[6]

The seminar's unwieldy array was balanced with helpful overviews by critics constructively for deconstruction (Culler) and against it (Abrams); by Holquist on Bakhtin, caught between belief and unbelief (Holquist, that is); by David Lodge's affably edited reader, *Modern Criticism and Theory*.[7] I never knew whether Anthro 413 would sink or soar, or where it would end. But I always knew where it would "begin," in Kenneth Burke's and perhaps

Edward Said's sense: with a 1987 essay by Aijaz Ahmad published just as the seminar here paraded began, and continued beginning.[8]

Ahmad

It has long been my possibly defensive habit to eschew any critical cutting edge—too transparent, I reason: too new-cliché.[9] But I gladly assigned Ahmad's "Jameson's Rhetoric of Otherness and the 'National Allegory' " hot off the press. Why?

Ahmad's essay took exception to Fredric Jameson's "Third-World Literature in the Era of Multinational Capital," with its universalizing decree, "All third-world texts are necessarily national allegories" (i.e., resistances reactive to colonialism). Ahmad tackled Jameson on his grandest ground—globe-spanning Marxism, extra-Western literary production, Three-World theory, the politics of canonicity—positioning himself thusly: "Now, I was born in India and I am a Pakistani citizen; I write poetry in Urdu, a language not commonly understood among U.S. intellectuals. So, I said to myself: '*All*? . . . *necessarily?*' It felt odd" (4). Ahmad deferred playing his card of "regional" credentials until his closing sections depicting Urdu literary history as an autonomous formation—one not determined by imperialist hegemony.

Between Ahmad's introit—"I-India-Pakistani-Urdu-poet" —and his quasi-nativistic case study (17–22), he made *general* arguments (*énoncés?*). I here reduce them to some bare-bones theory (garnished with Boasian asides to be augmented later).[10]

1. Ahmad denies "third-world literature" is an internally coherent object of theoretical knowledge (Boasians might call Ahmad's critical point "disaggregation").

2. Ahmad calls the worldwide translation industry "fulsome circuits for the circulation of translated texts" that spin speedily among select European languages but grind slowly "when it comes to translations from Asian or African languages" (5). He is skeptical of Jameson's belated opening toward Lu Xun and Ousmane. (Boasians might add that such token extensions of circuits to Asian and African text-productions still exclude much . . . Kwakiutl, to name one of thousands).

3. In Ahmad's view Jameson himself commits certain mystifications: a claim to be "essentially descriptive"; a reified dichotomy between capitalist and pre- or noncapitalist; a totalized opposition of post-

modernism/nationalism. Ahmad questions any uniformist logic of monolithic development; he emphasizes multiple ways even bourgeois political subjectivity (a cultural formation) "emerges"—in India/Pakistan, in Brazil, in South Africa. (Nothing could please "Boasians" more.) Ahmad even notes, also *contra* Jameson but not approvingly, "Bourgeois nationalisms of the so-called third world" have no "difficulty with postmodernism; they *want* it" (8).

4. Ahmad urges critical theorists to "forego the idea of a metanarrative"; and he faults Jameson for homogenizing differences despite professing preference for "an opulent sense of heterogeneity." Instead of Jameson's Three-Worlds Theory, Ahmad plumbs for one-world—charged with "the enormous cultural heterogeneity of social formations," yet "unified" in good Marxist fashion by "the ferocious struggle of capital and labor . . . now fundamentally global" (10).

Let me linger over item 4, anthropologically. Ahmad's proposal to "replace the idea of the nation with that larger, less restricting idea of collectivity" sticks close to current critical orthodoxy—we might call it Nation-Narration. True, Ahmad accentuates an "opulence" of nationalizing modes:

> The advantage of coming from Pakistan . . . is that the country is saturated with capitalist commodities, bristles with U.S. weaponry, borders on China, the Soviet Union [1987] and Afghanistan, suffers from a proliferation of competing nationalisms, and is currently witnessing the first stage in the consolidation of the communist movement. *(10)*

But even pluralized, this "problematic" still trails along a colonizer/colonized dichotomy, as do those first world/third world and second world/third world doubled dichotomies derived from it.

To overcome Jameson's suspiciously singular (Europocentric) models of hegemony, Ahmad may need to multiply not just nationalism but his critical *topoi*. One alternative I propose is region/religion (note my sly parallel in critical packaging—not *NATION-NArraTION*, but *REGION-REliGION*). Ahmad does remember to mention religions, and poignantly, but only in his case study: "The 'nation' [Pakistan] . . . came together with the partition . . . the most miserable migration in human history, the biggest bloodbath in the memory of the subcontinent, the gigantic fratricide conducted by Hindu, Muslim and Sikh communalists" (21–22). So relegated, religious divisions assume a local look rather than a general-theoretical look. Similarly, much culture theory today—both postmodernist and Marxist—concentrates unduly on "nation" (or the state mystified—"imagined"?—as such). It is assumed that the nation, narrated, is the privileged venue for generating obfuscations of Realpolitik (or *réelle*-power-knowledge). Religion gets safely tucked away—restricted theoretically to "meaning" rather than power.[11]

Ahmad, for example, asserts: "The kind of circuits that bind the cultural complexes of the advanced capitalist countries simply do not exist among countries of backward capitalism" (11). But this claim neglects Islam—circuited opulently indeed throughout Asia, Africa, and elsewhere. It also underestimates Catholic exchange-formations in Latin America, the Philippines, etc.—sometimes left wing, hardly pawns of the Vatican or "the West." Transnational circuitries among "countries of backward capitalism" are less monolithic than Ahmad implies, even before critics factor in borderlands of consumerist practice.[12]

In brief, while Ahmad—differently Marxian, we shall see, than Jameson—admirably complicates nation-narration theory, he remains a bit "blinkered" to region-religion, and possibly to consumption (versus production) as well. Moreover, except for his vignette of Urdu literary history, he makes little of languages overall. (My remarks here might be called "Boasian," possibly Weberian, or even De Certeauan.)[13]

> 5. Regrettably, Ahmad's essay placed its case study next-to-last rather than next-to-first; general theorists might never have gotten to it. Here is its crucial gist: Urdu religious prose dates from eighth-century translations composed from Arabic or Farsi; what began as a hybrid styled for North Indian upper-status groups remained hybrid through the nineteenth century, when courtly patronage and colonialist translation industries overlapped, as print formations opened toward compilations of colloquial language and journalistic reportage. Urdu "emerged" along divided subjectivities of translators, brokers, and go-betweens; ultimately *littérateurs* paid some attention to women's rights, but not reactively to a European presence. Emphatically: "The typical Urdu writer has had a peculiar vision, in which he/she has never been able to construct fixed boundaries between the criminalities of the colonialist and the brutalities of all those indigenous people who have had power in our own society. . . . There has never been a sustained powerful myth of a primal innocence, when it comes to the colonial encounter" (21). Now, Ahmad unavoidably forefronts lettristic elites; and he persists in modifying translation with "mere," even though (as Anthro 413 insisted) translation is always constitutive. Nevertheless, Ahmad's synopsis of "the rise of Urdu literary language" (an emergence not

so different from, say, *Hochdeutsch*) avoids reactionary counter-claims of supremacy and rejects universalized reductions. (This, again, is not an unBoasian achievement.) Urdu formations, in short, were never a metanarrative reactive to the Raj.

6. In closing, Ahmad exposes Jameson's unwitting complicity in an old critical strategy—hegemonization: "What is not possible is to oper-ate with the few texts [e.g., Lu Xun, Ousmane] that become avail-able in the metropolitan languages and then to posit . . . trans-parency in the process of determinancy . . . reduced to a single ideo-logical formation [with] all narratives . . . read as local expressions of a metatext" (23). Ahmad insists that a unitary determination is "in its *origins* a pre-marxist idea"; this anachronism he lays at Jame-son's feet. Still, some room remains for reconciliation. Like Jame-son, Ahmad rejects a "postmodernist intellectual milieu" (one he deems "doubtless of recent origin"), where "texts are to be read as the utterly free, altogether hedonistic plays of the signifier" (22). Here Ahmad's polemical "utterly" seems to join Jameson in refusing postmodernist language of "positional" free play.

Jameson's two-page response published with Ahmad's essay (26–27) has struck *all* stripes of students in Anthro 413 over the years—including Marx-ists, Weberians, sociobiologists, and cultural hermeneuts, whether fledgling or seasoned—as lame, even limp. And it would indeed be hard to deny that Jameson hedged—considerably—in pronouncing: "I believe that a *certain* nationalism does not *always* play an *exclusively* negative and harmful role in *some* socialist revolutions" (27; emphases added, for effect).

Nor had Jameson overcome a *certain* condescending air long associated with *some* colonialist discourse.[14] A few examples may prove revealing:

1. Jameson begins: "As for the term 'first world,' I hope it is not neces-sary to say that. . . ." What follows hardly matters; it is the lordly rhetoric that subjugates.

2. Jameson alludes to "our Roman eclecticism" and declares it "cur-rently expanding, I'm happy to say, to include a keen interest in contemporary Indian theory." One assumes he must mean, "since Chakrabarty."[15]

3. Jameson justifies his intervention as progressive for recognizing the challenge that "third-world literatures" pose to "even the most advanced contemporary theory." His remarks, which profess to reopen the issue of "Three-Worlds," actually reinstate such categorizing.

More progressively, Jameson does temper Ahmad's polemic against "utter postmodernism" with measured language about "situationals" or "relationals." Nodding to Barrington Moore, Jameson signals "radically *situational* difference in cultural production and meanings" and recommends "a *relational* way of thinking global culture" and "a comparative study of cultural situations" (26). Nothing wrong there; but then comes the tricky move. Jameson salvages a slip of turf shared with Ahmad, whose "Third-World" positionality (Jameson's term) he certainly wants to befriend . . . utterly. How? By defaming proponents of "sheer random difference," whose positivistic brand, Jameson reminds us, is "empiricist history of 'one damned thing after another.'" He fails, however, to second Ahmad's attack on "postmodern hedonistic plays of signification [more accurately, *signifiance*]—that other brand of "sheer random difference." *Pourquoi?* Was a new alliance shaping up in "the most advanced contemporary theory," circa 1987?

For whatever reason, at this particular historical juncture Jameson avoided demonizing postmodernism, choosing instead to scapegoat an older formation: Boasian anthropology. Let me quote directly his critical bromide with a slur:

> If Identity and Difference are fixed and eternal opposites, we have either a ceaseless alternation, or a set of intolerable choices: presumably there would be no great advantage gained by junking the category of "third world" if the result is that North America then becomes "the same" as the subcontinent, say. But nothing is to be done with sheer random difference either, which either leaves us back in Boasian anthropology or in the empiricist history of "one damned thing after another." The claim of the dialectic as a distinct mode of thought is to set categories like those of Identity and Difference in motion.   *(26)*

That peculiar dodge by Jameson has catalyzed this parry by me.[16] But who am I?—neither identifiably postmodernist nor Boasian; rather an avid dabbler in both persuasions, and in Jameson and Marx . . . and Ahmad.

It is not uncommon in ideological movements (including Marxist ones) to patch over any breach in solidarity (e.g., Ahmad *contra* Jameson) by an act of "othering"—round up the usual suspects: in this case Boasian anthropology. But Boasian anthropology—assuming it can be aggregated—is an odd thing to drag out in counterdistinction to Ahmad, if only because Ahmad sounds so much like its practitioners, at least when he gets specific, relational, radically situated (Jameson might say).[17]

Before tendering my paper's pivotal Ahmadian-Boasian comparison, I should confess that the appeal of Ahmad's essay (for me) stems less from its impressive expertise in global critique than from features of his exposition my account has thus far suppressed: its narrative shape, its ironies and professed awkwardness, its spiriting forth—earnestly? theatrically? (Who knows?)[18]—a moment of heartfelt contestation. Ahmad's variegated and vulnerable voice is rare these days among disciplines that regularly critique ideas of "culture." His complexity of tone recalls (to my ear) such upheavals as Jameson's earlier *Marxism and Form* (a personal favorite) more than that Jamesonianism subsequently *established*—with its cozy alienation from the "global American culture of postmodernism" and from Boasian anthropology too.

Against Jameson's latter-day "historical *énoncés*," Ahmad's essay "assemblages" discourse that wavers between a personal "book-voyage and reading navigation" and a "letter from an unknown Indian."[19] "Dear Freddie," he almost seems to write, "how could you betray your devoted reader and ardent fellow-traveler, relegating the likes of me to a Third-World metatexter?" True, much of Ahmad's essay becomes more routinely polemical when it charges Jameson with underestimating the "Third World" (by criteria of gender and race) encrypted in his "own" first world. (Oddly, Ahmad did not connect Jameson's long avoidance of *women* or *black* literatures [Ahmad's italics] to his relative intolerance of postmodernity's spaces—an argument worth pursuing.)[20] But after the polemic, Ahmad's closing pages resume a more affecting, personalized, contingent tone that dramatizes a fair-play turnabout of Jameson's Three-World categorizing. Ending, Ahmad hazards an experiment in culturally locating Jameson's "ostensibly first-world" text. I telegraph Ahmad's remarks:

> Jameson . . . a U.S. intellectual . . . able to juxtapose Ousmane and Deleuze so comfortably . . . debunks postmodernism; . . . theory marxist, politics socialist, thus second world; but deep into the third world, valorizing it . . . filiating himself with it. . . . Where do I, who do not believe in the Three Worlds Theory, in which world should I place his text: the first world of his origin [natality], the second world of his ideology and politics [1987, remember], or the third world of his filiation and sympathy? And if "all third-world texts are necessarily" this or that, how is it that his own text escapes an exclusive location in the first world?   *(24)*

Ahmad's final move is juster still, poetically speaking. After spotlighting Jameson's conveniently suppressed hybridities, he officiously counterasserts his "own" Marxist authority over Jameson's, proclaiming Jameson *"primarily* in the global culture of socialism," judging by "all his theoretical undertakings for many years" (24). Ahmad thus does unto Jameson something resembling what hath been done unto him, Ahmad (or the likes of him) by Jameson. He knocks or nudges Jameson off his critical high horse, hoists Jameson by the petard of his still-exclusivistic theory. Jameson's texts, despite their hybridities, get transmogrified into a metanarrative, an allegory of (in this case) the one world.

Ahmad may have anticipated all this in his essay's artful beginning, a narrative of betrayal couched in a possibly *faux-naif* cliché:

> I have been reading Jameson's work now for roughly fifteen years . . . and because I am a marxist, I had always thought of us, Jameson and myself, as birds of the same feather even though we never quite flocked together. But, then, when I was on . . . the sentence starting with "all third-world texts are necessarily . . ." etc., I realized that what was being theorised was . . . myself. . . . The farther I read the more I realized, with no little chagrin, that the man whom I had for so long, so affec-tionately, even though from a physical distance, taken as a comrade was, in his own opinion, my civilizational Other. It was not a good feeling.   (3–4)

Am I imagining things, or does Ahmad's hackneyed "birds of a feather" say-ing play to stereotypes of Anglo-Indian, or Anglo-Pakistani? It can conjure up a "colonial's English"—prone to parade the textbook trope, to rehearse copied colloquialisms, to display figurativeness "rather too" conspicuously. Such pre-sumed "second-English" sounds quaint to presumed "first-English" ears (so-called Anglo-English, whether Queen's English or Oxbridge English)—which jaded discourse, as I have already indicated, Fredric Jameson, although Amer-ican, can skillfully ape, and high-handedly. Does Ahmad's tired metaphor, so overworked by metropolitan critical standards, evoke the plangeant politics of "Third World" intellectuals who are expected to "translate" (pass?) into impe-rialist language-circuits? Is Ahmad's lament through a quaint cliché—"Marx-ists of a feather, unflocked"—meant as a discursive equivalent to familiar the-atrics of double consciousness, the subordinate obliged to satisfy expectations of the master?[21] Ahmad's feather image may represent a vocal equivalent of that stock gesture of horizontal head-wagging, fixated on by Anglo-English listeners when gazing upon Anglo-Indian speakers—speakers who are *still* hoping to be *heard*—once by colonizers, now by critics.

Of course, I may be overreading here. But that seems inevitable, given that I too, no less than Jameson, desire to filiate with Ahmad. Perhaps, then, readers will not begrudge me a momentary lapse out of theoretical *énoncé* into a personalized discourse of my own:

I, too, have been reading Jameson's works now for roughly fifteen years
. . . and because I am a dialectic *cum* semiotic comparatist, I had always
thought of us, Jameson and myself, as feathers of the same bird (pea-
cock-critique), even though our colors and stripes contrasted. But,
then, when I was on the phrase "leave us back in Boasian anthropology," I realized that the critic whose sense of dialectical form I once
embraced was in his own opinion, my disciplinary Other.

Specifically, my *Other Tribes, Other Scribes* (1982:152) appropriated from
Marxism and Form (1971:53) a forceful passage:

Dialectical thinking is thought about thought, concrete thought about
an object, aware of its own intellectual operations in the very act of
thinking, self-consciousness inscribed in the very sentence itself;
involving a conjunction of opposites, conceptually disparate phenomena; like the Surrealist image, the strength of the dialectical sentence
increases proportionately as the realities linked are distant and distinct
from each other.

I tried drawing Jameson's dialectics into active affinity with Durkheim plus
Weber, Mauss with Marx, Benjamin-on-Proust, late and poststructuralism,
Jacobean ethnology, Balinese narrative, early Romantic philology, hermeneutics with a difference (bumping among multiple cultures over struggling histories), and, yes, Boasian anthropology. Needless to add, upon encountering
Jameson's response to Ahmad, I found a portion of my interdisciplinary self
"othered." It was not, *frères et soeurs lecteurs-lectrices*, a good feeling.[22]

Dirlik

1987 became a charismatic critical moment in my parochial world. Yet I
abstained from following subsequent critical news of claimed syntheses
between antithetical Marxists (Jameson/Ahmad, etc.). I doubtless desired to
keep Ahmad sounding fresh, upstart, un*Aufhebung*ed: a David-voice challenging a Goliath of "serious critical theory." My tactical innocence of aftermath has lately been despoiled by signs of Ahmad's absorption into the
global critical canon, U.S.-style.[23] A 1994 article by Arif Dirlik—Turkish-
born, Duke historian, China specialist—helps me address Ahmad's fate
obliquely.

Dirlik's "The Postcolonial Aura: Third World Criticism in the Age of
Global Capitalism" savors discrepancies of self-positioning by far-flung

intellectuals "arrived" in first world academe. "Only partially facetious," Dirlik's nice touches include a winky debunking of some strategical reverse-snobbery by Gayatri Spivak: when challenged from India, she defended her credentials of marginality by noting her employment by a U.S. university outside the elite Northeast/West Coast circuit (her infiltration of Columbia came later). Although I differ from Dirlik theoretically, and even facetiously (though I like the Gayatri Spivak bit), his article helps me hurry on to hybridities—not only in Homi Bhabha's sense that Dirlik disavows, but in Edward Sapir's sense—my Boasian.[24]

Dirlik's list of "postcolonial critics" is imposing: "Edward Said, Aijaz Ahmad, Homi Bhabha, Gyan Prakash, Gayatri Spivak, and Lata Mani" (338). Dirlik does not homogenize these intellectuals, "widely different politically"; indeed, he credits Ahmad with grounding his critique of Jameson on the realities of capital, whose foundational status Prakash is chided for denying (338). Dirlik adds to such disaggregation a dash of negative polarization, aiming rather acrimoniously his unideterminant accent on capitalism against both Prakash and Bhabha: "Bhabha is exemplary of the Third World intellectual who has been completely reworked by the language of First World cultural criticism" (334).

For Dirlik, most scholars who assert "postcoloniality" are guilty of mystifying their own class position. Theirs is not a simple nostalgia for "comprador-intelligentsia" (per Tony Appiah), but a false consciousness, an ideology beduped—blind to its enabling infrastructure: globalcapitalism. Marxist Dirlik retains the culprit capitalism as foundational to history (331); Prakash, he charges, is postfoundational.[25] (So, by the way, am I; or rather antifoundational, possibly for reasons different from those of Gayan Prakash, a prized colleague in the same East Coast institution that I marginally inhabit.)

Again, Dirlik both disaggregates (Boasian move) and polarizes (Marxian move) his retinue of postcolonial critics. Nevertheless, a list he has indeed drawn up, with Ahmad categorically included on it, among differentiated voices. (Dirlik, I note, mentions Lyotard's notion of "postmodern" as "incredulity toward metanarratives"; but he never wonders where this leaves Ahmad, who couples such incredulity with glancing swipes at postmodernist critical "free play," while admitting that the "Third World"—*pace* Jameson—*wants* postmodernism. More muddles, or rather disaggregation.

One further irony. All sources that Dirlik cites *in this particular formation* (this article) are unilingual: English sources on China; English sources skeptical of the prefix "post" (a skepticism I happen to share, whether in English or not):

> *Postcolonial* is the most recent entrant to achieve prominent visibility
> in the ranks of those "post" marked words (seminal among them,
> *postmodernism*) that serve as signposts in(to) contemporary cultural
> criticism . . . *postcolonial* claims as its special provenance the terrain
> that in an earlier day used to go by the name of Third World. It is
> intended, therefore, to achieve an authentic globalization of cultural
> discourses . . . etc.   *(329)*

And it is English sources (e.g., Anne McLintock) that Dirlik here aims against
postcoloniality, which "in spite of its insistence on historicity and difference
. . . mimics in its deployment the 'ahistorical and universalizing tendencies' in
colonialist thinking" (344). (Another not altogether unBoasian critique!).

I leave aside Dirlik's linguistic credentials; for all I know, he is versed in
Chinese as a China scholar and Turkish as a natal Turk, among other languages. But the particular article in question, as he acknowledges, enters the
very formation that it polemically quizzes—viz., that capitalism-underpinned
staging of intelligentsia who, arguing auspices of Third Worldness, sidestep
their possible cooptation by global circuitry of standardized theoretical *énoncés* translated into Academic English (Marxism included). Yes, here Dirlik
indeed capitulates: I hear few contingencies, no accents, little hint of distinctive Englishes (including Turkish English, a proud tradition), comparable to
Ahmad's suspected seasonings of Anglo-Pakistani flavor and voice. To expand
his general category of "postcolonial critics," Dirlik deletes Ahmad's narrative
devices, erases his positional auspices for felt betrayal by Jameson, nullifies any
crosscultural specifics conveyed in his rhetorical turns and tropes.[26]

What becomes of real historical hybridities (including anyone's "Academic English") in Dirlik's article? They get thrown out with Homi Bhabha, as
so much bathwater. Dirlik, heavily citing Prakash, deems Bhabha "responsible for the prominence in discussions of postcoloniality of the vocabulary of
hybridity and so on" (333). "And so on"? And so forth:

> The postcolonial exists as an aftermath, as an after—after being
> worked over by colonialism. Criticism formed in this process of the
> enunciation of discourses of domination occupies a space that is nei-
> ther inside nor outside the history of western domination but in a tan-
> gential relation to it. This is what Homi Bhabha calls an in-between,
> hybrid position of practice and negotiation, or what Gayatri Chakra-
> vorty Spivak terms catachresis; "reversing, displacing, and seizing the
> apparatus of value-coding."   *(333)*

Let me—a practicing ethnographer—leave catachresis to upscale critics and
stick with the folksier synonym.

"Hybridity" receives priority in both Bhabha's and Prakash's sense of postcolonial subject positions. Dirlik ventilates their dream of escaping binary fixity, only to blow it away:

> In drawing attention to the language of postcolonial discourse, I seek . . . to deconstruct postcolonial intellectuals' professions of hybridity and in-betweenness. The hybridity to which postcolonial criticism refers is uniformly between the post*colonial* and the First World, never, to my knowledge, between one post*colonial* intellectual and another.   *(342)*

While there may be some truth to this observation, Dirlik's "never" sounds pretty absolute; it possibly ducks thorny dilemmas associated with the category "intellectual," and it may actually camouflage a refusal to dissolve (as Ahmad recommends) Three World distinctions.

Dirlik brings in Bhabha's theorized hybridity in order to deconstruct it. I bring in Bhabha in order to extend hybridities beyond some exclusivistic claims of "postcoloniality" in the aftermath of subaltern studies. Oddly, Dirlik and I may overlap here, share a slip of turf. Regardless, Dirlik deems his own plea to deconstruct Bhabhian hybridity *really* a counterdeconstruction of postcolonialists' deconstruction of Marxism:

> The approach of postcolonial critics is not to translate Marxism into a national (which is rejected) or local (which is affirmed) vernacular but to rephrase it in the language of post-structuralism, in which Marxism is deconstructed, decentered, and so on. . . . A critique that starts off with a repudiation of the universalistic pretensions of Marxist language ends up not with its dispersion into local vernaculars but with a return to another First World language with universalistic epistemological pretensions.   *(342)*

What side is one to take at this moment of de-deconstruction? Search me. I only want to observe, ethnographically, that, thus embroiled in critical critique, Dirlik mentions the "vernacular."[27] And mention of vernaculars at last gets this paper to where it has been going—to the in-betweenness, the plus-que-postcolonialist hybridities (relational ones, by the way) championed by "my Boasian." It is time to salvage Edward Sapir from Jameson's theoretical ash can.

Sapir

Edward Sapir himself (1884–1939) was no stranger to hybridity. Pomerania-born Jew, displaced in 1889 (age five) to North America, he mastered Eng-

lish as a second language over his fundamental (not foundational) German
and/or Yiddish; a poet-linguist, literary anthropologist, scientist-artist; a
Boasian with distinctive features, hyphenated (as a hypothesis) with
Whorf—unfortunately, I feel, although not to Whorf's discredit.[28] Sapir was
a gifted hearer of Native American *Sprache*, an aficionado of Croce, a reciter
of Heine, and a reader of Hebrew (Sapir 1920; Darnell 1990:403). None too
effective a careerist, he was stuck for years in Ottawa, passed through
Chicago, and died at Yale, when restrictions against his kind still obtained at
the Graduate Club where faculty "old boys" networked. Sapir then, hardly a
winner, may have felt less cozy in the "world" he inhabited—or worlds he
bridged—than prominent critics of our day, now that hyphenated identities
are (happily) the rage.

Before continuing with Sapir, let me stipulate that I second Bhabha in
not equating hyphenated identity and hybridity; as Bhabha remarks:

> Hybridity is the revaluation of the assumption of colonial identity
> through the repetition of discriminatory identity effects. It displays the
> necessary deformation and displacement of all sites of discrimination
> and domination. It unsettles the mimetic or narcissistic demands of
> colonial power but reimplicates its identifications in strategies of sub-
> version that turn the gaze of the discriminated back upon the eye of
> power.   *(1995:3)*

Continuing in this vein, Bhabha "theorizes" hybridity with a mixed metaphor: "a negative transparency." This much seems clear. Nevertheless, unlike
Bhabha (perhaps), I claim no ability consistently to distinguish hybridity
from hyphenation (old or new). Hybridity (*gibrid*, in Bakhtin's Russian,
according to Holquist and Emerson's glossary—wherever translated) may
"itself" categorically overlap not just with hyphenation but with linguistic
creoles, pidgins, and other modes of irreducible composites and alloys.[29] In
short, hybridity slides alongside *différance*, deferring, and pre-alienated positions that refuse "origins." One might theoretically deem hybridity (both
upbeat and abject varieties) the constitutively motley, the medley, the
inevitably tatterdemain—which brings me back to Sapir.[30]

Sapir's personal *mélange* and vulnerability resonate with his acute sense
of languages' global alloying throughout humanity's long haul (*durée*). It is
1920, and Sapir is apprehensive about "race" sentimentalists, or what different Marxists—Jameson, Ahmad, Dirlik, etc.—might *all* call racist ideologies
of supremacy, ones that coopt language-as-culture into their schemes. Sapir
combats such creeds with cold science, dry commentary, wit, style, and
cagily chosen cases of "mixings." We need to remember that Boasians cus-

tomarily disaggregated language from culture, and both language and culture from "race," a concept they de-essentialized, disfoundationed, radically overturned, or deconstructed, if readers prefer.[31] Indeed, by disaggregating, Sapir virtually detonates doctrines of superiority attached to language; behind fantasies of origin he discloses facts of borrowings, and beneath dreams of purity he reveals evidence of mongrels: "The man in the street . . . feels that he is the representative of some strongly integrated portion of humanity—now thought of as a 'nationality,' now as a 'race.' . . . If he is an Englishman, he feels himself to be a member of the 'Anglo Saxon' race, the 'genius' of which race has fashioned the English language and the 'Anglo Saxon' culture of which the language is the expression" (208). Sapir offers instead "a viewpoint that allows a certain interest to such mystic slogans as Slavophilism, Anglo-Saxondom, Teutonism, and the Latin genius but that quite refuses to be taken in by any of them" (209). He keys his argument that "a single language intercrosses with race and culture lines" to select examples aimed directly against prejudices of the day—both pedestrian and high-flying ones:

> The English language is not spoken by a unified race. In the United States there are several millions of negroes who know no other language. It is their mother-tongue, the formal vesture of their inmost thoughts and sentiments. It is as much their property, as inalienably "theirs," as the King of England's. Nor do the English-speaking whites [including Baltic, Alpine, Mediterranean] of America constitute a definite race except by way of contrast [he means ideological contrast] to the negroes.
> *(209)*

Sapir proceeds to assume the position of devil's advocate, and it loses, thanks to facts marshalled with understatement and flair, in order to thwart pernicious, common-sense notions prevalent in the English-reading public: "But does not the historical core of English-speaking peoples, those relatively 'unmixed' populations that still reside in England and its colonies represent a race, pure and single? I cannot see that the evidence points that way"(210). Sapir summarizes historical shifts and minglings among Norman, French, Celtic and so-called "Anglo-Saxon" peoples —certainly, for Sapir, an "invented tradition," and a bogus one. He underscores the manifestly mixed "Celtic" category and then shows that the presumably pure and singular— say, Baltic or "Teutonic"—is no less motley. Here are characteristic moments:

> Linguistically speaking, the "Celts" of today (Irish, Gaelic, Manx, Scotch Gaelic, Welsh, Breton) are Celtic and most of the German of

today are Germanic precisely as the American Negro, Americanized Jew, Minnesota Swede, and German-American are "English."

We cannot stop here. Not only . . . is English not spoken by a unified race at present but its prototype, more likely than not, was *originally a foreign language to the race with which English is more particularly associated.*   (211–12; emphasis added)

This demonstration pretty nearly declares hybridity "foundational" (or rather antifoundational)—despite the limitations of Sapir's epistemological historicism (he was, after all, Boasian). No language can be traced historically to a pure identity, to an unalienated condition. English was never "at home" to itself as a language, any more than Urdu was. Any language is equally alienable to anyone whose language it becomes. That position was certainly progressive in 1920, and it remains so today.

Please do not get me wrong. I attribute to Sapir few if any leanings toward some kind of postmodernist hybridity—if that is what Bhabha's postcoloniality is. For Sapir, any conventional relation between language and "identity" (he would have said "culture") is hybrid, perhaps even inherently hyphenatable. But his work retains distinctions between genuine cultures—harmonized wholes—versus spurious cultures, "spiritual hybrid[s] of contradictory patches."[32] Still, Sapir rejected any idea of language-based consolidation of unitary identity, including "nation" and "nationalism," anytime in anyone's history (208, 213). This stance should not be confused with "sheer random relativism" (whatever that may be), per Jameson; rather, Sapir's Boasian stance is situatedly relativist—relatively relativist, I like to say. Sapir directs categorical hybridity against any yearnings for purity by "race sentimentalists," whether naïve or premeditated.

Boasian Sapir also questions overextended theories of Brand X languages (and literatures) as metanarratives of this or that. Arguments by Ahmad on Urdu and Sapir on English (and Nootka, and Kwakiutl) would seem to flock together quite nicely, even though their feathers remain distinctive. But it is not so much a filiation as an affinity that emerges![33] Suggestions by Sapir that European metropole languages are no less foreign to their would-be "original" colonizers help cast a different light on Dirlik's most pessimistic message:

I think it is arguable that the end of Eurocentrism [proclaimed by post-colonialists] is an illusion [remember, Dirlik is writing in English] because capitalist culture as it has taken shape has Eurocentrism built into the very structure of its narrative, which may explain why, even as Europe and the United States lose their dominion of the capitalist

world economy, European and American cultural values retain their
domination.   *(Dirlik 50)*

That may be, but unless we learn to listen for hybridities that comprise such
cultural values—Anglo-Saxon ones, Urdu ones, and, yes, postmodern
ones—how can we be so sure?

Toward Listening Like Sapir

Sapir—my Boasian—helped enfranchise all history's *Sprache* as recombina-
torial, nonessential, hybrid. The Sapir of Whorf-Sapir considered world
view to be "grooved" (his word) by grammatical form and conceptualization
to occur according to unconscious categories that "drift" (his word) historically.[34] One trouble with Whorf-Sapir—this notorious hypothesis—is that
it sounds like a universal *énoncé* of absolute relativism, one apparently outside the contingencies it invokes, deaf to its own discursivity. All I can say is
that Sapir may be less culpable on these counts than many critics assume.
Indeed, his book *Language*, which extends to "literature" as well (ch. XI),
coins no such "hypothesis"; rather, it poses the grammar-grooves-conceptu-
alization theme narratively, and relationally. Sapir's text alludes to its
inescapable positionality in English (with Germanic residues), never claiming to pass into anything pure (not even Kwakiutl!).

These merits may be most manifest in chapter V, "Form in Language:
Grammatical Concepts." Sapir begins with a wittily simple sentence—"The
farmer kills the duckling." He unpacks its grammatical freight—definite,
agentive, number, tense, diminutives, etc. Seven pages later he charts seven-
teen involuntary grammatical components encrypted in the sentence, and
pauses to reassure readers with a Boasian moral: "Destructive analysis of the
familiar is the only method of approach to an understanding of fundamentally different modes of expression" (89; Shklovsky smiles).[35] Sapir then
opens English grammar, now defamiliarized, to "various classes of concepts
in alien types of speech" (89). These include near ones, such as German,
which still differs from English in aspects of case, gender, number (Sapir's
slight solecism in "*Der Bauer tötet das Entelein*" may be intentional).[36]

And they include far ones, such as Yana ("Kill-s he farmer, he to duckling?") and Chinese: "In . . . 'Man kill duck.' . . . there is by no means present for the Chinese consciousness that childish, halting, empty feeling
which we experience in the literal English translation" (92). Next comes the
signature Boasian move: not only defamiliarizing "own" but multiply

encountering "others," likewise defamiliarized (Shklovsky grins). On the verge of both analyzing (and defending) Chinese, Sapir's paragraph winds up suddenly elsewhere—interrogating *both* Chinese and English from yet another dramatically different grammar (like a Surrealist image, Jameson might once have said):

> Definiteness or indefiniteness of reference, number, personality as an inherent aspect of the verb, tense, not to speak of gender—all these are given no expression in the Chinese sentence, which, for all that, is a perfectly adequate communication. . . . In the English sentence too we leave unexpressed a large number of ideas which are either taken for granted or which have been developed or are about to be developed in the course of the conversation. Nothing has been said, for example, in the English, German, Yana, or Chinese sentence as to the place relations of the farmer, the duck, the speaker, and the listener. Are the farmer and the duck both visible or is one or the other invisible from the point of view of the speaker, and are both placed within the horizon of the speaker, the listener, or some indefinite point of reference "off yonder"? In other words, to paraphrase awkwardly certain latent "demonstrative" ideas, does this farmer (invisible to us but standing behind a door not far away from me, you being seated yonder well out of reach) kill that duckling (which belongs to you) or does that farmer (who lives in your neighborhood and whom we see over there) kill that duckling (that belongs to him)? This type of demonstrative elaboration is foreign to our way of thinking, but it would seem very natural, indeed unavoidable, to a Kwakiutl Indian.   *(93)*

So that's how Edward Sapir, a Boasian, keeps theories that grammar-grooves-world-view relational and nonunideterminant: situated within the translatedness of any effort to understand—defamiliarized own-language self included. (Sapir should, of course, be summarily reprimanded for failing to lament—technical-bourgeois linguist that he was—cruelty to ducks).

What an artful narrator was Sapir!—as worthy of rereading as, say, Benjamin and Bloch, inventively glossed by Jameson in *Marxism and Form* (again, my favorite). "Dear Freddie," this is why I find your slight of Boasian anthropology counterproductive to the "opulent sense of heterogeneity" you claim to commend to inclusive critique.

Another exclamation: What a cagey essayist was Sapir! Disguising his cross-language turn until after he has committed it, Sapir tries to hear the English sentence—dislocated from its own grammar and contrasted to German, Yana, Chinese—as if listening from within elaborate confines of Kwakiutl grammar. And Kwakiutl grammar—a prisonhouse with a difference, I'd say—is as mandatory to Kwakiutl speaking as tense and number are to English. (Pidgin English is, of course, otherwise "grammared"; and there is doubtless pidgin Kwakiutl—not to mention Chinook!)[37] Yes, Boasian Sapir tries listening back to his "personal" accented-English—as if hearing it from within Kwakiutl, whose grammar *requires* stipulating the horizon not just of the speaker but of the listener.

Now, one of Sapir's *spécialités* was grammars; but another was sound. Perhaps he was inspired by Kwakiutl grammar to positional listening; I have no idea. Regardless, this linguist-poet was indeed "into" the phonotext, a *topos* nicely framed by Garrett Stewart in *Reading Voices*.[38] It is Sapir's distinctively comparative emphasis on hearing that I would recommend to theorists of hybridities—whether postcolonial, postmodernist, or always-already.

Sapir's *Language* (1921) engages sound rather like Nabokov's *Lolita* (1955), or "Lo . . . li . . . ta"—the tongue-tip tripping along points of articulated contact, glottal chords attached to cartilages, forming for human organs of speech "what the two vibrating reeds are to an oboe or the strings to a violin" (Sapir 47). Heard-sounds entail *utterly* delicate differentials, including "a mysterious 'accent' to these foreign languages, a certain unanalyzed phonetic character, apart from the sounds as such, that gives them their air of strangeness" as heard by a "native speaker" (43). For Sapir, every speaker is native to the practice of what I would call "listening for foreignness."

The phenomenal nuance of sonic differences may strike critical theorists as idealized, even aestheticized, by Sapir; but there may be more radical implications in his speculations about how sound gets committed to evidence—both written and heard. Please read carefully:

> The conception of the ideal phonetic system, the phonetic pattern, of a language is not as well understood by linguistic students as it should be. . . . The unschooled recorder . . . is often at a great advantage as compared with the minute phonetician, who is apt to be swamped by his mass of observations. My experience in teaching Indians to write their own language . . . yields . . . valuable evidence here. I found that it was difficult or impossible to teach an Indian to make phonetic distinctions that did not correspond to "points in the pattern of his language," however these differences might strike our objective ear [Sapir means ideologically objective] but that subtle, barely audible, phonetic differences, if only they hit the "points in the pattern," were easily and

> voluntarily expressed in writing. In watching my Nootka interpreter write his language, I often had the curious feeling that he was transcribing an ideal flow of phonetic elements which he heard, inadequately from a purely objective standpoint, as the intention of the actual rumble of speech. (56)

Is Sapir idealizing here or "concretizing"? The same might be asked of his unnamed Nootka, the "native speaker" whom Sapir watches transcribing as if seeing him hear internally more than his graphics reveal. Sapir, then, not only "hears with his eyes"—to pinch a figure from *Reading Voices* (Stewart 37); he imagines another doing so (in Nootka) as well. Sapir's *Language* offers a translated speech act, one doubly inscribed (I note that both Nootka and Sapir are inscribing-listening), thus representing an intensive instance of imagined hybridity both across languages and among writing-hearing-sounding.

Diverse critical issues reopen in Sapir's composite cultural scene. What becomes of writing's relation not just to speaking, but to listening—hearing-oneself-speak otherwise (as attributed by Sapir to his Nootka)? The Nootka speaker-writer, with Sapir listening in, seems to "other" (differ?) phon*etic* notation into a phon*emics*, a phrasing keyed (in the musical sense) to his culture's sonic-*gamme*. Does, then, the Nootka both "parole" *langue*, Sapir cheering him on, and invade would-be historical *énoncé* with discourse— "cultural" discourse (Nootka speakings versus phon*etics*), along with "personal" discourse (one Nootka bloke encountering a peculiar linguist, who conceivably taught phonetic elements in German [Yiddish?]-accented "English," so to speak)? Who, moreover, is the locutor here, and who the *listener?* What is violated here, and by whom? Are we witnessing the violence of the letter or of the glottal stop? Another fleeting thought: What might have ensued in critical theory, had Derrida adumbrated not that "other" writing lesson (a reading with which I have long differed), but this writing lesson: the Nootka selectively correcting signifieds-for-sound against his inner speech flow, as Sapir writes having imagined it? (That will be my last head-wag toward mainstream deconstruction).[39]

Sapir's writing lesson (who, by the way, is learning here?) deserves becoming a mnemonic narrative, at least as I read it. May it remind us critically to listen to and for hybridities; to attend to locutor and listener (both ways); to acknowledge that hybridities have a ring to them—enacted as accent, whether regional ("dialect") or foreign, also underscored by Sapir. Again: "As for the languages of foreigners, [the average speaker] generally feels that, aside from a few striking differences that cannot escape even the uncritical ear, the sounds they use are the same as those he is familiar with but that there is a mysterious 'accent' to these foreign languages, a certain unanalyzed phonetic character, apart from the sounds as such, that gives them their air of strangeness" (43).

Accents resoundingly disrupt projects in universalist abstraction (so-called *énoncés*). Such inevitable embarrassments to universals—not to mention metanarrative—constitute the very stuff and substance of "culture" in one Boasian (-Sapirian) sense.

More questions: What about Ahmad's accent—as Sapir, or that Nootka, or I might imagine hearing it? How does Dirlik's theory *sound*? How do Prakash's positions ring? (Lordy me, I envy him their flow and control.) And Spivak's? (Very upscale!). Yours truly, by the way, hears much discourse of postcoloniality as a bit "British" sounding—ironically, "rathahh Raj." In the provisional guise assumed here of *local* American, I, like Ahmad, feel a tad . . . well . . . colonized STILL, whenever my reading feels subjected to Oxbridge inflection, including Jameson's mimicry thereof.

One of hybridities' signs is accent-heard—whether Jameson's, whether mine, whether a Nootka counterinscribing letters taught him by a Pomerania-born American Jew. How can our theories—many of them incorrigibly *visualized* STILL—bring hybridities' accents within earshot? Can we coax hybridity—Homi Bhabha's, Arif Dirlik's, Karl Marx's (there's an accent-laden scene!)—away from routine politics of identity and turnabout empowerment, away from constant reactive-hyphenating, away from traces of physiognomic distinctions lingering in profusions of polychrome shades, away from old-style dialectics and updated prefixing by "post"?[40] Bhabha has been saluted for factoring accent into theory: "Homi Bhabha on the other hand [the contrast drawn is with Spivak], through recovering how the master discourse was interrogated by the natives in their own accents, produces an autonomous position for the colonial within the confines of the hegemonic discourse, and because of this enunciates a very different 'politics' " (Ashcroft 1995:40). But does Bhabha truly "hybridize" accent itself into manifold aspects—including diversely "foreign" and "ultra-local"? Sapir, perhaps, began to.

The question, then, remains: Can theory veer away from trails and traces of purisms that still haunt postcoloniality—as liberation, as aftermath—and turn toward accented vernaculars, with "high critique" included? Or, to overdraw my semiotic dichotomy: Can hybridities be released from the Panopticon, the prisonhouse, or just the pigeonholes of *viewing* ("birds of a feather"), and accede to fluidities of specific *listening*? It won't be easy to loosen listening from routine politics of theoretical diatribe. And it may take a little humor.[41] One day, however, Sapir (resuscitated, I hope, along with some sister "Boasians") may finally flock together with

Ahmad, perhaps Bhabha, and even early Jameson—their diverse theoretical songs blended in an ALTERNATIVE NEW BEGINNING TO NOW-MAINSTREAM POSTCOLONIAL CULTURAL STUDIES. Needless to add, these closing *majuscules* of mine are really discourse only disguised as *énoncé*, unheard unless and until their hybridities are given not just "voice" (an abstraction) but, ironically, accent.

Codetta

The performance version of this essay delivered at Irvine concluded with a twist here deferred to a future study, due to limitations of space. Drawing from long-term work on early "show business" across cultures, I tried suggestively to address the thorniest instance of so-called hybridity in American popular entertainment: "blackface"—replete with hyphens, erasures, festivity, and abjection. Both saluting and questioning recent critique of this format by Michael Rogin (1992, 1994), Eric Lott, and others (much of it stressing identity politics of blacks/Jews/Gentiles/etc.), I asked listeners to join in hearing Al Jolson's *accented-voice* on a recording of "That Haunting Melody" made long before he donned blackface, but whose *sound* came to be associated with that objectionable style. Rather like Sapir listening to his Nootka, I strained to hear subtler distinctions within this prejudice-laden hybridity (running from minstrelsy through Tin Pan Alley to Hollywood) than those polarized identities that loom so large for Rogin (another of my favorite "Marxists").[42]

Sapir's work is a theoretical "old song," much as Jolson's "Haunting Melody" is a showbiz "old song." (Both Jolson and Sapir, by the way, were sons of cantors).[43] One might wish for Sapir a fate similar to one that Ethan Mordden—a wonderfully attentive listener—declares Judy Garland achieved for Jolson (many of whose standards she reprised): "She didn't revive old songs, she rejuvenated them" (1990:142). Rejuvenating Sapir (or the ways Sapir's ears could hear) can complicate studies of "culture" too inclined to *énoncés* locked into the business of making theory nouveau. Nor perhaps should we critics quite so contentedly lambaste nostalgia; accents from and for the past are tricky sounds to read.

NOTES

I wish to thank John Carlos Rowe and everyone directly and indirectly involved with the Critical Theory Institute for wonderfully open responses to an offbeat presentation and essay.

1. Kristeva, *Language: The Unknown* (1989), 11.

2. For example, Kristeva (1980), chs. 7, 1.

3. Evans-Pritchard (1965); D. Tedlock (1983); see also Boon (1982, ch. 4).

4. Benjamin (1969); see also Smith (1989); Derrida (1985, 1993); Steiner (1975, 1989); Cixous (1993).

5. See Pitcher (1971); Schmitz (1983).

6. Dabbydeen in Ricks and Michaels (1990); Culler (1976); Sapir (1921).

7. Culler (1983); Abrams, "The Deconstructive Angel," in Lodge (1988:264–76); Holquist (1990); Lodge (1988), including Miller, "The Critic as Host" (277–85).

8. Kenneth Burke's entire corpus, including (1966, 1970); Said (1975); see also Boon (1982); Ahmad (1987).

9. Hybridity may already be waning as a hot topic; it was, of course, never new; only the hyphens had changed. To indicate how "hybridity" gets standardized in postcolonial theory, I draw occasionally on a handy *Reader* (the genre of routinization) edited by Ashcroft et al. (1995).

10. See Boas (1940); for some interpretive intricacies of other Boasians and part-Boasians—particularly Robert Lowie, Ruth Benedict, and Margaret Mead—see Boon (1982, ch. 3; 1990, Postlude; 1995).

11. This paragraph alludes constructively to Bhabha (1990); it also alludes to Anderson (1983).

12. For some composite "transnational circuitries" across Indonesia generally (and Bali in particular), stretching through ninth-century "Indianizings," fourteenth-century Islamizings, various European colonizings, pro- and antimissionizings, and such formations as so-called Early Modern mercantilisms and so-called postmodern tourisms—"borderlands" all—see Boon (1977, 1990, 1992).

13. Weber (1958); De Certeau (1984, 1986); these approaches are interwoven in Boon (1990).

14. On this patronizing tone *as institutionalized* in Indonesian colonialist discourse, see Boon (1990, ch. 2); one great critical tirade (by a European) against colonialist condescension and oppression is *Max Havelaar*, Douwes-Dekker's 1860 novel in the form of a Menippean Satire (Multatuli 1982); see Boon (1990:15—16). The great critical tirade (by an Indonesian) against colonialist condescension and oppression, perpetuated in nationalist regimes, is Pramoedya Ananta Toer's epic (1990); this work was possibly inspired in part by Multatuli and/or possibly parodied its parody.

15. See, for example, Chakrabarty (1992), among many works in the "subaltern studies" manner.

16. Compare Rousseau's "*Lettre à M. d'Alembert sur le spectacle*": "I am at fault if I have on this occasion taken up my pen without necessity. It can be neither advantageous nor agreeable for me to attack M. d'Alembert. I respect his person; I admire his talents; I like his works"; and much later: "Never did personal views soil the desire to be useful to others which put the pen in my hand and I have almost always written against my own interests. . . . Readers, I may deceive myself, but I do not deceive you willingly." (1960:3, 132.)

17. For representative views of Boas's achievements, see Stocking (1974); see also Krupat (1990).

18. Compare Diderot's *Neveu de Rameau*, passim. On certain theatrics of critical contestation, see Bernstein, who emphasizes abjection even in Bakhtin. For a less downbeat, yet by no means chipper, sense of interpretive theatrics, see Greg Dening (1996), who appears to reconcile Turner, Geertz, Sahlins, and so forth, but actually keeps very subtle differences among, say, Geertz and Turner in play; see also Geertz (1983), ch. 1.

19. My book-voyage trope is hybridized from Jacobean scholar Samuel Purchas (see Boon 1982, ch. 5); my second trope composites Stephan Zweig and N. Chaudhuri, with apologies.

20. See Goldstein (1996) for sensitive insights in this area.

21. "Double consciousness" alludes to ideas of W. E. B. Du Bois (see Gates 1988), plus those of William James, whose abiding concern with split consciousness and "multiple personalities" dated from the case of Ansel Bourne; see Kenny (1986).

22. Jameson's slighting of Boasians may stem from his buying into the conventional view that their approach was "undertheorized." But for Jameson to ape this *avis* detracts from his own call for "radical situational difference in cultural productions and meanings." Truth to tell, Boasians (at least those linguistically inclined) were undertheorized only by unideterminant (I name not Marxist) standards. In some respects their work was precociously multideterminant—inclined toward disaggregation and (one might even say) hybridity. I shall amplify this claim, directly, via Sapir.

23. See, for example, Ashcroft (1995), where Ahmad is excerpted into the *Post-colonial Studies Reader*. For purposes of this paper, I must leave aside Ahmad's fuller body of work.

24. Dirlik (1994), 339–40. For Spivak, see Spivak (1988), and her contributions and commentaries indexed under her name in Ashcroft (1995). I am ignorant as to whether Spivak has helped sponsor translations of, say, Derrida into Hindi or other South Asian literariness. Still speaking of Spivak, below I opt for folksier versions of her high-theoretical slogans of and for catachresis.

25. See Appiah (1991); Prakash (1990, 1992)

26. Similarly, the extract of Ahmad in Ashcroft (1995:77–82) retains his nation-narration credentials but eliminates *hybridities* of his rhetorical devices, with their apparent play between as-if *énoncés* and personalized discourse.

27. For experiments in self-consciously "vernacularized" style and crosscultural comparison, see Boon (1992, 1998).

28. Sapir (1921); on Sapir's career, see Darnell (1990); fresh work on Whorf by J. Kelly, M. Silverstein, A. Hastings, and others is under way.

29. For translations of Russian *gibrid*, see Bakhtin (1981:429, 305ff, 358ff); on the "alloyed isle of Aru," see Boon (1990:19–23).

30. See also Boon (1982, chs. 3–4).

31. A clearinghouse of precedents and implications of Boasian stances against racism and exposure of the fallacy of race is Montagu (1964 [1942]); see also Shanklin (1995), a recent review of "anthropology and race" nicely credited by Appiah.

32. Sapir, "Culture Genuine and Spurious" (1949). In 1968, a beginning graduate student, I was troubled by Sapir's slighting of switchboard operators as somehow "spurious" (ultra-mediators, inherent go-betweens, only-connections-never-connected). To counter his assumptions, I invoked Judy Holiday's unforgettably genuine practice of

"Suzanswerphone" in *The Bells Are Ringing*. In 1997, I stick by my disaggregation of Sapir's lapse into invidious distinctions between genuine/spurious. See also Caffrey (1989:148); Handler (1986).

33. For theories of "filiation" and reception enacted by Roland Barthes and for ideas of "affinities" *filiated* from Goethe to Max Weber and others, see Boon (1990, 1982:151–52).

34. For "groove," see Sapir (1921:15); "drift" is the topic of ch. VII, Sapir's classic discussion of language moving "down time in a current of its own making" (15). Such systematic change amidst the "purposeless flux" of linguistic variations, although not evolutionary, "has direction" (155)—as in English's movement toward the uninflected, isolated "word," that registers in grammar, syntax, and phonemics. On such linguistic dynamics, see especially Friedrich (1979).

35. Shklovsky's 1917 "Art as Technique," where *ostrenanie* ("defamiliarization") debuted as a theoretical concept, is nicely framed, and juxtaposed with Saussure and Jakobson, in Lodge (1988:15–30). I like these bedfellows—*ostrenanie* indeed (Boon 1972).

36. Sapir uses "*tötet*" for "killing" a duck in German—an ungrammatically "humanistic" coinage! Other places where Sapir appears playfully to blend (hybridize) his gifted English prose back with his "language of origins" include: "The explanation of primary dialectic differences is still to seek" (149). One might parallel Sapir's "prosing" across the world's grammars to his poetic "hearing" anew lapsed semantics of compounds (e.g., the break-fast, in breakfast). Sapir experiences English's "drift" toward isolated, unmotivated (in the Saussurian sense) "sememes" (not Sapir's word) from the vantage perhaps of German/Yiddish still devoted to lexical compounding: hybrid *wörter* (see Sapir 1921:141, 132, 196, 93). Similarly, Sapir manages to disclose compositeness of "grammars" by reading them relationally and worldwide.

37. On Pidgins, Creoles, Chinook, and so forth—*loci classici* of contending with "hybridity" in anthropological linguistics—see Hymes (1961, 1964, etc.) and Romaine (1988); a handy overview of this and most other linguistic issues is Crystal (1987).

38. Stewart (1990); see also Attridge (1988, ch. 6) on "Lipspeech." I thank Hillis Miller for gingerly querying the "digs at deconstruction" in this paper. I offer them more as winks—extending my custom, when reading cultures comparatively, of *including* deconstructive positions *among others*. This has proved a strangely difficult task; in critical circles to which I remain dutifully tangential, "deconstruction" sometimes tended to *take over*. What, I want to keep asking, could have been more paradoxical?

39. For some reservations about Derrida's influential "take" on Lévi-Strauss's episode in *Tristes tropiques*, see Boon (1982:278–79). Oddly, Derrida's *Donner le temps* (1991) reiterates his earlier style of refusing even as-if yearning for lost-presence or pre-*écriture*. Here Derrida's ever-deferring prose strikes this reader as nearly "nostalgic" (winkingly, no doubt) for his own prior polemic; this go-round, however, the target is not Lévi-Strauss, but Marcel Mauss. For some thoughts on Mauss as a non-nostalgist, see Boon (1992, "Litterytoor 'n' Anthropolygee"); these thoughts have been assembled with related ones in Boon (1998).

40. To sample what one might call Marx's humorous "polylinguicity"—a "discursive hybridity"?—see Wilson (1972:251). Certain ironies of prefixing "post" are suggested in Boon (1990, Prelude) and pursued in Boon (1998, passim).

41. My allusions to the topic of critiquing "the visual" draw on Martin Jay (1986). Again, I broach vernacular "humor" and enact a bit of discourse alert to accent's "embarrassments"—both own and others'—in Boon (1992, "Cosmopolitan Moments," "Litterytoor 'n' Anthropolygee"; 1998).

42. On Rogin's sense of Melville's *Mardi* as America's equivalent to Marx's "Eighteenth Brumaire," see Rogin (1982), discussed in Boon (1998, "Rehearsal C").

43. On Sapir's father, see Darnell (1990:152).

WORKS CITED

Abrams, M. H. "The Deconstructive Angel." In David Lodge, ed., *Modern Criticism and Theory: A Reader*. New York: Longman, 1988, 265–76.

Ahmad, Aijaz. "Jameson's Rhetoric of Otherness and the 'National Allegory.'" *Social Text* 17 (1987): 3–27.

Anderson, Benedict. *Imagined Communities*. London: Verso, 1983.

Appiah, Kwame Anthony. "Is the Post- in Postmodernism the Post- in Postcolonial?" *Critical Inquiry* 17(2)(1991): 336–57.

Bakhtin, Mikhail. *The Dialogic Imagination*. Trans. C. Emerson and M. Holquist. Austin: University of Texas Press, 1981.

Benjamin, Walter. *Illuminations*. Trans. Harry Zohn. New York: Schocken, 1969.

Bernstein, Michael André. *Bitter Carnival: "Ressentiment" and the Abject Hero*. Princeton: Princeton University Press, 1992.

Bhabha, Homi, ed. *Nation and Narration*. London: Routledge, 1990.

——. *The Location of Culture*. London: Routledge, 1994.

Boas, Franz. *Race, Language, and Culture*. New York: Macmillan, 1940.

Boon, James A. *Affinities and Extremes: Crisscrossing the Bittersweet Ethnology of East Indies History, Hindu-Balinese Culture, and Indo-European Allure*. Chicago: University of Chicago Press, 1990.

——. "Cosmopolitan Moments: Echoey Confessions of an Ethnographer-Tourist." In Daniel Segal, ed., *Crossing Cultures: Essays in the Displacement of Western Civilization*. Tucson: University of Arizona Press, 1992.

——. "Litterytoor 'n' Anthropolygee: A Twainian Talk About Cultures, Vernaculars, and Humor, plus the Magical Essays of Marcel Mauss." *Swiss Papers in English Language and Literature*, vol. 6. Tübingen: Günter Narr Verlag, 1992, 197–229.

——. *Other Tribes, Other Scribes*. New York: Cambridge University Press, 1982.

——. "Ultraobjectivity, Cross-culturally: Interpretive Anthropology and the Arts of Rereading." In W. Natters et al., eds., *Objectivity and Its Other*. New York: Guilford, 1995.

——. *Verging on Extra-Vagance: Anthropology, History, Religion, Literature, Arts, . . . Showbiz*. Princeton: Princeton University Press, 1998.

Burke, Kenneth. *Language as Symbolic Action*. Berkeley: University of California Press, 1966.

——. *The Rhetoric of Religion: Studies in Logology*. Berkeley: University of California Press, 1970.

Caffrey, Margaret. *Ruth Benedict: Stranger in This Land.* Austin: University of Texas Press, 1989.

Chakrabarty, Dipesh. "Postcoloniality and the Artifice of History: Who Speaks for 'Indian' Pasts?" *Representations* 3 (1992): 1–26.

Cixous, Hélène. Letter published in section, " 'L'Affaire Derrida': Yet Another Exchange." *New York Review of Books,* April 22, 1993.

Crystal, David. *The Cambridge Encyclopedia of Language.* Cambridge: Cambridge University Press, 1987.

Culler, Jonathan. *On Deconstruction: Theory and Criticism After Structuralism.* Ithaca: Cornell University Press, 1983.

——. *Saussure.* Ithaca: Cornell University Press, 1976.

Darnell, Regna. *Edward Sapir: Linguist, Anthropologist, Humanist.* Berkeley: University of California Press, 1990.

De Certeau, Michel. *Heterologies: Discourse on the Other.* Trans. B. Massumi. Minneapolis: University of Minnesota Press, 1986.

——. *The Practice of Everyday Life.* Trans. S. F. Rendall. Berkeley: University of California Press, 1984.

Dening, Greg. *Performances.* Chicago: University of Chicago Press, 1996.

Derrida, Jacques. "Des Tours de Babel/Des Tours de Babel." In Joseph F. Graham, ed., *Difference in Translation.* Ithaca: Cornell University Press, 1985.

——. 1991. *Donner le temps.* Paris: Editions Galilée.

——. Letter published in " 'L'Affaire Derrida': Another Exchange." *New York Review of Books,* March 25, 1993.

Diderot, Denis. *Le Neveu de Rameau.* Ed. J-C. Bonnet. Paris: Flammarion, 1983.

Dirlik, Arif. "The Postcolonial Aura: Third World Criticism in the Age of Global Capitalism." *Critical Inquiry* 20(2)(1994): 328–56.

Evans-Pritchard, E. E. *Theories of Primitive Religion.* New York: Oxford University Press, 1965.

Friedrich, Paul. *Language, Context, and the Imagination.* Stanford: Stanford University Press, 1979.

Gates, Henry L. *The Signifying Monkey: A Theory of Afro-American Literary Criticism.* New York: Oxford University Press, 1988.

Geertz, Clifford. *Local Knowledge.* New York: Basic Books, 1983.

Goldstein, Judith L. "The Female Aesthetic Community." In George Marcus and Fred Myers, eds., *The Traffic in Culture: Refiguring Art and Anthropology.* Berkeley: University of California Press, 1997.

Graham, Joseph F., ed. *Difference in Translation.* Ithaca: Cornell University Press, 1985.

Handler, Richard. "Vigorous Male and Aspiring Female: Poetry, Personality, and Culture in Edward Sapir and Ruth Benedict." In *History of Anthropology,* vol. 4. Ed. George Stocking. Madison: University of Wisconsin Press, 1986.

Holquist, Michael. *Dialogism: Bakhtin and His World.* New York: Routledge, 1990.

Hymes, Dell H., ed. *Language in Culture and Society.* New York: Harper and Row, 1964.

——. "On Typology of Cognitive Styles in Language (with Examples from Chinookan)." *Anthropological Linguistics* 3(1)(1961): 22–54.

Jameson, Fredric. "A Brief Response" (to Ahmad 1987).

————. *Marxism and Form*. Princeton: Princeton University Press, 1971.

Jay, Martin. "The Empire of the Gaze: Foucault and the Denigration of Vision in Twentieth Century French Thought." In David C. Hoy, *Foucault: A Critical Reader*. Oxford: Basil Blackwell, 1986.

Kenny, Michael G. *The Passion of Ansel Bourne: Multiple Personality in American Culture*. Washington: Smithsonian Institution Press, 1986.

Kristeva, Julia. *Desire in Language*. Ed. Leon S. Roudiez. New York, Columbia University Press, 1980.

————. *Language: The Unknown*. Trans. Anne M. Menke. New York: Columbia University Press, 1989.

Lodge, David, ed. *Modern Criticism and Theory: A Reader*. New York: Longman, 1988.

Montagu, Ashley, ed. *Man's Most Dangerous Myth: The Fallacy of Race*. 1942; reprint, New York: Meridian, 1970.

Mordden, Ethan. "A Critic at Large: I Got a Song." *The New Yorker* October 22, 1990, 110–42.

Multatuli. *Max Havelaar*. Trans. Roy Edwards; ed. E. M. Beekman. 1860; reprint, Amherst: University of Massachusetts Press, 1985.

Pitcher, George. "Wittgenstein, Nonsense, and Lewis Carroll." In *Alice in Wonderland*. Ed. Donald J. Gray. New York: Norton, 1971.

Prakash, Gyan. "Postcolonial Criticism and Indian Historiography." *Social Text* 31/32 (1992).

————. "Writing Post-Orientalist Histories of the Third World: Perspectives from Indian Historiography." *Comparative Studies in Society and History* 32 (1990).

Ricks, Christopher and Leonard Michaels, eds. *The State of the Language*. Berkeley: University of California Press, 1990.

Rogin, Michael Paul. "Blackface, White Noise: The Jewish Jazz Singer Finds His Voice." *Critical Inquiry* 19 (1992): 417–22.

————. " 'Democracy and Burnt Cork': The End of Blackface, the Beginning of Civil Rights." *Representations* 46 (1994): 1–34.

Romaine, Suzanne. *Pidgin and Creole Languages*. London: Longman, 1988.

Rousseau, Jean-Jacques. *Politics and the Arts: Letter to M. d'Alembert on the Theater*. Trans. Allan Bloom. Ithaca: Cornell University Press, 1960.

Said, Edward. *Beginnings*. Baltimore: Johns Hopkins University Press, 1975.

Sapir, Edward. "Culture Genuine and Spurious." In *Selected Writings*. Ed. D. Mandelbaum. Berkeley: University of California Press, 1949.

————. *Language*. New York: Harcourt, Brace, 1921.

Schmitz, Neil. *Of Huck and Alice: Humorous Writing in American Literature*. Minneapolis: University of Minnesota Press, 1983.

Shanklin, Eugenia. *Anthropology and Race*. Belmont, Calif.: Wadsworth, 1995.

Shklovsky, Victor. "Art as Technique." In David Lodge, ed., *Modern Criticism and Theory: A Reader*. New York: Longman, 1998, 15–30.

Smith, Gary, ed. *Benjamin: Philosophy, Aesthetics, History*. Chicago: University of Chicago Press, 1989.

Spivak, Gayatri Chakravorty. *In Other Worlds: Essays in Cultural Politics*. New York: Methuen, 1988.

Steiner, George. *After Babel: Aspects of a Theory of Translation.* New York: Oxford University Press, 1975.

———. *Real Presences.* Chicago: University of Chicago Press, 1989.

Stocking, George, ed. *The Shaping of American Anthropology, 1883–1911: A Franz Boas Reader.* New York: Basic Books, 1974.

Tedlock, Dennis. *The Spoken Word and the Work of Interpretation.* Philadelphia: University of Pennsylvania Press, 1983.

Toer, Pramoedya Ananta. *Awakenings (This Earth of Mankind; A Child of All Nations).* Trans. Mark Lane. London: Penguin, 1990.

Weber, Max. *From Max Weber.* Trans. H. Gerth and C. W. Mills. New York: Oxford University Press, 1958.

Wilson, Edmund. *To the Finland Station: A Study in the Writing and Acting of History.* 1940; reprint, New York: Noonday, 1972.

Colonialism, Psychoanalysis, and Cultural Criticism: The Problem of Interiorization in the Work of Albert Memmi

Suzanne Gearhart

I. Cultural Identity and the Problem of the Unconscious

An important aspect of recent work in the area of cultural studies is that it no longer treats culture primarily as a reflection of deeper historical, economic, or sociopolitical forces. On the contrary, culture has come to be regarded as a dynamic, formative system in itself, with its own specificity and relative autonomy. And it would not be difficult to show that the "new culturalism" that has come into increasing prominence derives much of its impetus from the centrality of the problem of culture in the critique of and resistance to colonial domination. An important moment in the emergence of culture as a primary rather than secondary concern is Aimé Césaire's "Letter to Maurice Thorez," in which he broke with the Communist Party over the question of colonialism. Césaire asserted that he was no longer willing to attach less importance to his cultural solidarity with other West Indian and African peoples than to his social and political solidarity with other economically oppressed groups. With this letter, Césaire not only broke with European Marxists over the question of the significance of national liberation movements. He also testified to the need for a new sense of culture, one that would play a central role in the critique of and resistance to colonial domination.[1]

A large and growing body of scholarship testifies to the existence of a broadly shared sense of the critical importance of the problem of culture in the critique of colonialism and other forms of hegemony. Nonetheless, warnings about what Frantz Fanon called the "pitfalls of national consciousness" are becoming more frequent, insofar as national consciousness assumes a homogeneous notion of culture and cultural identity. In *Culture and Imperialism*, Edward Said continues to defend national consciousness, but with an important qualification that reveals that he has taken Fanon's warning seriously: "That many nationalists are sometimes more coercive or more intellectually self-critical than others is clear, but my own thesis is that, at its best, nationalist resistance to imperialism was always critical of itself" (219). While this is a defense of the value of national cultural consciousness in combating imperialism and colonialism, it also amounts to a concession that when it is not "at its best," nationalist resistance to imperialism is *not* self-critical. And in a later section of his book, Said, like others who have warned against the potential dangers of nationalism, praises Fanon for his farsightedness in criticizing the limited goals and outlooks of many of the movements of national liberation of the fifties and early sixties.[2]

There is thus even for Said a potential risk, both political and theoretical, involved in the cultural paradigm. It is the risk of creating or presupposing a new collective and individual identity based on national culture, one that would ultimately be as abstract, limited, metaphysical, and thus potentially as repressive in nature as the humanisms unmasked and criticized from the perspective of a critical concept of culture. Said himself makes this point when he characterizes what he considers to be the most positive aspect of national resistance as "anti-identitarian," while conceding that certain forms of resistance contain or are even dominated by an "identitarian" tendency.

It is with regard to the risks inherent in the concept of culture that Henry Gates, for one, has written of the importance of psychoanalysis for contemporary, culturally oriented studies of colonialism. In "Critical Fanonism," Gates analyzes the "fascination" Fanon holds for contemporary theorists in terms of the "convergence of the problematic of colonialism with that of subject-formation" (458). Because of Fanon's position at the intersection of these two problematics, Gates suggests, the attention being paid to his work can be read as the sign of a heightened interest in the potential role of psychoanalysis within that segment of cultural theory and criticism focused on the problem of colonial culture.

There are two important dimensions to Gates's discussion of the role of psychoanalysis in cultural studies. The first is critical and is evident in his analysis, which is at times ironic and humorous, of what might be called the "pitfalls of psychoanalytic consciousness." According to the logic of Gates's argument, perhaps the most important of these pitfalls is the risk of simply applying psychoanalysis to the field of colonial discourse, and thus reducing the colonial situation to the status of one more "case study." Clearly the risk in question is political, but it is theoretical as well, consisting in the denial of the uniqueness and specificity of the colonial situation. The second aspect of Gates's approach is more supportive of psychoanalysis, for he also suggests that psychoanalysis has a potentially critical role to play in terms of the further development of a theory of colonial discourse. He writes, for example, toward the end of his essay: "In the context of the colonial binarism, we've seldom admitted fully how disruptive the psychoanalytic model can be" (470).

The perspectives of Gates and Fanon thus explicitly raise the question of the role of psychoanalysis in understanding the problem of culture. Does it have a critical role to play, and is that role a "disruptive" rather than "destructive" one? Can psychoanalysis provide a more complex picture of the colonial situation than the one that colonialism itself has bequeathed to us— the picture of what Fanon called a "manichean" universe and of what Gates calls "colonial binarism"? If it can provide us with such a picture, can it do so without in any way legitimating colonialism itself and banalizing its destructive effects?

The question is difficult, because both in the general field of cultural studies, even in the branch of it devoted to the critical analysis of colonialism, and in the field of psychoanalytic theory, heterogeneity and even conflict are the rule, and unanimity the exception. As Gates argues in "Critical Fanonism," no single figure dominates the field of cultural studies or provides a definitive general theory of the colonial situation. By the same token, there is no single author whose work alone could be said to exemplify the convergence of psychoanalysis and the theory of colonial culture. It should not and cannot be forgotten that Octave Mannoni's theory of the "dependency complex" of the colonized and his equally questionable theory of the "inferiority complex" of the colonizers (as opposed to the supposed mental health of Europeans living in Europe) also lie at this convergence.[3] Even if one limits oneself to a consideration of theories that are oppositional, that is, that turn to psychoanalysis in order to better grasp and unmask the hypocrisy and destructiveness of colonialism, important differences can still be found. But despite the existence of any number of works that could be cited, I would argue that Albert Memmi's *The Colonizer and the Colonized* is of particular interest in terms of the possibility of a psychoanalytic theory that would be "disruptive," that is, critical but not destructive of the problematics of culture.[4]

Part of the interest of Memmi today lies in his being less familiar than the other major theorist of colonialism with whom he invites comparison—

Frantz Fanon.[5] Said, for example, gives Fanon a prominent position in *Culture and Imperialism* by devoting substantial space to a discussion of his work and perhaps even more by the importance he attaches to him as a figure who exemplifies Said's own critical project. Memmi, on the other hand, is mentioned only three times in passing. Homi Bhabha, another contemporary theorist who has sought to combine psychoanalysis with cultural theory in his analysis of colonialism, has focused on Fanon to the virtual exclusion of any of his contemporaries. Gates, who gives a somewhat more prominent place to Memmi, argues that we should avoid falling into the trap of feeling we have to choose between Memmi and Fanon. But to a great extent, as Gates also argues, colonial discourse theory *has* chosen, by electing Fanon as its representative or what Gates calls its "global theorist."

The fact that Memmi's work has often been overlooked, however, is only one reason for considering him here. A more important reason is the manner in which Memmi uses psychoanalysis to question as well as to refine, complicate, and affirm the role of culture in the emancipation of oppressed groups. Memmi's portraits of the colonizer and the colonized show both the cultural and the psychic identity of each to be a myth, and the ultimate effect of those portraits is to undermine all the more radically the ideological bases of colonialism. But these same portraits also provide the basis for a potential challenge to contemporary cultural studies, insofar as such studies continue to rely on the concept of a simple, unified subject of culture.

In saying this I hasten to add that such reliance, where it does exist, is in most cases implicit rather than explicit. In the work done in cultural studies today, the existence of a cultural "identity" is perhaps less likely to be affirmed than the idea that there is no unified subject. But it is also true that, despite the disclaimers, a unified form of subjectivity is being tacitly affirmed nonetheless in many instances where the individual is defined as a product of culture or cultural relations. Such relations may be specified in terms of a particular cultural group, a hierarchy between two or more groups, or multiple axes of conflict within a given cultural configuration. The subject "produced" or "positioned" by such relations may appear to be relatively complex. But in a fundamental sense the subject in question remains simple as long as the psyche is viewed as the mere reflection of cultural forces, however diverse, and its passivity and neutrality in the process of its own production are assumed.

By showing such psychic passivity to be a myth in the case of both the colonizer and the colonized, Memmi's psychocultural analysis looks beyond the binarism characteristic of colonial societies. But it also looks beyond a potentially reductive aspect of important examples of cultural studies, which interpret specific historical conflicts in terms of simple, culturally determined oppositions. Equally important, Memmi's *Portrait of the Colonized* shows that it is possible to look beyond such reductive interpretations and effectively challenge the view that relations of domination are stable and inevitable.

The issue of the relation between cultural studies and critical theory has been discussed frequently in recent years, and almost every writer who has treated it has assessed it differently. Such diversity in and of itself suggests that it would be fruitless to attempt simply to oppose or assimilate cultural studies and critical theory—assuming for a moment that it is possible to agree on what constitutes "cultural studies" and what constitutes "critical theory." While the analysis of Memmi that follows relates to these various assessments, its implication is obviously not that either assimilation or opposition is preferred. It does, however, reflect a view that Memmi's psychoanalytic approach to cultural questions is of interest from the standpoint of both cultural studies and critical theory, though the interest is problematic in each case.

Memmi's appropriation of psychoanalysis provides support for a critique of contemporary cultural studies, inasmuch as it represents Memmi's rejection of a purely cultural approach to what he himself nonetheless affirms are cultural questions. In this particular respect, Memmi's perspective converges with that of certain contemporary critical theorists who would argue that much of cultural studies relies in an uncritical manner on the concept of culture. But Memmi's work also provides support for cultural studies itself and for affirmations concerning the fundamental significance of culture, even though Memmi's concept of culture has been subjected to a critique from a psychoanalytic standpoint and hence refined and complicated. What is ultimately significant, however, is the potential role his work suggests psychoanalysis can play in enhancing the critical dimension of cultural studies and critical theory alike.

It is equally important to note, moreover, that in offering a critique of "colonial binarism," which in Memmi's terms is perhaps the ultimate creation of colonial society, Memmi's work also provides the grounds for a critique of psychoanalysis, insofar as psychoanalysis or at least certain aspects of it could be said to support the notion of a unified subject. For *The Colonizer and the Colonized* does not hold up psychoanalytic theory as a model. On the contrary, Memmi refers to psychoanalysis in critical asides that express his distrust of any theory—and he includes Marxism in this category—that treats what he calls "*le vécu*" or "lived experience" reductively, in terms of a single model: "Psychoanalysis or Marxism must not, under the pretext of having discovered the source or one of the main sources of human conduct, pre-empt [*souffler*] all lived experience [*le vécu*], all feeling, all suffering, all the byways of human behaviour, and call them profit motive or Oedipus complex" (*The Colonizer and the Colonized*, xiii). But despite these important reservations, Memmi's theory of colonialism does nonetheless imply the need for a (critical) psychoanalysis and suggests that such an analysis would have a potentially crucial role to play in the understanding of colonialism.

From a psychoanalytic standpoint, the key to Memmi's analysis of colonialism lies in his concept of lived experience and the role and nature of what I would call the process of interiorization that it implies. "*Le vécu*" is a term that had wide currency in the period in which Memmi wrote *The Colonizer and the Colonized*. It is usually used to stress the authenticity or validity of individual consciousness and the immediate experience of perception—as opposed to more abstract processes involving imagination and ideation and a subjectivity that is shared rather than unique and specific. For Memmi, the value of "lived experience" is crucial in understanding how colonialism works, as he asserts in a passage in the preface to the 1966 edition of *The Colonizer and the Colonized* in which he enumerates aspects of his book that had been overlooked even by its admirers (15). The precise significance of his concept of lived experience becomes evident when one considers the manner in which it is exemplified in each of the portraits that are the focus of Memmi's analysis of colonialism. Each starts out from the premise that neither the colonizer nor the colonized is "born": "The colonial situation produces [*fabrique*] colonialists, just as it produces the colonized" (56, translation modified).

In the logic of this affirmation, a description of the lived experience of colonialism would constitute the crucial moment in the analysis of colonialism, because it is only in terms of the lived experience that we can come to understand how the colonial situation creates or produces both the colonizers and the colonized. If an inclination to domination or to being dominated were inherent in individuals or groups "by nature," then their lived experience or interiorization of colonialism would be derivative of and thus irrelevant to understanding the colonial situation. At the same time, if colonialism merely shaped the colonial subject once and for all time, that is, if interiorization were not a process, then an analysis of the experience of colonialism would be equally irrelevant to understanding its nature. Even more, there would be no lived experience of colonialism, no ongoing history of the frustrations, humiliations, compromises, and rejections that according to Memmi make up life in colonial society.

The significance Memmi attaches to his notion of lived experience implies the need not only for a concept of interiorization to account for colonialism but also for a concept of the (or an) unconscious. That the process of colonialism implies a collective or cultural unconscious is evident in Memmi's argument that the behavior of individuals in colonial society does not originate in conscious, personal intentions. This is certainly true in the case of the colonizer who refuses colonialism, and it also turns out to be the case for the colonized and even for the colonizer who accepts colonialism. Insofar as it is interiorized unconsciously, the power of the colonial situation to determine the individual is as great as and perhaps even greater than the power of the individual to determine it. When Memmi writes that the "colonial phenomenon" [*le fait colonial*] is "an *objective condition*, which imposes itself on the two partners to colonization," that is, on both the colonizer and the colonized,[6] he is stressing not only the economic and cultural dimensions of colonialism, but also its unconscious dimension—that is, the power of colonialism to shape the colonizer and the colonized "from within," to make the subjective experience of colonialism coincide with the objective dimension of colonialism. He is thus rejecting any notion of an original, unified subject that would remain unaffected by the colonial situation and retain its precolonial specificity or nature in it. But he is also rejecting the idea that the subjective is merely a reflection or a product of objective conditions when he insists that the nature of colonialism lies in the way it is "lived" by the colonizer and the colonized.

In *La Relation poétique*, Edouard Glissant has written of the cultural and poetic significance of the phenomenon of *métissage*. In its limited form, *métissage* is a process that can result in a creation or hardening of cultural or linguistic identities, in a form of multiculturalism. But Glissant also argues that it exists in a "general form," which he calls *créolisation* and defines as a "*métissage* without limits." This generalized *métissage* is "an encounter and a synthesis of two *différents* . . . whose results are unforeseeable. . . . [It produces an] explosion of cultures [which] is not their scattering or their mutual dilution. It is the violent sign of their consensual, not imposed, *partage* [a term that signifies both partition and sharing]" (46–47). In its general form, then, *métissage* is a process that is eminently cultural and at the same time disruptive of cultural identities.

It is clear that the process of interiorization analyzed by Memmi is in an important sense quite different from *métissage*, insofar as its context is not the "consensual" one evoked by Glissant but a colonial context of violence, exploitation, and the imposition of one culture on another. But at the same time, Memmi's analysis shows that, despite the economic structure and political realities of colonial society and despite the manner in which indigenous culture is depreciated and deformed by colonial ideology, a process of *métissage* is already underway in the colony, and ultimately undermines colonial identities by means of the very mechanism of interiorization that provides colonialism with its cultural/psychological basis.

In the case of the colonizer, the role played by interiorization is evident in the various symptoms of an unconscious sense of illegitimacy, which is fundamental to understanding his outlook and behavior. Memmi dubs this unconscious attitude the "Nero complex," and he explains it by referring to the character of the same name who is the protagonist of Racine's *Britannicus*. In Memmi's view, the sense of illegitimacy, which is fundamental to this character (and to the colonizer), is significant not only because it results from a specific experience or series of experiences but also because it becomes itself a primary factor in shaping events:

> [Like the colonizer,] Nero, the exemplary figure of the usurper, is thus led [in an attempt to justify his illegitimate status] to persecute Britannicus outrageously. . . . But the greater the harm he does him, the more he comes to embody this atrocious role [of the usurper] that he has chosen for himself. And the more deeply he sinks into injustice, the more he hates Britannicus and tries to get at him.   *(77)*

In contrast to Freud's Oedipus, whose "fulfillment of a wish" brings about his punishment, Nero is a figure who is punished from the start by the (unconscious) sense he has of himself as a usurper. This unconscious sense is as much the *cause* of his crimes as their result.

The importance of the notion of interiorization can thus be seen first of all in Memmi's portrait of the colonizer, who in Memmi's terms sooner or later must and will accept the role played by Nero in Racine's tragedy and the unconscious sense of illegitimacy that goes with it. An objection that comes to mind immediately here is that it is not at all obvious that the sense of being an usurper Memmi attributes to Racine's perverse hero is shared by the colonizer who accepts colonialism. The glaring inequities of colonial society seem to suggest that the colonizer feels no insecurity whatsoever in relation to the colonized. But Memmi argues that many of the most destructive features of colonialism are incomprehensible unless we suppose that some such sense of illegitimacy exists even—or perhaps especially—in the case of the most ardent colonialist: "Human relations in the colony would perhaps have been better, less crushing for the colonized, if the colonialist had been convinced of his legitimacy."[7] Memmi's point here is not that colonial society could have been reformed in some way to make it better or more acceptable, as he clearly demonstrates in his analysis of the case of the "colonizer who refuses" and clearly asserts in his conclusion.[8] It is that a cultural/psychological factor—a "complex of the usurper"—is involved in the relation of the colonizer to the colonized, a factor that leads to an attempt to crush and depreciate the colonized in a manner that cannot be accounted for solely in economic or political terms.

In his preface, Memmi makes a somewhat different argument that points, nonetheless, to the same underlying complex. Whereas in the passage referred to above he argues that the savage quality of the colonizer's dehumanization of the colonized betrays the existence of a Nero complex, in a brief passage from the preface to *The Colonizer and the Colonized* he suggests that the equally puzzling *inconsistency* of the colonizer's treatment of the colonized is another indication of the existence and role of the colonizer's sense of illegitimacy: "How could the colonizer both take care of his [colonized] workers and periodically gun down a crowd of the colonized?" (x, translation modified). On the surface, the colonizer who accepts colonialism is a puzzling mixture of good and bad, but Memmi's analysis suggests that these two dimensions of his persona are intimately connected by his sense of illegitimacy, which in certain instances can lead him to violence and in other instances to gestures of atonement.

For Memmi, the proof that the Nero complex exists lies in the ultranationalism (which is proto-fascist when it is not explicitly fascist) and above all in the racism of the colonizer, whose purpose, Memmi argues, is not merely to facilitate economic exploitation but to *justify* it. The irony is that in attempting to justify inequality, both nationalism and racism thereby testify to the fact that it cannot be justified:

> How can usurpation try to pass for legitimacy? One attempt can be made by demonstrating the usurper's eminent merits, so eminent that they deserve such compensation [that is, the privileges of the colonizer]. Another is to harp on the usurped's demerits, so deep that they cannot help but lead to misfortune. And these two efforts are in fact inseparable. . . . Moreover, this complementarity is not all there is to the complex relation of these two movements. It must be added that the more the usurped is crushed, the more the usurper triumphs in his usurpation. As a result, he himself confirms his guilt and his own condemnation. Thus the play of the mechanism is accentuated, ceaselessly propelled, aggravated by its own rhythm. *(52–53, translation modified)*

The self-inflicted punishment of the colonizer thus does not diminish or inhibit the tendency to commit or to perpetuate injustices. Instead it exacerbates and even is at the basis of that tendency.

Memmi's analysis of the "Nero complex" should not in any way be con-fused with an argument on behalf of the colonizer, a plea to his readers to extend sympathy to the colonizer for the suffering he endures due to the pangs of conscience. Memmi's point is that colonialism cannot end if its true nature has not been grasped, and in this sense, there is not and cannot be a fundamental conflict between a critical analysis of the implications of the process of interiorization and the cause of resistance. Indeed, many forms of resistance to colonialism continue to posit an identity—in this case, the neg-atively evaluated identity of the colonizer, who is supposed, for whatever rea-son, to be free of ambivalence in his relation to the economic system imposed by the colonial power (or whose ambivalence is held to be irrele-vant to the nature of that system), and whose cultural position is held to be correspondingly unambiguous. But once we have understood the complex role played by interiorization in the creation of the colonizer, then the limi-tations of such forms of resistance become clear.

Memmi's insistence on the central role played by the interiorization of culture thus distances him from Marxism, which identifies the economic structure of colonial society as what determines its character "in the last instance."[9] In this sense it is highly ironic that Fanon, rather than Memmi, should have emerged as such a prominent figure in the field of cultural stud-ies, because in *The Wretched of the Earth* in particular, Fanon argues in a clas-sically orthodox Marxist fashion that the cultural dimension of the struggle for liberation should be, and in principle is, subordinate to its economic and material dimension: "The responsibility of the colonized man of culture is not a responsibility to the national culture but a global responsibility to the totality of the nation, of which culture is, after all, one aspect. . . . To fight for national culture is first of all to fight for the liberation of the nation, the *material* matrix that makes culture possible" (187, translation modified, my emphasis). Fanon did indeed warn of the "pitfalls of national consciousness," but he did so from a Marxist perspective in which the national and cultural dimensions of the struggles for colonial liberation were always secondary and relatively superficial.[10]

Memmi, it is important to note, does not dispute the economic basis of colonialism or reject Marxist analysis as a valuable tool in combating colo-nial exploitation. As he states in the preface to *The Colonizer and the Colo-nized*: "I have been criticized for not having based my portraits [of the colo-nizer and the colonized] entirely on an economic structure. But I have repeated often enough that the notion of *privilege* is at the heart of the colo-nial relationship—and that privilege is undoubtedly economic. Let me take this opportunity to reaffirm this point strongly: for me the economic aspect of colonialism is fundamental" (xii). But Memmi goes on to stress with equal force that "colonial privilege is not solely economic," and *The Colonizer and the Colonized* as a whole confirms that for Memmi the cultural and symbolic nature of colonial privilege is no less important than and in no way subordinate to its economic nature. Memmi's discussion of Marxism and colonialism does not substitute cultural factors for economic determinants; instead its ultimate effect is to undermine both the cultural and the economic as principles of identity.

Memmi's insistence on the importance of the cultural factor is crucial in defining his relation to and distance from Marxism. But it is equally important to stress that, as we can see in the case of the "colonizer who accepts," the cultural factor only becomes active through interiorization, a process that is never neutral or unambivalent, *even* when it serves the colonizer's economic interests. It is the colonizer's ambivalence about his own position that lies at the basis of much of what is most destructive and most tenacious in colonialism, and yet this ambivalence is not accessible to individual analysis or treatment, any more than to a transformation of economic relationships alone. This is because it arises from or is the sign of an interiorization of culture and of cultural stereotypes, which is an inherently paradoxical process that blurs the boundary between individual and society.

II. Interiorization and the Colonized

Given that the Nero complex is linked by Memmi to an initial "usurpation" of the place of the colonized by the colonizer, it is difficult to imagine, at least on the face of it, that there could be such a thing as a "complex of the colonized" and a corresponding interiorization by the colonized of the colonial situation. Indeed, this is exactly what Fanon argues in *The Wretched of the Earth*. It should be stressed that there are many points on which Memmi's and Fanon's analyses of colonial society overlap.[11] But in *The Wretched of the Earth*, Fanon also diverges crucially from Memmi on the issue of what I have been calling interiorization, specifically as it relates to the colonized.

In simplest terms, for the author of *The Wretched of the Earth* there is no such thing as an interiorization of colonialism by the colonized: "During colonization, the colonized ceaselessly liberates himself between nine o'clock in the evening and six o'clock in the morning," that is to say, in his dreams (41, translation modified). The concept of the unconscious is central to Fanon's interpretation of colonialism, but in his later work its importance stems from his view of it as a reservoir for the authentic subjectivity and freedom of the colonized. According to Fanon's logic, that subjectivity remains intact in the face of colonial experience, because it can withdraw from the political and social arenas and gather force in the unconscious—until the day when it can express itself freely and openly in the struggle for liberation.

It is in the light of passages such as these that I would take issue with the argument made by Homi Bhabha in two recent articles, "The Other Question: Difference, Discrimination and the Discourse of Colonialism" and "Remembering Fanon: Self, Psyche, and the Colonial Condition," where Bhabha has sought to synthesize Frantz Fanon's theory of colonialism with Lacanian psychoanalytic theory. There are many questions that could be raised about Bhabha's interpretations of both Fanon and Lacan. But the most important in connection with the issue of interiorization concerns Fanon's concept of the unconscious as it is articulated in *The Wretched of the Earth*. Obviously Fanon's perspective combines psychoanalysis with a political theory of colonial society. However, it can be seen in numerous passages from *The Wretched of the Earth*, similar to the one quoted above, that in Fanon's terms the basis of that synthesis is the ultimately more profound nature of social analysis as compared with psychoanalysis. In this sense, Fanon himself could be said to oppose a synthesis that would merge the two, because this would presumably rob sociopolitical analysis of its primary role in the critique and destruction of colonialism.

It is true that even in *The Wretched of the Earth* Fanon acknowledges that the colonized frequently exhibits self-destructive behavior in a variety of forms. But such behavior does not relate to the possibility—or actuality—of an interiorization of colonialism, according to Fanon. It is instead to be understood only as the discharge of libidinal or aggressive forces dammed up in the unconscious by colonial repression.[12] Fanon argues that colonial repression is imposed on the colonized from without by the colonizer group, and hence it is never really successfully imposed at all. This explains why Fanon sees what he considers to be manifestations of the unconscious such as voodoo, possession by spirits, and exorcism as being produced by colonialism and as destined to disappear in the struggle for decolonization and the postcolonial period.[13] Like dreams, these practices provide a way for the colonized to discharge the psychic forces that are inhibited but not essentially compromised by colonialism.

Of course the picture of colonial society in *The Wretched of the Earth* differs in important ways from the one painted in *Black Skin, White Masks*, even or perhaps especially as concerns the phenomenon of interiorization. From its opening paradox—"At the risk of arousing the resentment of my colored brothers, I will say that the black man is not a man" (10)—Fanon's focus is as much on the interiorization of the colonial situation as on the manner in which "the racist . . . creates his inferior" (93). And *Black Skin, White Masks* not only opens with this seemingly unequivocal affirmation of the (negative) importance of "interiorization," it also ends with Fanon's personal rejection of a "black identity" for himself, clearly on the grounds that such an identity would be a confirmation of some of the worst aspects of colonialism rather than a liberation from them: "I am a man, and what I have to recapture is the whole past of the world. I am not responsible solely for the revolt in Santo Domingo" (226).

But even in this early work, sociopolitical analysis takes precedence over psychoanalysis at certain key moments, and this despite Fanon's critical analysis of the Marxism of Jean-Paul Sartre (132–39). Fanon concedes that blacks do interiorize the image of themselves created by colonialism. But he argues that what he calls the black inferiority complex, which is the consequence of this interiorization, is the result of a double process that is "*économique d'abord,*" "in the first place economic," and only secondarily psychological (13, translation modified). In proposing this interpretation of the interiorization of the colonized, he thus anticipates the argument that he will later make in Marxist terms in *The Wretched of the Earth.*

In his "Frantz Fanon and the Notion of 'Deficiency'," Memmi discusses the differences between his own interpretation of the importance of interiorization and that expressed by Fanon in a passage from *The Wretched of the Earth:*

> I claim, to the contrary [of Fanon], that in every dominated man there is a certain dose of *denial of self,* in large part born of his suppression and his exclusion. . . . How . . . could one hope for the contrary? When objective conditions are so heavy, so corrosive, how can one believe that there will be no destruction, no distortion of the soul, the physiognomy, and the conduct of the oppressed. You can't get out of it by saying that "the colonized is dominated, but not domesticated."[14] I apologize to the memory of Fanon, I say this not in order to diminish his courage and his conviction in a struggle for which he gave his life, but he sidesteps the issue. . . . In reality I think that . . . Fanon was perfectly cognizant of these effects [of colonialism] on the personality of the colonized; he could not not have noted them. But they embarrassed him and revolted him, because, like many defenders of the colonized, he had in him a certain dose of revolutionary romanticism.
>
> (*Dominated Man,* 86–87, translation modified)

As conveyed by the language Memmi quotes from *The Wretched of the Earth*, Fanon pictures the colonized as possessing an identity derived from his unconscious desire for freedom. In contrast, Memmi proposes a portrait of the colonized as split by a denial of self, because he has interiorized the law of a colonial society that rests on the devalorization of indigenous customs and peoples and in this way has confirmed the primary nature of the process of interiorization.

One could, of course, argue that there is nothing specifically unconscious and therefore nothing particularly radical about such a split and the conflict it presupposes. Both are clear and even self-evident in the lived experience of colonialism, where they take the form of an obvious choice for the colonized between assimilation and revolt. In Memmi's terms, however, the choice between these two options is simple and clear-cut only in appearance. His analyses of each, which form the two aspects of his portrait of the colonized, show them to be interconnected at many points. It is quite true that, on the surface, the desire for assimilation seems to imply a rejection of one's own group and a positive identification with the colonizers, which the colonizers themselves would welcome and want to foster. Memmi writes that, as such, the "love of the colonizer" exacts a terrible cost from the colonized, who, if he chooses assimilation as his means of liberating himself from colonial repression, can do so only at the price of "a systematic hostility towards himself" (124, translation modified).

Nonetheless, the project of assimilation reveals its profoundly ambiguous nature from the standpoint of both the colonizers and the colonized when the latter encounters what Memmi calls "the colonizer's rejection" (124, translation modified). In fact, Memmi argues, the colonizers never wanted assimilation, and the criticisms they make of those colonized who are assimilated—if they are successful they are labeled as "apes" who only know how to imitate (124)—reveal as much. Assimilation turns out to have a negative, critical significance in relation to the colonizer as well as to the colonized group.[15] That a possibility of assimilation exists means that the colonizers do not hold positions of privilege because of cultural qualities that are a birthright rather than an acquisition or usurpation. In this respect assimilation represents as much an attack on the foundations of the colonial system as a rejection of the indigenous culture.[16]

The other option open to the colonized is equally ambiguous in its significance. On the surface, the position of the colonized who rejects the colonizer and his culture and valorizes his own is much more coherent and even "healthy." It is important to note here that as Memmi goes on to discuss the complex significance of this choice, he does so only after affirming its necessity, inevitability, and dignity. But the ambiguities of the self-affirmation of the colonized are for Memmi nonetheless very real. The colonized who refuses his victimization by colonialism will accept himself as separate and different, but he cannot do this, Memmi argues, without accepting as his own a character that has been "delimited and defined by the colonizer" (136, translation modified). The colonized who revolts defines himself in terms of a tradition and religion that have been systematically devalorized by the colonizer, but in doing so he conforms more than ever to a stereotype produced by colonialism.

Of equally ambiguous significance is the colonized's transformation of this negative stereotype into a positive one. This transformation results in the fabrication of what Memmi calls a "*countermythology*. The negative myth thrust on him by the colonizer is succeeded by a positive myth about himself suggested by the colonized. . . . To hear the colonized and often his friends, everything is good, everything must be retained among his customs and traditions, his actions and plans; even the anachronous or disorderly, the immoral or mistaken" (139). Not only is the countermyth of the colonized just that—i.e., a myth that continues to define itself as the negation (and therefore as the confirmation) of the myth of the colonized created by the colonizers, it also leads to the same kind of violence as the symmetrical myth of the superiority of the colonizer, and therefore also to bad faith: "Realizing that these attitudes are essentially reactive, [the colonized] suffers from the pangs of bad faith. Uncertain of himself, he gives in to the intoxication of fury and violence. Uncertain of the necessity of this return to the [pre-colonial] past [which he typically idealizes], he reaffirms it aggressively. Uncertain of being able to convince others, he provokes them."[17]

III. Interiorization and the Struggle Against Colonialism and Racism

In *Civilization and Its Discontents*, Freud identified guilt as the source of the malaise associated with civilization. He went on to argue that unlike the suffering of the neurotic, which can be cured, there is no cure for this widespread suffering, inasmuch as the disease is one caused by civilization itself. In *The Colonizer and the Colonized*, Memmi similarly concludes his diagnosis of colonialism by considering the remedy for the situation he has been describing in his portraits of *The Colonizer and the Colonized*. Like Freud, he avoids putting himself in the position of the doctor of (colonial) civilization.[18] Unlike Freud, Memmi unequivocally states that there *is* a remedy for the disease of colonialism, and that, moreover, this remedy is inevitable: the disappearance of "contemporary colonization" (146).

But while in one sense the cure for colonial guilt is a simple matter, in another it is highly problematic, as Memmi indicates: "The liquidation of colonization is nothing but a prelude to complete liberation, to self-recovery" (151). In contrast to Fanon's insistence on the "absolute violence" of independence and the absolutely new beginning it creates for the newly liberated society, Memmi underscores its crucial but nonetheless far from totally determining character.[19] That the attitudes created by colonialism can and do survive the demise of colonial law, institutions, and even a colonial economic system is clearly suggested by Memmi, so that at the end of *The Colonizer and the Colonized* the idea of a "cure" appears in all its potential difficulty and elusiveness.[20]

Memmi does not explicitly provide us with the portrait of the free individual who has rid him- or herself of the last vestiges of colonial guilt—his implication being that in this case a portrait is not possible precisely because such an individual's actions and attitudes will have ceased to be structured and determined. But Memmi does permit us to distinguish between the former colonized who is simply independent (and the former colonizer who has withdrawn from the colony, but who continues to view colonialism in a positive light) and the free individual. From Memmi's perspective we can see the typical and particularly despicable ultranationalism of the actual or former colonizer not as a precondition of colonialism but as one of its most destructive effects. And we can see the more legitimate but nonetheless problematic nationalism of the colonized not as the resuscitation of the precolonial past, but as an effect of the colonial situation itself:

> In order to free himself from colonization, the colonized had to start from the position of his oppression, the deficiencies of his group. In order that his liberation may be complete, he must free himself from those conditions, which are of course inevitable, of his struggle. A nationalist, because he had to fight for the emergence and dignity of his nation, he must conquer himself and be free in relation to that nation. He can, of course, assert himself as a nationalist. But it is indispensable that he have a free choice and not that he exist only through his nation.   *(151–52)*

Memmi's portraits of both the colonizer and the colonized focus on the ambivalence necessarily connected to the process by which contradictory attitudes underlying the position of each partner to the colonial relation are interiorized. In doing so, he reveals the profoundly destructive psychological and social effects of such ambivalence when it must be disavowed.

What is at stake for Memmi, then, in his critique of the particularly destructive nationalism of the colonizer and the much more legitimate but still problematic nationalism of the colonized is not so much the freedom of the individual in relation to the nation—though Memmi never denies the importance of individual freedom. It is the idea of a culture that would not take the form of a suppression of the ambivalence implied by the process of interiorization, a process which is implicitly integral to all forms of human culture, even the most open and "least colonial."[21]

Memmi's analysis of the specifically cultural dimension of colonialism makes it clear that colonialism does not necessarily end when the means of economic production have been reappropriated by a new nation or even, it appears, by the most disadvantaged groups within the new nation. Given colonialism's specifically cultural dimension, it is unfortunately possible for it to survive the colony even in the most revolutionary of societies. Memmi's analysis of colonialism as well as his own subsequent work on the problem of racism strongly suggest that it is not enough to transform the economic or political structure of a society in order to change its culture. There is implicitly a need for a revolution in culture—not a "cultural revolution"— that will not necessarily follow from political and economic "liberation." At the same time, Memmi's analysis of the interiorization of culture suggests that the cultural forces that create and promote racism are not directly accessible to transformation. This is because, first of all, insofar as they are unconscious, their roots lie beyond the reach of traditional efforts of education and enlightenment. And second, it is not at all clear who the teacher or teachers of antiracism should be, since the cultural forces that promote racism are not just in others, but in all of us—as Memmi's portraits of the colonizer and the colonized, taken together, clearly confirm. It is in this spirit that Memmi, in an "Attempt at a Definition," writes of racism: "I have been forced . . . to abandon once and for all that *sociology of good intentions*, or psycho-pathology, which looks on racism as a monstrous and incomprehensible aberration on the part of certain social groups or a sort of madness on the part of certain individuals. . . . There are *bases* for racism within the individual human being and within the social group" (*Dominated Man*, 194–95).[22]

It could be argued that at this point in his analysis Memmi reaches a limit where, in an effort to understand racism and colonialism, he has connected them so closely with so-called normal attitudes and typical cultural situations that he has in effect legitimated them. Memmi himself appears to respond to such an objection when, in a subsequent work, he underscores

once again the central importance for him of the concept of "lived experience." In a postscript to *Dominated Man*, Memmi rejects the view that the
effects of colonial culture, of cultures in which minorities are oppressed, or
of industrial culture, even if they are destructive to some extent of all the
groups comprising them, are *equally* destructive of each group:

> I must, however, merely recall that this way of considering the misfor-
> tune of humanity as a whole is not as novel as it may appear. I don't say
> it is totally false or useless. For my part, I have shown that the colonizer
> *also* pays a price for colonization, and the White American, I am con-
> vinced, will not emerge unscathed from his confrontation with the
> Black. In a word, there exists an alienation of the oppressor as well. . . .
> However, does this alienation common to all men, this permanent mis-
> fortune, eclipse the various specific misfortunes, the particular oppres-
> sions from which each human group suffers? I don't believe so at all. . . .
> I ask, on the contrary, if it wouldn't be more appropriate even here to
> proceed to differential analyses. Not everyone suffers from the failure of
> industrial civilization in the same way and to the same extent. . . . Even
> in the midst of industrial civilization, finally, the question remains: who
> is actually oppressed, and to the advantage of whom?   *(210–11)*

The Colonizer and the Colonized reveals the importance of keeping before us
the universal significance of the colonial condition. At the same time,
through his emphasis on the importance of lived experience, Memmi also
demands that we keep before us the particularity of each instance of oppression, which can only be grasped in terms of a process of interiorization
whose reality lies as much in its cultural and individual specificity as in its
generality or universality.

In *Dominated Man*, Memmi describes the general project on which he
is still working: a "major book on oppression, which I am always planning,
which I might never achieve, but towards which I advance every day" ("Preface"). This ultimate work, or at any rate the idea of such an ultimate work,
is necessitated by Memmi's entire critical project, since it is only in terms of
such a "global theory" of oppression that the full significance of the situation
of the colonized can be understood. But in Memmi's terms such a work must
remain unfinished, a mere possibility. In *Dominated Man*, Memmi turns his
attention once again to the colonized, but he also goes on to analyze the
experience of "the Black man," "the Jew," "the worker," "the domestic ser-
vant," and what from Memmi's perspective is perhaps the most difficult of
all oppressions to analyze, because he recognizes an obligation to consider it
from the standpoint of an oppressor—that of "the woman." Implicitly,

Memmi's aim in taking up these additional cases of oppression is not to create an exhaustive inventory of all the possible types of oppression but rather to suggest that no single instance of oppression can be privileged, that is, considered primary or inclusive of all the others.

Despite his explicit refusal to consider oppression from the standpoint of a global theory or model that would privilege a single form of it as the most inclusive or exemplary, Memmi's work as a whole does nonetheless implicitly privilege a model that is singular in an important respect. As the title of the sequel to *The Colonizer and the Colonized* suggests, the model in question is offered by the situation of "dominated man." Though this sequel includes an essay on "the woman," when one considers Memmi's work as a whole, it is difficult to avoid concluding that the framework for his analysis of oppression remains by and large a humanism, understood as an androcentrism, that is obvious in his language ("dominated *man*," the portrait of the " *colonisateur*," not " *colonisatrice*," and of the " *colonisé*," not " *colonisée*," etc.) and choice of subject matter. It is true that his essay on the woman delineates specific characteristics of feminine oppression that do not clearly relate to his previous discussion of either economics or culture, thus suggesting the need for an opening up or a revision of his theory of (colonial) domination. But given that the picture Memmi offers of the woman is only a sketch, it is difficult to deny the limitation imposed on Memmi's analysis of oppression by his complicity with a traditional, male-centered humanism. Like the humanism of Senghor, Fanon, and others, Memmi's conception of oppression in terms of the situation of dominated *man* may be the aspect of his thought that ties it most closely to a specific historical context whose limitation in this regard seems as evident to us today as ours in this or other respects may seem one day to future generations.

There is, however, another important potential objection to Memmi's analysis of the colonial situation. It would be that in depicting the subjective experience of the colonizer and colonized as determined by the objective nature of the colonial situation, Memmi has indeed revealed the universal significance of the colonial experience and the corresponding naïveté of those who feel that because they do not live in a nominally colonialist society they have no involvement in and no responsibility for colonialism. But, such an argument would continue, Memmi has to pay dearly in order to make this point, because his portraits of *The Colonizer and the Colonized* also posit serious limitations on human freedom or even deny it altogether, insofar as Memmi shows the subjective experience of each conforming to and being determined by the objective nature of the colonial situation. According to this view, Memmi's portrait of colonialism would provide the basis for a radical critique of national identity and subjectivity, but in the process it would also negate the idea of freedom upon which opposition to colonial injustice is founded.[23]

Memmi's description of the self-condemnation felt by the various parties to colonialism needs to be considered once again in the light of this objection. As we have seen, this self-condemnation points to the existence of a split in each subject of colonialism, and this split, in turn, implies that the subject is both free and not free, that he or she is both the subject and the object of his or her (own?) condemnation. In other words, the split in the subject implies not merely a negation but rather a problematization of human freedom. In this sense, Memmi's portrait of colonial society provides a critique of the identity of both the colonizer and the colonized, without simply negating the freedom that is the basis of the resistance to colonialism.

While it does not offer an explicit portrait of the free human being and sustains the thesis of human freedom only problematically, *The Colonizer and the Colonized* is nonetheless unequivocally the expression of Memmi's engagement in the struggle against a racism that is as much an expression of culture as of an economic system. But its methods and strategy also reflect the notion that culture demands and gains its force through a process of interiorization, because what this work ultimately proposes is not merely what I would call a refutation of the arguments of racists or nationalists who are represented as opposing their myths to a reality they purportedly seek to mask. As Memmi argues, what makes colonialism and racism so destructive and resistance to them so difficult is their power to mold or create a reality that conforms to an important degree to their myths. In the absence of any "reality" or "essence" that could be opposed to the myths of colonialism, how is it possible to show that they are indeed myths and to combat their destructive power? In the chapter of *The Colonizer and the Colonized* entitled "Mythical Portrait of the Colonized," Memmi opposes colonial myths through a critique that explores their internal contradictions, in particular, their contradictory depiction of the colonized.

According to Memmi, the inconsistency of what he calls the "myth of the colonized" can be seen at every turn. To listen to the colonizer, the colonized "is simultaneously inferior and wicked, lazy and backward" (83). Taken together, these negative characterizations contradict each other and as a result reveal that each one is false. A related feature of the myth of the colonized is that it invariably transforms what in any other context would be virtues into weaknesses—as Memmi argues was the case with "Arab hospitality," which became, for the colonizers, the sign of the "irresponsibility and extravagance" (83) of the colonized. If one wants to make sense of or find a consistency to the various contradictions in what could be called the logic of the discourse of racism, Memmi argues, "it is useless to seek this consistency anywhere except in the colonizer himself. At the basis of the entire construction, one finally finds a common motive: the colonizer's economic and affective needs, which he substitutes for logic, and which dictate and explain each of the traits he assigns to the colonized" (83, translation modified). In the "Mythical Portrait of the Colonized," we can see that the analysis of the internal contradictions of colonialism does not suffer because it does not rest upon a theory or assumptions concerning the identity of the colonized. On the contrary, it takes its force from its critical perspective on identity.

The critical effects of *The Colonizer and the Colonized* thus lie not in the manner in which Memmi captures the essence or identity of each of the parties to the colonial relation, but rather in the persuasiveness with which he depicts a process of *métissage* that is inherent in the colonial situation and that the binary logic of colonialism is powerless to suppress. That such a process of *métissage* is the inevitable result of colonialism, and that it ultimately works as much or even more against the colonial system as for it, is indicated by Memmi in an autobiographical note in the preface to *The Colonizer and the Colonized.* Memmi stresses that as a Tunisian national, he was, like all other Tunisians, a victim of colonial oppression: "A second-class citizen, deprived of political rights, refused admission to most civil service departments, etc." (xiii). But Memmi also avers that his situation was not completely identical to that of Muslim Tunisian nationals. As a Jew, he was raised within a group whose members "endeavored to identify themselves with the French" (xiv). As a result of this complex set of identifications, his portraits of the colonized and the colonizer are both, as Memmi himself declares, in part portraits of himself. For he was "a kind of half-breed [*métis*] of colonization, who understood everyone, because he was not totally of anyone [*parce qu'il n'était totalement de personne*]" (xvi).

In his portrait of himself as the *métis* of colonialism, Memmi clearly suggests that the interiorization of culture he describes neither presupposes nor creates an identity that would subsume all the individual portraits within a single figure. Instead, interiorization and *métissage* need to be understood as processes that are both cultural and unconscious, processes that do not coincide with or belong to "anyone." In this sense, I would argue that a portrait of colonial society such as Memmi has provided can serve as the basis for a powerful critique of (neo)colonialism and racism and also elucidate the processes of interiorization-as-*métissage* that are inherent in all cultures, and that even the most repressive of colonial regimes cannot suppress. Memmi's *The Colonizer and the Colonized* testifies to the idea that there is a crucial role for the concept of culture in understanding one of the most important social phenomena of our time, but that cultural analysis can only realize its critical potential if we understand the way in which culture is disruptive, rather than simply constitutive, of all forms of identity.

By analyzing colonial culture in terms of the tension and the overlapping between the psychic and the cultural, Memmi's work exemplifies an open, undogmatic approach to cultural and social issues from which humanists and social scientists still have something to learn today. It has been argued that every discipline is in a sense forced to construct its own object. The (re)emergence of culture as an object of critical reflection has unquestionably opened up many new areas to investigation and critique, but it also has contributed to the construction of the cultural and the psychic as new or renewed interdisciplinary objects. In certain cases the psychic and the cultural have been conceived as two discrete and opposed terms. In others, one term has been posited as dominant or inclusive of the other. In contrast, Memmi's use of psychoanalysis to simultaneously challenge and affirm the determining role of culture testifies to the critical importance of challenging the construction of discrete objects of this type, whether they originate within a given discipline in the humanities or social sciences, on the borders between them, or in the newly opened spaces in which critical theory, cultural studies, and other interdisciplinary practices have arisen.

NOTES

1. The official purpose of the letter was to announce Césaire's resignation from the Communist Party. Even in resigning, Césaire stresses that he does not "make light of" the "*solidarités*" offered to "Negroes" by the Communist Party, which include "the French proletariat and, via communism . . . all the world's proletariats" (14–15). But he also stresses the legitimacy of the cultural ties of African and West Indian peoples with each other, regardless of whether they are communist or not, saying that these ties increasingly appear to form "a living brotherhood" rather than "what looks like the features of the coldest of all chilling abstractions" (15).

2. In recent essays, Lisa Lowe and Christopher Miller each refer to Fanon in order to make a similar point. See Lowe, "Literary Nomadics in Francophone Allegories of Postcolonialism: Pham Van Ky and Tahar Ben Jelloun" (1993) and Miller, "Nationalism as Resistance and Resistance to Nationalism in the Literature of Francophone Africa" (1993).

3. See his *Prospero and Caliban: The Psychology of Colonization.* This work was first published under the title *Psychologie de la Colonisation* (Paris: Editions du Seuil, 1950). If we were in any danger of forgetting this work, Fanon's devastating and accurate critique of it, in *Black Skin, White Masks,* would prevent us from doing so.

4. Albert Memmi's *The Colonizer and the Colonized* was originally published in

French under the title *Portrait du colonisé précédé de portrait du colonisateur* in 1957 and was republished in 1961, 1966, and 1985. It was written in Tunis and Paris in 1955–1956, and sections of it appeared in *Les Temps Modernes* and *L'Esprit* before it was published in book form.

5. Like Fanon, Memmi was born and grew up in French colonial society. The son of a Jewish artisan, he lived with his family in the Jewish ghetto in Tunis and attended lycée on a scholarship. An early autobiographical novel, *The Pillar of Salt*, which was orig-inally published in French in 1953, describes the painful economic circumstances of his own and other Jewish families, along with his alienation from both his own social and cultural milieu and that of the colonizer. By the mid-fifties Memmi had moved to Paris, where he was later to teach philosophy at the University of Paris X.

6. *Portrait du colonisé*, 15, my translation. The passage corresponding to the one in which this phrase appears in the original French is found on p. xi of the English transla-tion. The phrase itself, however, was omitted by the translator.

7. Ibid., 76. The corresponding passage appears in the English translation on page 51, but with the omission of "less crushing for the colonized," which corresponds to the French "moins accablantes pour le colonisé."

8. Though Memmi confesses that he had originally hoped colonial culture could be improved (he writes of an "*aménagement*") and the rights of the colonized recognized by the colonizer, he ultimately concluded such an "improvement could not take place because it was impossible. Contemporary colonization carried an inherent contradiction which, sooner or later, would cause it to die" (146).

9. In *La Guerre des Algériens*, a collection of essays written between 1956 and 1963 in connection with his role as a member of the political group *Socialisme ou barbarie*, Jean-François Lyotard provides numerous details that document many of Memmi's argu-ments, even though Lyotard's position as expressed in these essays also differs in certain important respects from that of Memmi. Several of these essays have been translated into English and appear in a collection of Lyotard's *Political Writing*. In one of them, "A New Phase in the Algerian Question," written in 1957, Lyotard writes in regard to the conflict between nationalism and the left: "The position of the Soviet bloc with respect to the Algerian question remains unchanged for the time being; it explains the persistent inac-tivity of the French Communist Party on the French scene [*sur le plan métropolitain*]. The aim is to keep Algeria as much as possible in the sphere of French economic, politi-cal, and cultural domination, in order to improve the prospects of the Algerian branch of the French Communist Party" (187, translation slightly modified). This passage confirms Memmi's view of the complicity of Communists in both North Africa and in France, not to mention in the Soviet Union, with French nationalists. Communists saw the decolo-nization movements as hostile to their interests for the same reasons that they were hos-tile to French national interests.

10. Given the predominantly cultural nature of Said's project in *Culture and Impe-rialism* and Fanon's contrasting views concerning the subordinate position of culture in the struggle for decolonization, it is interesting to consider the manner in which Said attempts to integrate Fanon into his own perspective. In Said's terms, Fanon is a central figure in the history of cultural resistance to imperialism, because he, "more dramatically and decisively than anyone . . . impugns imperialism for what it has created by acts of

powerful rhetorical and structured summary" (268–69). Despite Fanon's polemic against culture, Said is able to rescue him for his own cultural project by suggesting that the power of Fanon's work is primarily rhetorical and narrative (and therefore cultural). In doing so, Said evades the problem posed by Fanon's explicit allegiance to Marxism and the manner in which it dictates and dominates his view of culture. Fanon can still be seen as a uniquely "decisive" figure in spite of the fact that Said in a later passage criticizes "Western Marxism," along with European theory in general, because they "haven't in the main proved themselves to be reliable allies in the resistance to imperialism" (278).

11. Fanon's critique in *Black Skin, White Masks* of O. Mannoni's psychoanalytic interpretation of colonialism relates to this point in particularly forceful terms. In it, he exposes and rejects the intellectual and moral hypocrisy of the idea that the colonizers represent an abnormal or neurotic group of Europeans and that the destructive nature of colonialism can be explained as a consequence of this abnormality. Fanon argues that in making such an argument, Mannoni not only evades his own responsibility as a European for colonialism, but also fails to see that the colonial situation cannot be simply treated as a particular case, as one manifestation of the Oedipus complex among others.

12. "This collective self-destruction, which is very concrete in tribal struggles, is one of the ways in which the muscular tension of the colonized is released" (43, translation modified).

13. "During the struggle for liberation, we shall see a singular disaffection for these practices (i.e. 'vampirisme,' possession by djinns, by zombies, etc.)" (46).

14. "Il est dominé, mais non domestiqué," *Les Damnés de la terre*, 19. A different translation of this passage appears in *The Wretched of the Earth*, 42.

15. The negative, critical significance of assimilation is highlighted by André Breton in his preface to the 1947 edition of Aimé Césaire's *Cahier d'un retour au pays natal*, where he writes of the author: "C'est un Noir qui manie la langue française comme il n'est pas aujourd'hui un Blanc pour la manier" ("He is a black who handles the French language like no white today can"), 80. For Breton, this epic poem and also the review *Tropiques*, which Césaire founded during the Occupation, gave voice to a politics which, unlike that of the French press, exemplified the most clear-sighted and courageous opposition to fascism. Breton sees Césaire's masterful use of the French language as a similarly forceful challenge to the politics of racism, as the perfect cultural counterpart to his political project.

16. Memmi's view of assimilation is sustained and amplified in Ferdinand Oyono's *Houseboy*. Like Memmi, Oyono shows the ambiguity of assimilation in the figure of his hero, Toundi, when he depicts the violence directed at this model houseboy by his colonial masters. In a recent essay, Christopher Miller argues that Toundi's apparent passivity in relation to the colonial system and his conscientious performance of his household duties have a critical impact. In this sense, his passivity is *only* apparent. It "must . . . not be taken at face value. It is a strategy of resistance. This rather obvious point has nonetheless been missed by some critics of *Une vie de boy*, who have seen in Toundi nothing but the 'passive' victim of the colonizer's violence" (84).

17. *Portrait du colonisé*, 154. The third sentence in the quoted passage has been omitted from the English translation, 139. A perspective similar to that of Memmi's on the ambiguous significance of both assimilation and rejection of the culture of the colonizer

can be found in Herman Lebovics's *True France: The Wars over Cultural Identity, 1900–1945*. Lebovics discusses the situation of Vietnam under French colonialism and draws conclusions from it that he applies to the situation of the French colonies generally: "The radical (essentially metaphysical) separation of the identities of oppressor and oppressed is neither good theory nor good history. Traditions, even top-down invented ones, can become battlefields in culture wars. Once implanted, they change, perhaps even becoming weapons of the colonized against the metropole. Moreover, the resisters often also invent some of their own traditions, which may bear little relation to history. Nor is it useful to see the struggle as one between the little identity defending itself against the grand one. Serious penalties are attached to the heedless pursuit of difference and diversity as *the* key to liberation and autonomy" (123–24).

18. Toward the conclusion to his text, Freud first warns against the theoretical dangers inherent in applying concepts that have been effective in one context—in this case the psychological or psychoanalytic—to another—such as the social or the cultural. He then goes on to write of the difficulties of a practical implementation of psychoanalytic solutions to social problems: "And as regards the therapeutic application of our knowledge, what would be the use of the most correct analysis of social neuroses, since no one possesses the authority to impose such a therapy upon the group?" (*Civilization and Its Discontents*, 144).

19. "National liberation, national renaissance, the restoration of nationhood to the people, commonwealth: whatever may be the headings used or the new formulas introduced, decolonisation is always a violent phenomenon. . . . Without any period of transition, there is a total, complete and absolute substitution. It is true that we could equally well stress the rise of a new nation, the setting up of a new state, its diplomatic relations, and its economic and political trends. But we have precisely chosen to speak of that kind of *tabula rasa* which characterises at the outset all decolonisation" (*The Wretched of the Earth*, 29).

20. In "Critical Fanonism," Henry Gates concludes his discussion of the relation between culture and psychoanalysis with a comment that simultaneously affirms the importance of Fanon's attempt to come to grips with the problem of colonialism and also distances his own perspective from that of Fanon, in particular as concerns his view of the "absolute violence" of independence: "We too, just as much as Fanon, may be fated to rehearse the agonisms of a culture that may never earn the title of *post*colonial" (470). This concluding statement recalls another comment made earlier in the essay in which Gates connects an awareness of the ongoing nature of the decolonization process with a recognition of the crucial relevance of psychoanalysis to the theory of colonial society: "Freud's pessimistic vision of 'analysis interminable' would then refer us to a process of decolonization interminable" (466).

21. It is in terms of Memmi's suggestion that ambivalence is an integral part of the cultural process that Homi Bhabha's attempt to synthesize the theory of colonial discourse with Lacanian psychoanalytic theory appears most problematic. Though many specific questions could be raised about Bhabha's interpretation of Lacan, an overriding one is whether or not, given the cultural theory that subtends Lacanian psychoanalytic theory, a Lacanian model can be used to address the problem posed to the theory of culture by the colonial experience. "The Function and Field of Speech and Language in Psy-

choanalysis," for example, contains passages referring directly to the work of Lévi-Strauss and to the social organization of "the Pacific Argonauts," an allusion to Malinowski's *Argonauts of the Western Pacific* (61, 68). These passages attest to the existence of a Lacanian anthropology and a view of culture that equates its most authentic embodiments—what Lévi-Strauss called the culture of "peoples without history"—with the Symbolic. According to such a view of culture, the ambivalence accompanying the interiorization of culture would be experienced only in the context of those cultures Lacan designates as "modern," and not in the context of these ancient, Symbolic cultures. In the terms of Lacan's anthropology, societies in which there is social repression represent deviations from a Symbolic norm in which culture and individual are fully and freely integrated in and through language. In this sense, it is questionable whether Lacanian theory, any more than Marxist theory, can account for the interiorization of culture in terms other than those of an "abnormal anthropology."

22. In a subsequent book, *Dependence: A Sketch for a Portrait of the Dependent,* Memmi goes even further in the direction of depsychopathologizing colonialism when he considers the complex relations between domination and the phenomenon he calls "dependency."

23. It should be noted that this was clearly not the view of prominent figures in the African independence movements such as Léopold Senghor and Alioune Diop, for whom the *Portrait du colonisé* represented an important step in the decolonization process. Their judgments of *Portrait du colonisé* are quoted in the editor's note to the 1954 edition. According to Senghor: "Albert Memmi's book will constitute a kind of document to which historians of colonization will have to refer" (my translation, 10). This assessment is echoed by Diop: "We consider this *Portrait* to be the best of the works published on colonial psychology" (my translation, 10).

WORKS CITED

Bhabha, Homi. "The Other Question: Difference, Discrimination and the Discourse of Colonialism." In Russell Ferguson, Martha Sener, and Trinh T. Minh-Ha, eds., *Out There: Marginalization and Contemporary Culture.* Cambridge: MIT Press, 1990.

——. "Remembering Fanon: Self, Psyche, and the Colonial Condition." In Barbara Krugers and Phil Mariani, eds., *Remaking History.* Seattle: Bay Press, 1989.

Breton, André. Preface to Aimé Césaire, *Cahier d'un retour au pays natal.* Paris: Présence Africaine, 1983.

Césaire, Aimé. *Letter to Maurice Thorez.* Paris: Présence Africaine, 1956.

Fanon, Frantz. *Black Skin, White Masks.* Trans. Charles Lam Markmann. New York: Grove Press, 1967.

——. *Les Damnés de la terre.* Paris: François Maspero, 1968.

——. *The Wretched of the Earth.* Trans. Constance Farrington. New York: Grove Press, 1965.

Freud, Sigmund. *Civilization and Its Discontents. The Complete Psychological Works of Sigmund Freud,* v. 21. Ed. James Strachey. London: Hogarth Press, 1953.

Gates, Henry L. "Critical Fanonism." *Critical Inquiry* (11)(3)(Spring 1991).

Glissant, Edouard. *La Relation poétique.* Paris: Seuil, 1992.

Lacan, Jacques. "The Function and Field of Speech and Language in Psychoanalysis." In *Ecrits: A Selection.* Trans. Alan Sheridan. New York: Norton, 1977.

Lebovics, Herman. *True France: The Wars Over Cultural Identity, 1900–1945.* Ithaca: Cornell University Press, 1992.

Lowe, Lisa. "Literary Nomadics in Francophone Allegories of Postcolonialism: Pham Van Ky and Tahar Ben Jelloun." *Post-Colonial Conditions: Exiles, Migrations, and Nomadisms. Yale French Studies* 1(82)(1993).

Lyotard, Jean-François. *La Guerre des Algériens.* Paris: Galilée, 1989.

——. *Political Writings.* Trans. Bill Readings and Kevin Paul. Minneapolis: University of Minnesota Press, 1993.

Mannoni, Octave. *Prospero and Caliban: The Psychology of Colonization.* Trans. Pamela Powesland. Ann Arbor: University of Michigan Press, 1990.

Memmi, Albert. *The Colonizer and the Colonized.* Trans. Howard Greenfield. Boston: Beacon Press, 1967.

——. *Dependence: A Sketch for a Portrait of the Dependent.* Trans. Philip A. Facey. Boston: Beacon Press, 1984.

——. *Dominated Man: Notes Towards a Portrait.* New York: Orion Press, 1968.

——. *The Pillar of Salt.* Trans. Edward Roditi. Chicago: J. P. O'Hara, 1955.

——. *Portrait du colonisé précédé de portrait du colonisateur.* Paris: Gallimard, 1985.

Miller, Christopher. "Nationalism as Resistance and Resistance to Nationalism in the Literature of Francophone Africa." *Post/Colonial Conditions: Exiles, Migrations, and Nomadisms. Yale French Studies* 1(82)(1993).

Oyono, Ferdinand. *Houseboy.* Trans. John Reed. London: Heinemann, 1966.

Said, Edward. *Culture and Imperialism.* New York: Knopf, 1993.

NINE

Textual Agents: History at "The End of History"

Mark Poster

An Electronic Context

As the twenty-first century approaches, the discipline of history faces a greatly altered landscape. The manner in which the profession defines the situation in which it finds itself and the quality of its response will no doubt seriously affect its future viability. If it misreads the historical conjuncture or if it responds in limited, defensive ways, its prospects will surely be diminished. I present this essay to fellow historians with the intention of furthering a discussion about the conditions of a discipline confronted by new possibilities and new alternatives. As far as I can determine, very little discussion is taking place, both within the academy and outside it, about the methods and topics of historical analysis in relation to a changing world. As professionals, historians do not reflect on the conditions of their knowledge production in anything like a systematic way, and as a result, I fear, their work resonates less and less with general social and cultural concerns because their foundational assumptions and intellectual gestures connect less and less obviously with impulses of contemporary life.

The problem is how to define the changes in the context that is most pertinent to the discipline of history. Some commentators point to global political and economic trends: the disappearance of communism from Europe and that region's emerging unification; the rise of strong economies in Asia; the shrinking size of the planet through improvements in transportation and revolutions in communication; the relentless deterioration of the ecology; the burgeoning of transnational corporations. Just as worthy of attention are the cultural and social changes: increased populations and their volatile geographic movements; vast gaps in the conditions of the wealthy and the poor; deteriorating urban centers and spreading postsuburban agglomerations; the disintegration of bourgeois, literate culture and its replacement by massified visual culture; the fragmentation of cultures in the advanced societies into an uncertain mixture of mutually hostile or indifferent groupings of fundamentalists, xenophobics, gangs, the homeless, nostalgics, new agers, postnuclear families, and new social movements all encompassed by a commodification of even the least recess of the life world and its legitimation by greedy invocations of a mythic free market. Finally, academia itself is rocked by privatization under the euphemism "technology transfer," vocationalization, multiculturalism, challenging new technologies of teaching and research, interdisciplinarity, and a potpourri of methods and theories that many find troubling, even frightening. Lists of novelties such as this one are easy to compose, but the question remains which items are substantial rather than ephemeral and which may serve as a stimulus to the formulation of new issues for historical investigation.

Not everything in this paragraph of changes is either horrible or directly relevant to the discipline of history. Yet enough items are pertinent enough to evoke a spate of apocalyptic discourses about the end of history or the birth of postmodern society, issues that I shall discuss below. For the moment, however, I want to draw the reader's attention to one particular contextual novelty that I consider central to the renewal of the discipline of history: the introduction, during the course of the nineteenth and twentieth centuries, of electronic systems of communication, from the telegraph and the phonograph to the telephone and radio, film and television, VCRs and fax machines, the computer and the Internet, and finally the emerging integration of all these technologies. I argue that these technologies reconfigure the sense of space and time in a manner that calls into question basic assumptions of the discipline of history.[1]

The assumptions I have in mind concern the figure of the individual in the modern period. Modern historiography assumes a discursive author who is culturally situated in linear time and perspectival space. Modernity constitutes the individual in a horizon of time and space such that lawful causalities govern people, events, and things. Modern individuals are able to be characterized as rational and autonomous in good part because of their cultural imbrication with this configuration of space-time. Both the historian and the historical topics he or she writes about are inscribed in such scenes, fields, or narratives, and these are taken for granted as basic conditions of life.

Electronic communications systems drastically restructure this modern space-time matrix. In the words of Paul Virilio, "Point of view, the omnipresent center of the ancient perspective design, gives way to the televised instantaneity of a prospective observation, of a glance that pierces through the appearances of the greatest distances and the widest expanses."[2] Virilio characterizes electronic communications such as television as introducing simultaneity and immediacy, qualities of experience that reorganize the individual's sense of position in time and space. When one receives impressions via broadcast technology from Kuwait, halfway around the globe, as they occur and when, using newer technologies such as video conferencing on the Internet, one responds with the same instantaneity, then Euclidean space and linear time lose their credibility and cultural force. With the restructuring of space-time complexes so also is transformed the general relation of human beings to machines. In these electronic communication systems, which are new skins of language, or new wrappings of signification, an interface is constructed between the human and the machine that connects them and configures them in new assemblages. The old distinctions collapse: subject/object, living/dead, human/machine, inside/outside, observer/observed, sender/receiver. Again to quote Virilio: "The theoretical and practical importance of the notion of interface, that drastically new surface that annuls the classical separation of position, of instant or object [is changed] . . . in favor of an almost instantaneous configuration in which the observer and the observed are roughly linked, confused, and chained by an encoded language" (52). With this altered cultural context the very conditions of being an individual appear as historically constructed and thus as a topic of historical investigation.

Agents versus Texts

With such new cultural formations spreading every moment to more and more social locations, having increasing influence on the identities of individuals, we may well ask how the discipline of history is to account for them and come to terms with them. Some evidence of historians' response is found in their reaction to theoretical developments in the 1970s and 1980s known as poststructuralism. I shall review and criticize this reaction not to defend poststructuralism but with the aim of lowering the level of polemics and indicating how a more open attitude to recent cultural trends might benefit the discipline.

The salient position of historians in recent debates over poststructuralism is to defend the notion of agents over the theory of texts. They complain that poststructuralism (or literary theory, or postmodernism) reduces everything to texts. The notorious citation from Derrida, "There is nothing outside the text" (*il n'y a pas de hors-texte*), has become for many the rallying point of the defense of history. This statement proves, the argument runs, that all this theory stuff is bankrupt because it ignores experience in favor of discourse, dissolves agency into textuality, substitutes nihilism for social commitment. In Brian Palmer's words, "Critical theory is no substitute for historical materialism; language is not life. . . . Left to its own devices, poststructuralist theory will always stop short of interpretive clarity and a relationship to the past premised on political integrity and a contextualized situating of historical agents within structures of determination."[3] Palmer's Marxist complaint is fairly representative of most social and political historians in its suspicion that poststructuralism somehow occludes life, reality, politics. Just beneath the surface of the raging argument lurks the hydra of moralism: history is threatened, for these commentators, by dandies; ironists; overly clever, self-promoting, irresponsible, careerist academic stars. Actually, this defense of history attains little more than the conventional position of respectability. It is too easy to show that Derrida in the above quotation does not mean that reality consists entirely of texts, which is surely not a position worthy of much attention anyway. Instead, deconstruction privileges a certain principle of interpretation that it finds in what it constitutes theoretically as "texts," for instance, as compared with "books." It is also easy to show how disciplinary training in history systematically draws attention away from the obvious fact that historians produce a discourse or text and that they do so primarily by performing operations upon other discourses they call documents and, finally, that these aspects of disciplinary work are not innocent trivialities but major characteristics of the kind of writing known as "history."[4]

Derrida's statement that there is "nothing outside the text" attempts to substitute his notion of writing for interpretive schemes that pretend to have access to a full reality. The phrase appears in his works first in relation to the interpretation of Rousseau, where Derrida insists that the notions of "real life" and "natural presence" are not suitable approaches. Acts of interpretation require a sense of distance from their object.[5] Derrida's insistence on the separateness of the interpreter from the object interpreted is the theme of the next appearance of the phrase five years later in the context of a critique of idealism, the Hegelian effort to center reality in the interiority of consciousness. Since historians cite the phrase in order to condemn poststructuralism wholesale, it is worth reproducing it in its context:

To allege that there is no absolute outside of the text is not to postulate some ideal immanence, the incessant reconstitution of writing's
relation to itself. What is in question is no longer an idealist or theological operation which, in a Hegelian manner, would suspend and
sublate what is outside discourse, logos, the concept, or the idea. The
text *affirms* the outside, marks the limits of this speculative operation,
deconstructs and reduces to the status of "effects" all the predicates
through which speculation appropriates the outside. If there is nothing outside the text, this implies, with the transformation of the concept of text in general, that the text is no longer the snug airtight inside
of an interiority or an identity-to-itself . . . but rather a different placement of the effects of opening and closing.[6]

Derrida's "nothing outside the text" is a critique of idealist strategies of mar-
ginalizing everything outside consciousness. Deconstruction introduces a
materialist notion of differential textuality to save exteriority, the outside,
the other from the pretensions of a colonizing concept of mind.[7]

    In the defense of agency over texts, the historian attempts to preserve
the unity and the validity of the *experience* of historical figures. This bespeaks
the fine intention of celebrating the capacity of individuals to resist oppression and the historian's role in preserving the memory of that resistance. The
historian does not want to be reminded that texts intervene between
him/herself and the historical moment, that texts have multiple meanings,
and that reading texts is not only an act of decoding but also an interpretation, one that relies in part upon the historian's own situation. Reminders of
these complications may annoy some historians and appear as efforts to discredit progressive political positions, as trivial digressions from the giant task
of preserving the memory of oppression so as to aid the project of emancipation. On the contrary, the insistence on the text is the only interpretive
stance that is able to resist the hegemonic figure of "the individual," because
only when the individual is understood as discursively constructed is the
false naturalness of the modern, bourgeois individual disrupted. It may be
paradoxical to some but it is nonetheless the case that critical historiography
proceeds only by dispelling the view of the agent as the unified center of
meaning. For this reason many antiracist and feminist critics have risked the
dangers of "the linguistic turn" not in spite of but because of their commit-
ments to radical politics.[8] Only by attending to the role of language can one
comprehend the operations through which gender and race are socially constituted.

    Instead of entering further into the epistemological and moral debate over the relative importance or intrinsic truth of text and agency for the discipline of history, I shall perform a historicist operation upon these terms. I shall argue that one way to assess the merits of the two positions is to study the historical transformation of the context in which the terms are deployed, especially in the last fifty years. I contend that the importance of the poststructuralist attention to language for the discipline of history derives not so much from the logical value of the arguments of poststructuralists or from their demonstrations and exemplifications (although I regard these as largely successful) but from the trend toward the extension of textuality throughout social space, on the one hand, and the increasing reduction of agency to a dim ideological hope, on the other. For what has occurred in the advanced industrial societies with increasing rapidity over the course of this century is the dissemination of technologies of symbolization or language machines, a process that may be described as the electronic textualization of daily life and the concomitant transformations of agency, transformations of the constitution of individuals as fixed identities (autonomous, self-regulating, independent) into subjects that are multiple, diffuse, fragmentary. The old (modern) agent worked with machines on natural materials to form commodities, lived near other workers and kin in urban communities, walked to work or traveled by public transport, and read newspapers but engaged as a communicator mostly in face-to-face relations. The new (postmodern) agent works mostly on symbols using computers, lives in isolation from other workers and kin, travels to work by car, and receives news and entertainment from television.

The new individual agent uses not only the telephone, radio, movies, and television but also computers, fax machines, copiers, stereos, portable music players, VCRs, remote telephones, and the Internet. All the second group have been installed in the home since the 1970s, a dramatic, even astonishing, reorganization of this space. The home has been segmented into multiple cultures and even more significantly respacialized.[9] Each home is now plugged into vast systems of symbolic exchange, interfaced with global networks of electronic communications. As a result individuals are now constituted as subjects in relation to these complex information systems: they are points in circuits of language-image flows; they are, in short, *textualized agents*. Their perceptions are organized by information machines. Their sense of time is edited and recombined by systems of digitized sequencing: real time on tape, movies on demand, fast forward, instant replay, pause, slow motion. Their conversations are delivered by satellite, crossing the globe as easily as one crosses the street. Their knowledge is stored in electromagnetic archives that render reproduction literally immaterial, instantaneous, and, in principle, nearly cost free. Individuals who have this experience do not stand outside the world of objects, observing, exercising rational faculties, and maintaining a stable character. The individuals constituted by the new modes of information are immersed and dispersed in textualized practices where grounds are less important than moves. Certainly not all individuals are affected equally by these trends; there are disparities introduced by hierarchies of race, gender, class, and age. Such inequalities in the dissemination of textual agency need to be studied, heeded, and addressed politically.

Historians appear to me to be doing badly in this debate with the theorists not because they are wrong in some objective or logical sense but because history has changed. The argument for the authentic experience of agents—the voice of the people—the argument that the role of the historian is to represent this agency no longer speaks to the situation of individuals or groups in the advanced societies. E. P. Thompson's moving tribute to agency as authentic experience, while eloquent, has lost its critical edge:

> I am seeking to rescue the poor stockinger, the Luddite cropper, the "obsolete" hand-loom weaver, the "utopian artisan" . . . from the enormous condescension of posterity. Their crafts and traditions may have been dying. Their hostility to the new industrialism may have been backward-looking. Their communitarian ideals may have been fantasies. Their insurrectionary conspiracies may have been foolhardy. But they lived through these times of acute social disturbance, and we did not. Their aspirations were valid in terms of their own experience.[10]

Thompson's book, *The Making of the English Working Class*, became a model for U.S. socialist historians who took it as a vindication of the working class today because it refutes the "condescension" of those historians who celebrate industrialization while ignoring its tragic costs. The "experience" of Thompson's obsolete artisans operated for these New Left historians to fortify the hopes for industrial democracy in the 1960s. But as Marx says, one must write history and struggle for freedom in relation to the circumstances in which one is born, and these circumstances have changed deeply and continue to do so whether historians recognize it, embrace it, or bemoan it. The past may become a coherent anchor of resistance or aid to critique only in relation to a given present and from its point of view. Can the past still serve as an arm of resistance? If so, what shape does this past have? What is the role of historical discourse in an age defined by altered, postmodern circumstances? Which past or whose past needs to be remembered in order to face more clearly the difficulties of today? How must this past be theoretically structured so as to make it an object about which knowledge can be formulated and produced? The issue is not whether it is possible to write a history of the conditions of the early industrial working class but whether it is pertinent. Is it not rather more important today to understand the early conditions of print and electronic communications and how these have altered the configuration of identity? If so, we require theories that allow us to understand such cultural processes, theories that constitute the historical field around the issue of identity formation.

Tell the Truth

One of the few efforts to confront the issue of a postmodern history is *Telling the Truth About History*, written by three highly respected and rightfully distinguished historians, Joyce Appleby, Lynn Hunt, and Margaret Jacob. I shall evaluate their endeavor to define the present situation of historical writing, to assess the ability of existing paradigms to cope with it, and to offer new directions for the discipline. My goal here is neither to praise nor to blame this book and these authors but to further the development of a critical historiography. Yet I must praise the authors once at the outset for taking up such an important task when so few others dare to do so. The vitality of the discipline of history, it seems to me, depends upon serious engagements with important intellectual trends and consequent epistemological readjustments in research topics, curricular design, and writing strategies. The laudable aim of the authors of *Telling the Truth About History* is to "provide general readers, history students, and professional historians with some sense of the debates currently raging about history's relationship to scientific truth, objectivity, postmodernism, and the politics of identity."[11] They know full well that historians are woefully inadequate in examining the nature of their own discourse, the general traits of their own kind of truth. It is not at all unusual that professional meetings of historians include few discussions of the nature of historical truth.[12] Appleby, Hunt, and Jacob are fully aware of historians' limited response to these issues as well as the discipline's great theoretical deficit. Unfortunately, they are too quick to provide historians with an alibi for this shortcoming: "Professional historians have been so successfully socialized by demands to publish that we have little time or inclination to participate in general debates about the meaning of our work" (9). This passage performs a very dangerous shift in the focus of the book, exonerating historians from self-reflexivity and setting into motion conditions for a limiting defensive posture toward "general debates about the meaning of our work."

The pressure to publish does not in itself exclude "general debates about the meaning of our work." One may publish exactly such works as Appleby, Hunt, and Jacob have done here. What hides behind this argument is the disciplinary rule against self-reflection, the injunction to produce works that add to the font of knowledge rather than question its worth. Language that suggests theoretical reflection, or mentions or discusses difficult concepts from current debates, is generally regarded as inappropriate for inclusion in the texts of historians. In a debate with Dominick LaCapra about the value of self-reflective intellectual history, for example, David Hollinger grudgingly admits some worth to histories of the canon of great texts but warns against the danger of trivialization and "loss of meaningful contact with the concrete" in purely methodological writings. Hollinger continues: "We then find ourselves talking about what others have said about what historians should do, and speculating about what might happen if historians followed this or that general approach. When we cross this perimeter, then, we move from 'discourse about discourse about discourse' to discourse about discourse about discourse about discourse."[13] If Hollinger's views may be taken as representative of the profession, the discipline has very successfully socialized its members to regard "general debates about the meaning of our work" as futile diversions from the "real" labor of gathering, sorting, and representing so-called facts. Yet when the context of historiographical production has altered, as I believe it has today, it becomes time to take stock. It may well be, as one commentator put it, that "The time has come that we should *think* about the past, rather than *investigate* it. . . . A phase in historiography has perhaps now begun in which meaning is more important than reconstruction."[14] The question of history's "truth" is now urgent, elevating self-reflexive writing, "discourse about discourse about discourse," into a matter of serious concern. Appleby, Hunt, and Jacob therefore deserve our thanks for boldly broaching the question of postmodernism and the current state of the discipline.

Historians have indeed been socialized by the discipline of history to avoid questions about the meaning of their own work. Any study of the nature of the truth about history must surely face the issue of what kind of truth historians produce and what mechanisms of self-criticism are built into disciplinary training. One might expect that a book on the topic of historical truth would raise questions about the validity and vigor of current disciplinary practices, that a major concern of such a volume would be a search for methods to evaluate disciplinary protocols. One might expect in fact that a theory such as Foucault's discourse analysis would be a natural choice in this quest. In part, the authors do just that, arguing that Foucault and Derrida have much of value to teach the historian. But the brunt of their position is that external forces have reshaped the environment in which history is written and taught, that these external forces have an ambivalent impact upon the profession, and, finally, that the discipline must preserve and conserve, as much as it is able, the standard of objective truth. The impression one gains from the book is that without the incitement of these external forces the internal protocols of historical work would not require examination. Although I agree with them that external forces are bearing down on the discipline I differ from them over which forces are most cogent and, above all, how these stimulate self-reflexive critique. While I regard changes in our context as opportunities for new research directions, Appleby, Hunt, and Jacob react, I believe, too defensively.

The title of the book, *Telling the Truth About History*, points to the subject very well: the question that needs to be asked is, What is the status of the knowledge produced in the discourse of history? Is this knowledge objective and universal or something less than that? Peter Novick's *That Noble Dream* demonstrated conclusively that historical knowledge has long been grounded in claims of objectivity that he characterizes as a "collection of assumptions" and "attitudes," including "a commitment to the reality of the past and to truth as correspondence to that reality; a sharp separation between knower and known, between fact and value, and, above all, between history and fiction."[15] Appleby, Hunt, and Jacob argue that this "absolutist" position about truth is no longer tenable, and that Foucault and Derrida are the ablest critics of that stance and the surest guides to a path beyond it. At the same time, they reject what they take to be the alternative of Foucault and Derrida to the absolutist position on truth—postmodernist relativism—seeking instead a new middle ground in the "qualified objectivity" of "practical realism."

The title of their book indicates the performative dynamics of the problem: that historical discourse is intertwined with power; that it has power effects; and that it is produced and deployed in a field of power relations.[16] For "telling the truth" is what our parents and grade-school teachers urged upon us when we were children, as the authors perhaps are ironically hinting. "Telling the truth" was presented to us as a solemn moral duty. We learned that it is *good* to tell the truth, that truth is a moral as well as epistemological act. And we learned this lesson from people who had authority over us and were much more powerful than ourselves, people we loved and feared deeply. We learned that truth was good in situations where we had little choice but to agree. Further we often learned this lesson in messy or ambiguous circumstances when our self-interest might have indicated otherwise: that the truth would hurt us or hurt someone we cared for; that the truth was another person's understanding of what happened that we were being coerced to adopt and repeat; that this same truth meant one thing to one person and something quite different to another. In these experiences, however understood, we were constituted as subjects who must tell the truth, as subjects for whom telling the truth is not simply an epistemological achievement but a moral and political one as well.

I do not know if the title resonated this way for the authors, but their argument certainly gives precedence to the moral and political force of "telling the truth about history" over the properly epistemological level. Regardless of its epistemological value, truth is for them a *moral* goal: "We are arguing here that truths about the past are . . . worth struggling for" (7). The problem with moral positions such as this is that they often hide or shield problems and uncertainties; they prevent certain questions from being brought into the open. The reader is coerced into consenting to the morally correct point of view as other positions are demeaned and presented in a bad light. In the case of *Telling the Truth*, historical truth is defended against the "cynicism" and "nihilism" of relativists who apparently attack it. The authors ominously warn the reader, "Every time people go down the relativist road, the path darkens and the light recedes from the tunnel" (193). One dramatic theme coursing through the book, then, is the moral defense of the truth against those who would relativize it. What is hidden by this moral posture, I contend, is the extent to which the discourse of history may itself be implicated in the state of affairs the authors wish to criticize. By externalizing the source of the problem to grand political trends (multiculturalism) and, in their eyes, questionable theoretical developments (postmodernism), they make it impossible to assess the extent to which the kinds of truths produced by historians are complicit, intentionally or not, with dangerous political and cultural conditions.

Telling the Truth is trapped in a deep ambivalence. Appleby, Hunt, and Jacob want to argue that recent democratizing political trends are positive and that the discipline of history ought to further such trends. At the same time they assert that these trends undermine objective truth and promote nihilism:

> Our central argument is that skepticism and relativism about truth, not only in science but also in history and politics, have grown out of the insistent democratization of American society [the inclusion of

workers, women, and minorities in the political process]. . . . We endorse the insights and revisions made possible by democratization, [i.e.,] healthy skepticism . . . [and] a multicultural approach to human history . . . but we reject the cynicism and nihilism that accompany contemporary relativism. (3–4)

The simple presence of large numbers of ethnic minorities in the classroom makes untenable Eurocentric and universalizing approaches to Western history. The discipline of history had been implicated in these repressive tendencies by its commitment to absolute, universal, objective truth. How, then, to rid the discipline of its Eurocentric epistemology but still maintain a posture toward the truth that is compatible with democratic politics? Here is the intellectual drama of *Telling the Truth*, the pivot of its successes and limitations.

The authors adopt a peculiar strategy: they argue that Derrida and Foucault best articulate a critique of Eurocentric "absolutist" knowledge, that Derrida and Foucault are postmodernists, and that postmodernism, drawing conclusions from its critique, goes too far in the direction of relativism and nihilism by reducing reality to language. To save history for democracy, the authors claim, one must depart from the postmodernists and return to a revitalized objective truth. While I agree with the first proposition, I disagree with the second and third. I shall take up these arguments in turn.

The label *postmodernist* for Foucault and Derrida is of course inappropriate in that neither accepted it and both no doubt would reject it. Derrida, for instance, explicitly rejects the label *nihilist*, a term Appleby, Hunt, and Jacob associate with postmodernism. In an interview with Richard Kearney published in 1984, Derrida responded sharply to the charge that deconstruction sees language as referring only to itself:

> It is totally false to suggest that deconstruction is a suspension of reference. Deconstruction is always deeply concerned with the "other" of language. I never cease to be surprised by critics who see my work as a declaration that there is nothing beyond language, that we are imprisoned in language; it is, in fact, saying the exact opposite. . . . I totally refuse the label of nihilism which has been ascribed to me and my American colleagues. Deconstruction is not an enclosure in nothingness, but an openness towards the other.[17]

But the labeling of Foucault and Derrida as postmodernist is not in itself a problem for me because the same demurrals have been made by the French thinkers in relation to the term *poststructuralist,* which I regard nonetheless as a valid and useful label for both of them. The difficulty with the term *post-modernist* is that, applied to these thinkers, the term loses its meaning as a designator of a new cultural trend or even a principle of social organization. By missing the chance to understand postmodern culture in particular as an important part of the contemporary conjuncture, one that relates to multi-culturalism and therefore to the fate of democracy as the authors understand it, Appleby, Hunt, and Jacob fail to come to terms with the relation of history to these developments. Postmodernity becomes for them a series of intellectual mistakes, theoretical exaggerations, ideological threats. If they understood postmodernism as a dominant *cultural* trend they might have had to bring into question certain habits of disciplinary practice. They might at that point find Foucault and Derrida's critiques of the absolutist knowledge produced by the *modernist* historian more appealing. For Appleby, Hunt, and Jacob want their politics of democracy along with their objective historical knowledge, except as it requires to be updated for the needs and conditions of women and minorities. They have not examined seriously enough the crisis of the discipline produced by these changes as well as those associated with postmodern culture.

Appleby, Hunt, and Jacob raise several arguments against the postmodernists. The success of their project for a renewal of historical writing hinges on the strength of this critique. They claim first that the postmodernist "argument against the unified self . . . undermine[s] the premises of multiculturalism. Without an identifiable self [note the slippage from "unified" to "identifiable" self—do they imply that the only "identifiable" self is a "unified" one?], there would be no need to worry about differing cultures, ethnic pride, and battered identities" (202). Multiculturalism for them depends upon a unified/identifiable subject, upon a grounded, essentialized notion of the individual as rooted in a tradition or culture. Yet many of the leading theorists of multiculturalism associate such a view of the subject with a wrong-headed, conservative stance. Stuart Hall, a founder of the Birmingham cultural studies movement, contends that only a nonunified concept of identity allows a proper understanding of "the traumatic character of 'the colonial experience.' "[18] He then defines identity in the language of Ernesto Laclau and Derrida: "Cultural identities are the points of identification, the unstable points of identification or suture, which are made, within the discourses of history and culture. Not an essence but a *positioning*" (395). The decisive issue for Hall and many other theorists of multiculturalism is that only a "postmodernist" understanding of the individual as complex, unstable, and constructed allows for a properly *historical* grasp of minority experience.[19] Only if the self is not already unified is its construction in history possible. The cultural-political mechanisms of this construction were the explicit aim of Foucault's writing in the 1970s. Appleby, Hunt, and Jacob play to unfortunate nationalist tendencies in some ethnic movements by their insistence on the self as unified. They also display an unfortunate ignorance of the state of the debate with multiculturalist discourse, a failing no doubt shared widely among historians who assiduously avoid these theoretical discussions.

Appleby, Hunt, and Jacob next charge the postmodernists with a loss of will: "Postmodernists are deeply disillusioned intellectuals. . . . Postmodernism is an ironic, perhaps even despairing view of the world" (206–7). Postmodernists are portrayed as members of a white, male, European mandarin class whose historical moment has passed. Their somber ideas are reflections of social and cultural decrepitude. Certainly the writings of Derrida and Foucault are contemporary with the decline of working-class politics, the crumbling of European empires, and the emergence of social movements like feminism and multiculturalism that do not take as their center the subject positions of white male intellectuals. Yet empirically both Foucault and Derrida (along with Althusser, Deleuze, Guattari, Lyotard, de Certeau, and many others) participated in radical politics, organized movements and institutions, and were quite active in world affairs. Among contemporary French intellectuals perhaps only Baudrillard exudes the *Weltschmerz* bemoaned by the historians, although even here the case is arguable. The postmodernists do, however, critique the modernist view of the intellectual, with its claims of authority to universal truth, its pretension to discern the shape of human history, past and future, and its husbanding of "the truth."

Thus Appleby, Hunt, and Jacob are right to condemn the postmodernists for offering no vision of the future: "Postmodernism cannot provide models for the future when it claims to refuse the entire idea of offering models for the future" (237). And they are right to characterize the postmodernists as opposed to totalizing narratives: "Postmodernism attacks meta-narrative" (232). Yet they fail to see that these self-imposed limitations on discursive forms are precisely correctives to the "absolutisms" that they themselves complained about earlier in their book. The postmodernists place restrictions on discourse at those points where, in the modern period, it has led into justifications of political power (Lenin's view of the role of theory in relation to the working class or the legitimation of the unified nation in the United States by historical writing, as Appleby, Hunt, and Jacob themselves so ably demonstrate) or the cultural suturing of hegemonic identity (supports for the rational male subject). They do not recognize the postmodernist strategy of substituting what Foucault called "a specific intellectual" for the universal one of the modernist past. The historians continuously make erratic and dubious judgments about the postmodernists, displaying a serious lack of understanding of the latter's work. For instance, they accuse the postmodernists of opposing the narrative form as "inherently ideological and hence obfuscating" (232). "Obfuscating" suggests an opposite of transparency when instead Derrida and Foucault search for the way narrative structures the meaning of a text without the promise of total clarity. Even worse, Appleby, Hunt, and Jacob banish the postmodernists from the house of history: "In the final analysis, then, there can be no postmodern history" (237). This terrible gesture of exclusion forecloses the possibility that aspects of the thought of Derrida and Foucault might prove useful or even crucial for a reconstruction of the discipline of history or the development of a "new cultural history," a project once highly touted by Lynn Hunt. It also dismisses without examination those historians who explicitly turn to these thinkers for support.

The final criticism of Foucault and Derrida by the historians points directly to the question of "the truth." For Appleby, Hunt, and Jacob, notwithstanding their rejection of epistemological "absolutisms," transparent knowledge of the world is the only basis for truth: "If postmodern theories are taken seriously, there is no transhistorical or transcendent grounds for interpretation, and human beings have no unmediated access to the world of things or events" (225). The historian must have, for them, a privileged position of observation and on that basis establish the truth of the past. This is the nub of the disagreement. If the historians are correct then the critique of logocentrism or Western epistemology by Foucault and Derrida would be superfluous, even a waste of time. Historians, in their "unmediated" relation to events, need only busy themselves with recording the people's wrongs along with the wrongs of the people. But Appleby, Hunt, and Jacob have already shown us that historians never have such a lofty perch. They have shown how American historians of the early nineteenth century, for example, eagerly and with the best (revolutionary) intentions, produced "the nation" for the nation, happily excluding women, blacks, and Native Americans. They have shown that historical writing has discursive effects that by no means reflect an "unmediated" relation to events. Thus their argument falls flat that Derrida and Foucault deflect historians away from producing truth toward examining the truths they do produce: "Were this version of postmodernism applied to history, the search for truths about the past would be displaced by the self-reflexive analysis of historians' ways of fictively producing convincing 'truth-effects'" (227). What could be more "fictive" as a "truth-effect" than the sign of the unified nation in the early national period of American history in the writings of historians? And what could be more useful than a self-reflective analysis of this discursive production? The discipline of history, it would appear, is perfectly ripe for an extended period of "self-reflexive analysis" as it confronts the confusion of deep cultural transformations.

Appleby, Hunt, and Jacob misinterpret Foucault and Derrida's stance against totalizing discourse as a depoliticizing move when in fact it is an attempt to renew the work of critique. The strategy of the little narrative or detotalized discourse, the effort to decouple monographic works from grand narratives, is precisely an attempt to produce a truth that delegitimates modern cultural and social forms. Some cultural historians have already forged ahead in this direction, offering a microhistory that disrupts linear narratives. The effort here is to discover a form of writing that does not mimic the cultural presuppositions of the subjects being discussed, a sort of ethnographic alienation effect within historical writing itself.[20] This writing is only relativist if absolutism is presumed as the governing norm. Certainly microhistory, like Foucault's discourse analysis and Derrida's deconstruction, cannot claim unconditional objectivity, but it does assert claims of truth, conditional and finite, but truth claims nonetheless. What Appleby, Hunt, and Jacob fail to understand is that the strategic hermeneutics of Foucault and Derrida are not designed to discredit discursive truth but to fortify it by removing legitimizing, foundational gestures that undermine its credibility.

The issue of the excess relativism of Derrida and Foucault can only be measured against the degree of change required in the protocols of the discipline. I suppose it would be pleasant to continue to espouse the same terms as in the past (objectivity, science, truth), if with a touch of skepticism; in Thomas Haskell's terms, to prefer "a sensible moderate" stance toward epistemological issues.[21] But the issue raised by the postmodernists and studiously ignored by historians is to reveal the true historicity of historical knowledge, not to show that it is therefore weak, relative, and insignificant: these are critical judgments from within the modern episteme of absolutism. The point of Foucault and Derrida's arguments against objectivist, mimetic, representational truth is that truth matters quite a bit and that only a deconstructed analytic position can reveal the dangers it contains without completely falling back into them, which remains a hazard—*the* hazard, perhaps—of disciplinary discourse. Appleby, Hunt, and Jacob's strategy of colonizing the term *postmodern* with the figures of Derrida and Foucault and then criticizing their ideas by citing for the most part the work of writers like

Sande Cohen[22] and Elizabeth Ermarth[23] prevents them from contextualizing their own discursive intervention. For we are indeed entering a period of cultural life that does not fit within modernist horizons, a postmodern period in that sense, in which social life is increasingly textualized, in which language undergoes the drastic rewrapping of the mode of information or electronic technologies. At this time the discipline of history needs new cognitive maps, new strategies of analysis and new thought experiments, and it is very likely that the most profound and serious thinkers of the recent past—Foucault and Derrida—will be most helpful in this endeavor. The very charges the historians made against the postmodernists—linguistic determinism and the reduction of the social and natural world to language and of context to text (230)—are exactly our best bets (of course, not as formulated in the terms of the critique) for rethinking disciplinary protocols. The attack on texts in the name of agency becomes instead a search to make sense of a world of textual agents.

The End

Historians are not shaken by talk of an end to history. For most historians history is a real sequence of events that will end only with the last gasp of the last human being. History and humanity are coterminous. In a sense, the grounds for this position are impeccable. We may freely grant that human experience has a temporal dimension that may at any time be represented as historical discourse. And yet no one may care. Only in some cultures are such discourses regarded as significant. It is worth recalling that the kind of writing produced by members of the American Historical Association is a recent phenomenon—a century old—and may well not last another. The question I wish to raise then is not the end of history as an aspect of human experience but the end of history as a discipline. Arguments are being raised more and more frequently that the kind of writing done by historians does not address the concerns of the day, that it is being done better by individuals trained in other disciplines, or that it supports an outmoded and dangerous institution: the nation-state. Should the discipline of history continue and, if so, on what basis? In order to respond to this question I must first clarify the issues of that other end, the debate over the end of history.

The question of the end has no doubt been raised from the beginning. Its recent incarnation is certainly animated by Francis Fukuyama's 1989 essay "The End of History" and its expansion in 1992 into a book, *The End of His-*

tory and the Last Man, as well as by the general debate over postmodernity in such works as Gianni Vattimo's *The End of Modernity* (1985) and Jean Baudrillard's *The Illusion of the End* (1992). Leading practitioners of the main standpoints in the dispute over history and postmodernism have written major essays in response to Fukuyama: for Marxists, Perry Anderson's "The Ends of History" (1992), and for poststructuralists, Jacques Derrida's *Specters of Marx* (1993). In reviewing this literature, one largely overlooked by the authors of *Telling the Truth About History*, I shall glean and sift arguments about the current state of history (Has it come to an end?) in relation to the current state of the discipline of history (How ought it respond to the situation?). In other words, these debates may help to define the present conjuncture and in that way may have an important impact on determining the directions the discipline of history might pursue.

In what many might regard as a departure from his earlier work, Derrida's *Specters of Marx* evaluates Marxist theory and in so doing reviews Fukuyama's discussion of the end-of-history theme. Certainly the occasion of a conference on Marx in the spring of 1992 at the University of California, Riverside, to which Derrida was invited to present a keynote address, helps to explain the shift of attention to Marx. But this interest may be connected as well to the collapse of East European communism and the demise of the Soviet Union in the late 1980s. It may also be linked to Derrida's concern with politics and related issues since the 1988 revelations about the early writings of his friend Paul de Man. Since that time Derrida's courses at the University of California, Irvine—on themes such as friendship, the witness, the secret—as well as his published writings—on European unification[24] and on Benjamin's *Moscow Diaries*,[25] for instance—suggest an increasing interest on his part in world affairs and political theory. But none of this prepares the reader of *Specters of Marx* for Derrida's explicit pledge of allegiance to and avowal of affinity with Marxism ("of a certain kind"), with democracy, with the Enlightenment, and with the project of emancipation. Over the years Derrida made clear his preference for these keystones of the political Left. Yet Derrida's systematic avoidance of direct, propositional statements as contradictory to the spirit of deconstruction renders particularly dramatic his unambiguous declaration of allegiance.

As the reader might anticipate, Derrida elaborates in *Specters of Marx* what surely had been taken as a minor literary image by commentators on Marx—the figure of the ghost—into a central problem of historical materialism. The ghost, for Derrida, indicates a rich, provocative turn in Marx's discourse but also an opportunity partly lost or defeated by the persistence in his writing of logocentrism or ontology:

Marx continues to want to ground his critique or his exorcism of the spectral simulacrum in an ontology. It is a—critical but pre-deconstructive—ontology of presence as actual reality and as objectivity. This critical ontology means to deploy the possibility of dissipating the phantom, let us venture to say again of conjuring it away as representative consciousness of a subject, and of bringing this representation back to the world of labor, production, and exchange, so as to reduce it to its conditions.   *(170)*

Derrida boldly proposes to improve upon Marx, to eliminate his "predeconstructive" limitation, to "radicalize" him, and calls for "a new International" that will instantiate "a new Enlightenment for the century to come. And without renouncing an ideal of democracy and emancipation, but rather by trying to think it and put it to work otherwise."[26] These dramatic gestures are warranted, Derrida argues, by several unique features of the historical context:

1. the existence of deconstruction as a tool of analysis that, he states, "has always pointed out the irreducibility of affirmation and therefore of the promise . . . of justice" (90);

2. the massive existence of "violence, inequality, exclusion, famine" resulting in unprecedented oppression, starvation, and even extermination (85);

3. the astounding centralization of power in the nation-state by dint of vast "concentrations of techno-scientific capital" (85); and

4. the spread of "new tele-techno-media" that transform public space and politics, infusing them with "ghosts" or "the spectral" (102).

Given this definition of the conjuncture, of the urgency of mass misery and the concentration of destructive power in state and corporate institutions, Fukuyama's celebration of the final victory of liberal capitalism appears worse than naïve. And this is exactly how Derrida regards *The End of History and the Last Man*. For Derrida, Fukuyama first commits the scholar's sin of ignoring relevant texts concerning the question of the end of history.[27] Fukuyama is indeed ignorant of the fascinating discussion in France in the 1950s and 1960s of the very issues he raises today.[28] In addition, Derrida shows how Fukuyama confuses two versions of the concept of the end: the ideal and the fact. Is democracy as an ideal triumphant over the globe or is it so in fact? In the final analysis, Fukuyama emerges as a poor reader of the Hegelian tradition of the concept of the end of history and a

poor analyst of the political situation of the present and the relative realization of anything like justice, so that his discourse is little more than a dangerous apology for the status quo. With regard to my earlier discussion of
Telling the Truth About History, it is worth noting that deconstruction, or
postmodernism, emerges in *Specters of Marx* as neither pessimist, lost in
texts, nihilist, nor relativist. Derrida presents an analysis of the *context* and
adopts a clear, although somewhat undefined, political position. Through
the analysis of Marx's image of the ghost and the discourse of Fukuyama
about the end, Derrida, as postmodernist, engages fully with the political
issues of the day. One may object to the claims Derrida makes for deconstruction as the basis for a new international and for the renewal of a nonre-
ligious "messianic" spirit that will serve as a political beacon in the new millennium and as the true inheritor of Marx.[29] But one may not accuse Derrida of cynicism, apoliticism, and the like.

A reading of *The End of History and the Last Man* largely confirms Derrida's judgment of its weaknesses.[30] Fukuyama infuses new energy into the
cliché "glib generalization." He manages to combine Hegel, Marx, Nietzsche, and Kojève—thinkers scorned and thought dangerous by Anglo-
American liberal and analytic traditions of thought—into a celebratory
medley for the folk tune of U.S. capitalism and democracy. Under the cloak
of the "speculative" tradition of continental philosophy, Fukuyama toots the
fanfare of the end of history as the victory of Western ideals: "At the end of
history, there are no serious ideological competitors left to liberal democracy."[31] The advance of science, the expansion of wealth, the collapse of
communism, and the spread of democratic institutions and values denote,
for Fukuyama, the achievement and culmination of "History" as a grand
narrative or total theory, not, let it be noted, "history" as the sequence of
events that never ends (xii). Feminism and postcolonial theory are not even
considered as possible worthy competitors to liberalism. Putting them with
socialist visions and ecological standpoints—in short, granting the lack of
competitors—by no means guarantees that new positions will not emerge in
the future, that liberalism in any form is adequate as an ideological framework for the realization of freedom in the present context, or that such freedom or any substantial version of it has in fact been realized by any, much
less by all, societies.

What escapes Derrida's notice in Fukuyama's imagined narrative ending
is an unbearable, unrelenting, and completely unself-conscious masculin-
ism. There are no worthy competitors, announces *The End of History*, so the
game is over and the game is won, as if world history were a football game.
In order to decorate this crude, muscular position in refined garments of dis-

course, Fukuyama turns to Kojève's reading of Hegel's struggle for recognition, finding in it a "thymotic" competition for prestige, a prideful, willful insistence on self-worth (xix) that bristles with testosteronic overtones, which allegedly drive the engines of history toward the telos of democracy. The realization of democracy relies, he contends, on an "irrational" self-assertion of its value and a lusty struggle for the victory of that vision. With history concluded, a new problem emerges for "the last man [sic]": "*megalothymia* finds outlets increasingly in purely formal activities like sports, mountain climbing, auto racing, and the like" (318). Fukuyama has apparently read not a single work of feminist theory (he cites none), or he might learn from some of this literature that his "end of history" is easily comprehensible as the end of the white, male metanarrative, the end of the heroic bourgeois epoch, and the emergence of a time in which the nonthymotic types are able to maintain full agendas without filling time by auto racing.[32] Fukuyama's celebration of the end punctuates more than anything else the era of unself-conscious patriarchy. For feminists the struggles over abortion and child care are history, and they are not over. If, for Fukuyama, there are no compelling political visions beyond liberal capitalism, it may be that this is so only from the vantage point of the Western masculine imagination and its obsession with the battle of nation-states. At the end of Fukuyama's history it is not clear if one is to celebrate the victory over communism or mourn the disappearance of the struggle against it: masculine *thymos* now has nothing left to accomplish. Meanwhile, the effects of the enormous gains of the women's movement have not even begun to be felt as new forms of gender relations, family structures, and child-rearing patterns are being invented and put into place, transforming fundamental aspects of culture and society.[33]

The other great achievement of *The End of History and the Last Man* is the transformation of what might have been a crisis of U.S. liberal-conservative politics into a self-congratulatory festival. The disappearance of East European and Soviet communism and the consequent evaporation of the cold war (and what an awesome opportunity for thymotic release that provided!) opened the danger of a political vacuum: in this case the end meant the literal vaporization of the enemy. So much of U.S. political culture and economic success in the postwar era hinged upon the competition with the Soviets that their sudden, unexpected absence threatens not only economic instability but deep political disorientation. Instead of facing the consequences and possibilities of a political life without this ultimate enemy, Fukuyama provides a grinning, blissful, comedic narrative; he writes the "Hollywood ending" of American cold war history. His book is a distraction for U.S. public life faced with the prospect of self-examination and reevaluation on the occasion of the end of the cold war. Now that the resources and energy previously allocated to that struggle (whatever its legitimacy) are no longer needed, what shall be done with them, and what have we learned from the experience?

Fukuyama defines his theoretical accomplishment as the demonstration of "a coherent and directional Universal History of mankind" (xxiii). Like Hegel's owl of Minerva taking flight at dusk, Fukuyama inscribes his Universal History after the fact, at the end. The end of history as a struggle for recognition, a "thymotic" contest, a rise of democracy allows Fukuyama the luxury of asserting the viability of the perspective of a universal history. The worldwide victory of liberalism gives epistemological force, in his eyes, to the discourse of universal history. The argument of postmodern theorists, to the contrary, is that "the end" means exactly the opposite: it means that such long-range or total histories are *not* possible. Of course the end for the postmodernists is different from that of Fukuyama, but the contrast in reactions to the same periodizing gesture is worth noting: both characterize the present as an "end," but each draws very different conclusions.

The literature on postmodernism is now enormous and the definitions of the term various and contradictory. I have raised the issue here in relation to the discipline of history and the way postmodernism serves as a new context for its self-reflection. With that in mind, Lyotard's now-classic use of the term *postmodern* as "incredulity toward metanarratives" is most pertinent.[34] If he is correct, it is no longer possible to do exactly what Fukuyama asserts he has done: to present a coherent view of the human past as a single story. Lyotard's argument is that changes in the nature, production, and distribution of knowledge (the use of the computer in particular) render incoherent the grand narratives of the Enlightenment, where human history is a single tale of the progress of freedom. Instead, justice is furthered if the principle of difference inherent in "small narratives" is legitimated. Rather than a march toward a monolithic culture of rational, fixed identities, what is emerging in history, for Lyotard, is a multiplicity of incompatible points of view, a tapestry of diverse subject positions. Fredric Jameson's equally classic response to Lyotard is that postmodernism is better understood as the "cultural dominant" of "late capitalism." In this way, he preserves the claims for a Marxist grand narrative while admitting with Lyotard drastic novelties in the cultural configuration of the present.[35] Both cases confront an end (for Lyotard, that of modernity itself; for Jameson, of modern culture only), but in neither case is history as such theorized as terminated. What characterizes the writing about postmodernism contra Appleby, Hunt, and Jacob is not a gloomy end of all things but a periodization and an articulation of a beginning, that of the postmodern.

Many theorists have discerned difficulties with the postmodern position. Gianni Vattimo, for instance, points out that Lyotard's announcement of the demise of totalizing history is itself a totalization. In addition, the thesis of postmodernity is flawed by the contradiction that the periodization of the "post," signaling a new epoch is a characteristically *modernist* intellectual gesture, the announcement of a new set of concepts in opposition to prevailing ones.[36] Yet for Vattimo there is a sense of a deep change, of a new experience of history as precisely an "end of historicity." Arnold Gehlen prefers the term *posthistoire* for this perception that individuals no longer inscribe their own lives in a grand historical narrative the way the modern bourgeois once did, individuals no longer orient themselves and fix their identities in the tale of human progress.[37] The incredulity toward metanarratives is then not so much an epistemological critique of totalizing narratives as an empirical judgment about experience or culture or daily life in highly industrialized societies. At this point it becomes clear that what is at stake is not so much the nature of the past and the status of discourses about it as a change in the present and the consequent impossibility of maintaining earlier forms of discourse about the past. The postmodern antitotalizing totalization is thus less a contradiction than an expression of the paradox of present conditions of living, writing, and observation.[38] To enunciate the postmodern is to refuse the modern and at the same time to invoke a modern form of discourse.[39] Put simply, one cannot formulate a description of the postmodern without at least implicitly referring to the totality of the past. The discipline of history must then develop discursive strategies that detotalize the past while recognizing a moment of totalization in its own epistemological position.

Whatever logical traps are entailed in the postmodern thesis, all theorists point to the role of electronic information machines, a new technoculture, as a salient determinant of the end of history. In Paul Virilio's words, "We are in fact switching from the extensive time of history to the intensive time of momentariness without history—with the aid of contemporary technologies."[40] However regrettable it may appear to some, daily life increasingly includes electronically mediated communications that position participants or audiences in a space-time continuum that is discontinuous and simultaneous rather than linear, dispersed and ubiquitous rather than perspectival. These are the cultural constituents of television, film, computer communication, and the rest, and they have already deeply transformed the characteristics of subjectivity of those exposed to them. This mode of infor-

mation is spreading throughout the institutions of modern society and turning them inside out, making them postmodern.

In Koselleck's terms, historical time is generated by "the tension
between experience and expectation which, in ever-changing patterns,
brings about new resolutions."[41] Postmodernity is such a new resolution of
these constituents of temporality. Modernity (*Neuzeit*), Koselleck argues,
constructs the pattern as a gap between past and future, a difference between
experience and expectation in which what is anticipated diverges more and
more from what has been. The future receives value as the past is discarded.
In the premodern temporality of a "peasant-artisan world," Koselleck points
out, expectations fed completely on the experiences of the ancestors; what
was anticipated was what had already happened as the past pervaded the present.

If we look at postmodern temporality from Koselleck's framework, the
present may appear to some to be a continuation of *Neuzeit* because technical innovations continue to orient experience toward the future. Yet a change
may be said to have occurred: in the context of electronic communications
the future is now. The present comes to be infused with the future, and the
tense that best expresses the modern individual's historical sense is the future
perfect, a future that has already been since it is embedded in the present.
The distance between experience and expectation has collapsed as the present implodes into the future. One has a sense not that the future is immi-
nent, a horizon that enables one to look both forward and backward, but
that it has already happened. The linearity of modernity was sustained by the
gap between past and future, a tension that gave the modern the sense of
being propelled directionally, of forging ahead. In postmodern temporality,
nonlinear and simultaneous, the future is here. In postmodernity, technical
innovations do not serve to distance one from the past but to thicken an
already subsisting technical world.

The academy in general and the discipline of history in particular are
not immune from the effects of electronically mediated communication.
Increasingly, written letters and even telephone calls are disappearing in
favor of electronic mail, a technology that has its own parameters—encour-
aging spontaneity, for instance—that introduce changes in quality, not only
in quantity or speed. In some disciplines, such as branches of physics, publication is now primarily in the electronic form, bypassing print. Although
relatively uncommon in the humanities, numerous scholarly journals are
published either first or only in electronic form.[42] In addition to communication and publication, the sources of research—archives, text, and documents—are increasingly being made available in electronic form. This again

means instantaneous, global access, altering forever the material conditions of doing research. But this conquest of time and space incurs qualitative change as well. Researchers are equalized by being able to publish their own work, and canons are evaporated as each researcher establishes his or her own archive, his or her own hierarchy of documentation. In addition, hypertext programs enable readers to restructure the text by making their own pathways through it, rearranging the order of significance that was once materially inscribed in the book by mechanisms of tables of contents, chapters, paragraphs, indexing, and so forth. Each reader becomes in a sense an author. Also, the relation of the word to the image and the sound is changed with their general digitalization. Once in computer-readable format, words, sounds, and images are easily combined in the same work—or text—such as what now appears on CD-ROMs. The verbal culture associated with historical work through the mere material constraints of reproduction is becoming integrated with a visual and aural culture that has not even begun to be explored in academic work.[43]

If these changes in the habits of research are not drastic enough, equally and perhaps even more challenging innovations are beginning to be instituted in the domain of teaching. Distance learning is now being set into place as the communications infrastructure almost capable of real-time transmission of text-image-voice. In addition, a multitude of mechanisms have emerged in network technology—listserves, bulletin boards, MUDs, MOOs, and WOOs—that enable easy interaction outside the classroom. In fact, the institutions of the classroom, the textbook, and the teacher are all open to deep transformations as a result of the new technologies. How, then, is history to be taught, researched, and generally disseminated under the new conditions? And are not these conditions themselves alterations in history that the discipline of history must account for?

These changes in the domain of academia are not merely incremental technical novelties but revolutions in the material conditions of scholarly production and practice. In this tiny region of contemporary society something radically new is in the process of formation. Restricting ourselves solely to this area, we can see how ludicrous Fukuyama's announcement of the end appears. While it is true that the full implications of the innovations have hardly begun to be concretized into general practices and routinized in institutions (for that matter, these innovations have not ceased to be invented and introduced; more likely, they have just begun) so that a new vision of higher learning (a postmodern vision?) is not available at this time, the conclusion that nothing new is on the horizon is simply folly. What has happened outside the masculinist focus of Fukuyama is that the center of change has temporarily shifted from political and economic forms to cultural and scientific domains. Once these transformations have reached a critical mass of sedimentation, fundamental reorganizations of the economy and the political system are likely to follow.

The question of a postmodern politics and the question of history's place in a postmodern society need to be approached with as much openness and imagination as possible. The caution and backward-looking reach of Appleby, Hunt, and Jacob and the urge to announce the end in Fukuyama belie the enormous transformations that are surely already in process. A society with women's significant participation, much less equality, an earth in danger of serious ecological disturbance, a biosphere increasingly open to scientific alteration, a sociosphere bathed in electronic communication, a global ordering and ethnic intermixing of a depth never before imagined possible: in this conjuncture, this edge of a human reconfiguration, the discipline of history has a vital role to play not only in exorcising ghosts but also in contributing to a cognitive mapping that envisions a new democracy.[44] The postmodern world will be one of multiple realities, virtual realities, little narratives, cyberorganisms, and nonlinearities. A conception of truth equal to such a world is required, a mobile and self-conscious epistemology conversant with virtual realities as well as social oppression, nondefensive, and nonthymotic in spirit, gaining its foothold not in the period of the Christian religious wars, as Appleby, Hunt, and Jacob recommend, but in the emerging adventure of the conditions in front of us.[45]

NOTES

1. Stephen Kern, *The Culture of Time and Space: 1880–1918* (Cambridge: Harvard University Press, 1983).

2. Paul Virilio, *The Lost Dimension*, trans. Daniel Moshenberg (New York: Semiotext[e], 1991), 31. This is an English translation of *L'éspace critique* (Paris: Christian Bourgeois, 1984).

3. Bryan Palmer, *Descent into Discourse: the Reification of Language and the Writing of Social History* (Philadelphia: Temple University Press, 1990), iv.

4. For an excellent example of an analysis that indicates the materiality of the text as opposed to reading documents as "the direct, untampered expressions of a unified . . . mind" see Harold Mah, "Suppressing the Text: The Metaphysics of Ethnographic History in Darnton's Great Cat Massacre," *History Workshop* 31 (Spring 1991): 1–20.

5. Jacques Derrida, *Of Grammatology*, trans. Gayatri Spivak (Baltimore: Johns Hopkins University Press, 1974), 158–59 and 163. See also David Carroll, *Paraesthetics* (New York: Methuen, 1987), 167–68, which helped me locate some of the Derrida references.

6. Jacques Derrida, *Dissemination*, trans. Barbara Johnson (Chicago: University of Chicago Press, 1981), 35–36.

7. He reminds readers of this in a third use of the term ten years later: "*Text*, as I use the word, is not the book. . . . I . . . recast the concept of text by generalizing it almost without limit, in any case without present or perceptible limit, without any limit that *is*. That's why there is nothing '*beyond* the text.' " ("Critical Response," *Critical Inquiry* 13 [Autumn 1986]: 167).

8. For antiracist theory see Stuart Hall, "Minimal Selves," *Identity: The Real Me* (London: ICA, 1987), 45; for feminism, see Joan Scott, "Experience," in Judith Butler and Joan Scott, eds., *Feminists Theorize the Political* (New York: Routledge, 1992), 22–40. Scott has engaged in numerous debates with historians over this issue. For example, see her debate with Bryan Palmer, Christine Stansell, and Anson Rabinbach in *International Labor and Working-Class History* 31 (Spring 1987): 1–36, and her debate with Linda Gordon in *Signs* 15(4)(Summer 1990): 848–60.

9. See Rob Kling, Spencer Olin, and Mark Poster, eds., *Postsuburban California: The Transformation of Orange County Since World War II* (Los Angeles: University of California Press, 1991).

10. E. P. Thompson, *The Making of the English Working Class* (New York: Vintage, 1963), 12–13. See also the excellent analysis of this most important work by Joan Scott in *Gender and the Politics of History* (New York: Columbia University Press, 1988), ch. 4.

11. Joyce Appleby, Lynn Hunt, and Margaret Jacob, *Telling the Truth About History* (New York: Norton, 1994).

12. Peter Novick, *That Noble Dream: The "Objectivity Question" and the American Historical Profession* (New York: Cambridge University Press, 1988), 593, notes that the 1986 meetings of the AHA had no such discussions. It might be noted that the convention of 1988 had a panel on "The Old History and the New" with contributions by Theodore Hamerow, Gertrude Himmelfarb, Lawrence Levine, Joan Scott, and John Toews. This was published in the *American Historical Review* 94(3)(June 1989) as a "forum." This issue also boasted an essay by Allan Megill and another forum on intellectual history with contributions by David Harlan and David Hollinger.

13. David Hollinger, "Discourse About Discourse About Discourse About Discourse? A Response to Dominick LaCapra," *Intellectual History Newsletter* 13 (1991): 18.

14. E. R. Ankersmit, "Historiography and Postmodernism," *History and Theory* 2 (1989): 152.

15. Novick, *That Noble Dream*, 1–2.

16. On this issue, see the important essay by Hayden White, "The Politics of Historical Interpretation: Discipline and De-Sublimation," *Critical Inquiry* 9 (September 1982): 113–37.

17. "Dialogue with Jacques Derrida," in Richard Kearney, *Dialogues with Contemporary Continental Thinkers* (Manchester: Manchester University Press, 1984), 123–24.

18. Stuart Hall, "Cultural Identity and Diaspora," in Patrick Williams and Laura Chrisman, eds., *Colonial Discourse and Post-Colonial Theory: A Reader* (New York: Harvester Wheatsheaf, 1993), 394.

19. Of this very large literature, see especially Homi Bhabha, *Local Cultures* (New York: Routledge, 1993); Rey Chow, *Writing Diaspora* (Bloomington: Indiana University Press, 1993); Ernesto Laclau, ed., *The Making of Political Identities* (New York: Verso, 1994); and "The Question of Identity," *October* 61 (special issue)(Summer 1992).

20. See, for example, Edward Berenson, *The Trial of Madame Cailliaux* (Berkeley: University of California Press, 1992), 8, and Natalie Davis, "Stories and the Hunger to Know," *The Yale Journal of Criticism* 5(2)(1992): 161, where she calls for "microhistories" of the discipline of history.

21. Thomas Haskell, "Objectivity Is Not Neutrality: Rhetoric vs. Practice in Peter Novick's *That Noble Dream*," *History and Theory* 29 (1990): 141.

22. Sande Cohen, *Historical Culture: On the Recoding of an Academic Discipline* (Berkeley: University of California Press, 1986).

23. Elizabeth Ermarth, *Sequel to History: Postmodernism and the Crisis of Representational Time* (Princeton: Princeton University Press, 1992).

24. Jacques Derrida, *The Other Heading: Reflections on Today's Europe*, trans. Pascale-Anne Brault and Michael Naas (Bloomington: Indiana University Press, 1992).

25. Jacques Derrida, "Back from Moscow in the U.S.S.R.," in Mark Poster, ed., *Politics, Theory and Contemporary Culture* (New York: Columbia University Press, 1993), 197–235.

26. Jacques Derrida, *Specters of Marx: The State of the Debt, the Work of Mourning and the New International*, trans. Peggy Kamuf (New York: Routledge, 1994), 170.

27. See Perry Anderson's informative intellectual history of the concept of the end of history, including discussions of Hegel, Kojève, and Fukuyama in "The Ends of History," *A Zone of Engagement* (New York: Verso, 1992), 279–375.

28. See Mark Poster, *Existential Marxism in Postwar France* (Princeton: Princeton University Press, 1975), for a review and analysis of these discussions.

29. For an example of such an objection by a Marxist, see Aijaz Ahmad, "Reconciling Derrida: 'Specters of Marx' and Deconstructive Politics," *New Left Review* 208 (November/December 1994): 88–106. Ahmad does not confront Derrida's critique of the logocentrism in Marx, but he does raise important questions about the ability of deconstruction to critique its own history and avoid a rhetoric of innocence. For a more favorable and probing reading of Derrida's book by a Marxist theorist, see Fredric Jameson, "Marx's Purloined Letter," *New Left Review* 209 (January/February 1995): 75–109.

30. Anderson disagrees sharply with this judgment ("The Ends of History," 333).

31. Francis Fukuyama, *The End of History and the Last Man* (New York: Avon Books, 1992), 211. The original essay appeared as "The End of History?" *The National Interest* 18 (Winter 1989): 3–18.

32. See for example Wendy Brown, *Manhood and Politics: A Feminist Reading of Political Theory* (Totowa, N.J.: Rowman & Littlefield, 1988), 180–83, for an analysis of the masculine view of politics in relation to tests of will in defiance of life.

33. Anderson puts the issue this way: "The emancipation of women has achieved more gains in the West over the past twenty years than any other social movement. . . . At the same time, it remains massively far away from real sexual equality, whose ultimate conditions are still scarcely imaginable today" ("The Ends of History," 356–57). The question is to what extent "scarcely imaginable" is a function of masculine bias.

34. Jean-François Lyotard, *The Postmodern Condition*, trans. Geoff Bennington and Brian Massumi (Minneapolis: University of Minnesota Press, 1984).

35. Fredric Jameson, *Postmodernism, or, The Cultural Logic of Late Capitalism* (Durham: Duke University Press, 1991).

36. Gianni Vattimo, *The End of Modernity*, trans. Jon Snyder (Baltimore: Johns Hopkins University Press, 1991), 4.

37. For a critical discussion of this discourse, see Lutz Niethammer, *Posthistoire: Has History Come to an End?*, trans. Patrick Camiller (New York: Verso, 1992). For a comparison of the postmodern to posthistoire, see Allan Stoekl, " 'Round Dusk: Kojève at 'The End,' " *Postmodern Culture* 5(1)(September 1994).

38. For an analysis of the paradox of the position of the observer, albeit without the constructivist or historicist framework of postmodernity, see Niklaus Luhmann, "The Paradox of Observing Systems," *Cultural Critique* 31 (Fall 1995): 37–56.

39. For a different characterization of this conundrum, see Jean Baudrillard, *The Illusion of the End*, trans. Chris Turner (Stanford: Stanford University Press, 1994).

40. Paul Virilio, "The Last Vehicle," in D. Kamper and C. Wulf, eds., *Looking Back on the End of the World*, trans. David Antal (New York: Semiotext[e], 1989), 118. Also see Virilio, *The End of Modernity*, 6.

41. Reinhart Koselleck, *Futures Past: On the Semantics of Historical Time*, trans. Keith Tribe (Cambridge: MIT Press, 1985), 275.

42. Kathleen Burnett, "The Scholar's Rhizome: Networked Communication Issues" (kburnett@gandalf.rutgers.edu) explores this issue with convincing logic.

43. For a discussion of the use of hypertext in the humanities, see George Landow, *Hypertext: The Convergence of Contemporary Critical Theory and Technology* (Baltimore: Johns Hopkins University Press, 1992).

44. For critique of Derrida's politics of the ghost, see Sue Golding, "Virtual Derrida," in Jelica Sumic-Riha, ed., *Philosophic Fictions* (Slovenia: Academy of Philosophy, 1994–95).

45. Appleby, Hunt, and Jacob, *Telling the Truth About History*, 271, where "new thinking" includes "a return to the intellectual center of the Western experience since the seventeenth century."